What People Are Saying About Elmer Dixon

"Elmer Dixon values what matters most to him: justice, inclusion, maximizing potential, building relationships, love of family and faith.

In his new book, Elmer shares his life's journey with stories about these ideals, including when he co-founded the Black Panthers in Seattle, to the present day where he leads his own consulting firm, teaching and training business leaders and college students about multicultural communications, diversity, conflict management, and more. He shares what it takes to bring people together from all walks of life to achieve personal and organizational success.

I have learned many lessons and hard truths about myself from my work with Elmer Dixon and so can you, when you read *Die Standing: From Black Panther Revolutionary to Global Diversity Advocate.*"

—S. Gary Snodgrass
EVP & Chief Human Resources Officer (Retired)
Exelon Corporation

"Elmer Dixon is and has been, without question, a man committed.

Committed to whom: To the People.

Committed for what purpose: To convince the people and their leadership to take responsibility to free themselves from the oppression and domination of illegitimate authorities.

Committed why: In order for the people to pursue Freedom, Justice, and Equality.

It should be understood that to be a member of the Black Panther Party was a very serious matter. Elmer knew then, and he knows now, that to be a member of the Party, means and meant that you were willing to die to end the oppression of the people.

Power to whom: Power to the People!"

—Dr. Albert W. Black, Jr.
Sociology and African American Studies Professor
University of Washington

"Elmer Dixon's revealing memoir reminds us that American democracy is a process, one that requires awe-inspiring resilience and a steadfast commitment to truth and justice. His engaging debut examines the fundamental barriers inherent in the struggle for freedom that defined the America of Dixon's youth.

Through beautifully constructed prose and honest storytelling, Dixon reveals his everlasting contributions to the Black Panther Party and the nation. His story serves as both an inspiration for younger generations and a primer on how to facilitate the creation of an inclusive democracy."

—Terry Anne Scott, Ph.D.
Director
The Institute for Common Power

"*Die Standing* is a superb biography written by Elmer Dixon. It chronicles his life in an easy to understand, storytelling style. It begins while Elmer is a 17 year old revolutionary and cofounder of the Seattle Chapter of the Black Panther Party in 1968, and ends with him describing what he has learned from his formidable life experiences as one of the most highly sought after lecturers in the United States as well as in many other countries around the world.

His training and teachings have significantly influenced students, professional staff, community organizers and leaders who have gone on to build truly anti-racist workplaces, with reduced misogynistic behavior and created more equitable and just living environments in every community where participants in his workshops and seminars live.

Mr. Dixon is a gifted trainer who has influenced the social and conscious development of half a million people all over the world. I genuinely expect that if enough people will read his book that the number of people he will have inspired to fight for self-improvement, fair play and democracy in dozens of countries around the world will increase tenfold. *Die Standing* is a book you must read!"

—Larry Gossett
Martin Luther King Jr. County Councilmember (1994-2019)

"When I was a teenager in 1970s Ireland, it felt at times as if I was the only Black person in the country. Of course, that wasn't the case. There were hundreds of Black kids like me hidden away in the institutions run by the religious orders. But it did feel lonely. My Blackness was completely devalued and isolated. Imagine then the impact that the iconic images of the Black Panthers had on me! Seeing young Black men and women in the characteristic Black leather coats and berets with shotguns balanced nonchalantly on their hips or their clinched fists held upwards as if they were challenging the very heavens themselves, offered me a sense of pride in my Blackness, something which was denied to me in every other part of my life here in a monoracial Ireland.

But the Panthers were more than just a defiant uniform as exemplified by the life work and experiences of Elmer Dixon. They were a community who offered solutions at a practical, communal level. This community engagement by Panthers like Elmer always seemed to me to be a greater defiance to the indifferent white society than raised fists and guns, in the States but also closer to home in the UK and in Ireland.

Elmer and the Panthers served as models for community-based solutions to poverty and inequality in Irish communities and their efforts to monitor and document police brutality help inform and folded into the work of Irish civil rights and anti-racism groups. As an isolated Black woman—who also wanted her own black beret and leather coat—I was particularly drawn to Elmer's message of internationalism and solidarity as a model for building transnational movements and alliances against systems of oppression and exploitation.

Elmer's and the Panthers' legacy and activism became an important source of inspiration, solidarity, and strategies for social justice and equality for similarly marginalized individuals, groups, and communities outside of the States, in the form of Black Panther movements in Israel, Bermuda, Australia, India, the UK, and New Zealand. And perhaps we can also include this unusual Irish chapter of the Panthers, whose membership at that time was this single Black teenage girl."

—Dr. Philomena Mullen
Assistant Professor Black Studies
Department of Sociology, Trinity College Dublin
Irish Research Council Government of Ireland Postgraduate Scholar

"During the late 1960s and early 70s, I witnessed Elmer Dixon as a young man with a profound commitment to help keep his community safe and assist people in need. As a leader of the Seattle Black Panther Party, he was respected by many and feared by others, including some in the Black community.

After understanding the mission of SBPP, Gloria Martin and I persuaded the Executive Director and the employees of the Central Area Motivation Program (CAMP) to make donations to the SBPP free breakfast program—they all had jobs.

I also challenged others who criticized the SBPP by simply asking them, 'How many children are you feeding? Where are your medical clinics? When is the last time you sought justice and challenged police misconduct?'"

— Eddie Rye, Jr.

"*Die Standing* is a most appropriate title for Elmer Dixon's reflections. His life is about standing—standing up, standing for, standing with. His outspoken commitment to critical values of human respect, justice, and equity, and his collaborative energy invite us to stand with him, to reflect on our own stories as we turn the pages of his lifetime of engagement.

While my earliest memory of Elmer is the well-known photo of him carrying an arm on the state capitol steps, it is my heart's desire that we will live, inspired by his story, and die, however, whenever, and wherever we do, standing together in spirit, letting our lives speak out to the last for what we believe in—Comrades with open, caring arms."

— Dr. George F. Simons
Creator of Diversophy®

"My Comrade and Brother, Elmer Dixon—a true 'Servant of the People'—gives an exceptionally heartfelt look into his life's journey, filled with abundance of courage and love for humanity.

For example: Brother Elmer co-founded the Seattle, Washington chapter of the Black Panther Party, where he worked diligently and with great effort assisting with implementing the many free community survival programs for the underserved communities.

Such as our: Free Breakfast for School Children and The People's Free Health Clinic and the many other outstanding quality of life free services and programs to the community.

Thank you, Brother Elmer. What great lessons you share to be enlightened and inspired by."

— Emory Douglas
Revolutionary Artist / Minster of Culture
Black Panther Party 1967/1982

DIE STANDING

from Black Panther Revolutionary to Global Diversity Consultant

ELMER DIXON

DIE STANDING: From Black Panther Revolutionary to Global Diversity Consultant

For information about this title or to order other books and/or electronic media, contact the publisher:

Two Sisters Writing & Publishing®
TwoSistersWriting.com
18530 Mack Avenue, Suite 166
Grosse Pointe Farms, MI 48236

ISBN 978-1-956879-39-1 (Hardcover)
ISBN 978-1-956879-40-7 (Paperback)
ISBN 978-1-956879-41-4 (eBook)

Printed in the United States of America
All the stories in this work are true.

Cover and Graphic Design: Illumination Graphics.

Author photos: The Dixon Family Collection.
Archival photos reprinted with written permission from: the Museum of History and Industry in Seattle (MOHAI); the Stanford University BPP Collection, care of David Hilliard; Stephen Shames; and Alan Copeland c/o Dr. Joseph Copeland.

DEDICATION

This book is dedicated to my fallen Comrades and my life partner, my wife, Dee Dee.
In memory of our son Merrill.

CONTENTS

ACKNOWLEDGMENTS

In the fall of 2010, I delivered a keynote speech to SIETAR France (Society for Intercultural Education Training and Research) on the Black Panther Party. Following my talk, two women approached me, asking if I would consider coming to Amsterdam to speak because children there learn about the BPP in school, and this would be an opportunity for them to continue their learning.

As I responded, I reflected on an experience I had just prior to leaving for Europe. A young Black student at a college where I was preparing to speak asked me, "What was the Black Panther Party? Were they like the Black KKK?"

For years before this moment, I had been asked to write a book about my life as a Panther. That student's questions made me realize more than ever that now was the time.

Misinformation about who we were and what we stood for continues to be rampant, led by narrow-minded people, and fed by lies that demonized the Party.

So, I began the long journey of telling my story, hoping to add to the stories of many of my Comrades, about life as a Panther. Mine is but one example that thousands of former members of the BPP could tell.

There are so many people to thank who helped me along the way, providing encouragement and assistance.

One person at the beginning was Dr. Terry Anne Scott, who at the time was a professor at the University of Washington's Ethnic Studies Department. She would invite me to guest lecture in her AFRAM class and began recruiting students as interns to work with me on my book. This was the impetus for me to get started. She and other profs, including Brukab Sisay and LaTasha Levy, provided a constant flow of interns who provided research, conducted interviews, and recorded me. The list is too long to recite them all, but a few who deserve extra recognition include Mariama Suwaneh, Jarrett Finau, Ryan Mansour, Rimaujhia Greenlee, Faiza Khalid, Alejandro Isiordia, Alyssa King, Abbi Heath, Edom Bogale, and "the fabulous three:" Anissa Jackson, Mikaela Southern, and Jessica Kirk.

A big thank you goes to Joanne Williams and TaRessa Stovall, who introduced me to my amazing editor and publisher Elizabeth Ann Atkins of Two Sisters Writing & Publishing®. TaRessa recalled walking into a Panther PE class when she was just 13 and remembered her encounter with me as respectful and caring; we became lifelong friends. TaRessa and Joanne outlined the initial strategy for writing my book and I am forever grateful for their support.

I can't thank Elizabeth and Two Sisters Writing & Publishing® enough for her dedication to editing and preparing my manuscript for publishing. Her tireless efforts brought my story to life.

And thank you to the team at The Museum of History & Industry (MOHAI), BPP photographer Stephen Shames, and David Hilliard for granting access to the Stanford University BPP Collection for providing photos. And to Deborah Perdue of Illumination Graphics for creating the book cover and preparing the manuscript for printing.

Much gratitude also goes to my marketing team, Deanna Shoss and my intern Saara Kamal.

Many thanks to my Comrades who shared their stories and experiences: Leon "Valentine" Hobbs, Melvin Dickson, Billie Jackson, and Kathy Jones, all now deceased. To Leonard Dawson, Willie Brazier, Jake Fiddler, Vanetta Molson, Carolyn Carter, Kathy "Nafasi" Halley, Joyce and James Redmond, my lieutenants, Wayne Jenkins, Steve Phillips and Larry Tisino (deceased), and Ron Johnson (deceased), who was with me to the end. And a special thanks to former BPP Chairman Bobby Seale. We spent long hours on the phone talking about the old days.

And a big thanks to my family: to our mother who at 98 still has a sharp memory of the family history; and to my dad for the long conversations we had when he was sick years ago before he died, sharing old family stories. To my brothers Aaron and Michael and sister Joanne for their unwavering support. Many thanks to my cousins Mark and Vincent Taylor for sharing their recollection of family history, and to our great cousin, Clara Miles, whom we affectionally called "Sister," for sharing stories of growing up with our grandfather Elmer Dixon, Sr., also known as "Gratdada."

It is also important to remind us all to never forget our Comrades who were and are still locked away in prisons across the country, and to remember their sacrifices. These Comrades include The Angola Three, who spent decades in solitary confinement, some longer than 40 years. Chip Romaine Fitzgerald spent more than 50 years incarcerated, dying in prison as the longest-imprisoned Comrade at the time of his death. They all continue to inspire me to not only finish this book, but to keep on fighting for justice, equity, and inclusion.

And most of all, my gratitude goes to my immediate family, starting with my incredible wife Dee Dee, who has stood by my side for more than 50 years, always encouraging me and lifting me up when I was down. And to our children, our son Merrill, who passed away far too young and like many of his generation was a target of the so-called war on drugs. And to our daughters Samora, Frelima, Angola, and our adopted daughter Genise for their love and support over the years. And to our nine grandchildren and six great-grandchildren—you are the future, the reason we fought "the good fight."

Long live the spirit of our fallen Comrades and all those who stood up and continue to stand up against racism, sexism, and oppression. Long live the spirit of revolutionary struggle.

"The main purpose of the vanguard group should be to raise the consciousness of the masses through educational programs and other activities. The sleeping masses must be bombarded with the correct approach to struggle and the party must use all means available to get this information across to the masses."

— Huey P. Newton
The Correct Handling of a Revolution

FOREWORD #1
BY BOBBY SEALE

Elmer Dixon's story as a Black Panther Party revolutionary is important today because many of the issues challenging our community we fought to resolve in the late 1960s, remain brutally problematic now, some 55 years later.

Black people's lives are still threatened by police brutality, economic oppression, the prison industrial complex, and the lack of political representation and power to change the abysmal status quo.

Elmer was, and continues to be, a powerhouse on a mission to change all of the above, through his work as a co-founder of Seattle's Black Panther Party in 1968, and today as a global diversity consultant.

I first met Elmer in the spring of 1968 following the brutal murder of my friend and Comrade Lil' Bobby Hutton. He and his brother Aaron along with other students from Seattle had traveled to San Francisco State University to attend the West Coast Conference of Black Student Unions.

"We're going to fight until our blood runs in the streets," I told the students during my keynote speech that electrified and terrified the students into taking action to join the Black Power Movement.

After the speech, Elmer and his brother Aaron made a beeline to talk with me.

Elmer Dixon is important to the history of the Black Panther Party because he joined the Movement at this critical time. Martin Luther King, Jr. had just been murdered on April 4, 1968, in Memphis, Tennessee, and two days later, Little Bobby Hutton was riddled with police bullets in Oakland, California, while in police custody. He was the first of many Panthers shot dead by police.

I asked the Seattle contingent, including Elmer and Aaron, to attend Lil' Bobby's funeral, where they saw hundreds of Panthers in our berets and leather jackets, united for the cause of protecting Black people, building our communities, and advocating for political power for Black and all oppressed people.

I wanted them to see the movement we were building firsthand and to experience what becoming a Black Panther Revolutionary was about: giving one's life to the revolution and being prepared to make the ultimate sacrifice for freedom. The whole Black community had come to stand in solidarity with the Party and when Elmer stared into the coffin of this fallen Comrade—who was also 17 years old—Elmer committed his life to the cause, pledging that he'd rather *Die Standing* as a revolutionary, than live on his knees, succumbing to the status quo of police violence and economic oppression of our people.

Two weeks later, I traveled to Seattle to organize the first chapter of the Black Panther Party outside of California and the second chapter overall. The initial meeting was at Elmer and Aaron's parents' home, packed with young brothers and sisters who wanted to enlist in our Party and become part of this revolutionary movement we were building. Overnight, 300 people immediately joined the Seattle chapter and during this fast-moving period, I traveled from Seattle to the East, establishing chapters and branches of the Party all across the country.

Under my guidance, Elmer, and his brother Aaron, who was named Defense Captain of the chapter, along with other dedicated Comrades, implemented the Black Panther Party's organizing strategy using our 10-10-10 program and the principles drawn from the Ten-Point Platform and Program, which I wrote in 1966 with our Party's co-founder, Huey P. Newton.

Our mission aimed for change at the top of America's power

structure, and at the bottom, where Black people were struggling to survive racism, poverty, and violence in our streets.

As the chapter's Field Lieutenant, Elmer understood our mission and committed his young life to making it a success. In charge of security for the chapter, he organized the police alert patrols and helped launch many of our community survival programs—referred to as survival programs—pending revolution. His dedication to the struggle is but a reflection of the dedication of hundreds of members of the Black Panther Party: an army of revolutionaries determined to shift the imbalance of power in this country and bring real Power to the People. That is what we stood for, and this is what Elmer continues to stand for.

Just as I continued my mission rooted in the Black Panther Party, Elmer Dixon continues to work to ensure fairness and inclusion, not only for Black people, but for all people, regardless of race, gender or sexual orientation. His experience with the Black Power Movement that started with us back in 1968 formed a powerful foundation for his work as a global diversity consultant today.

The world is a better place because of the work that Elmer Dixon did as a Black Panther Party leader on the streets and in our communities, and today in corporate boardrooms and on university stages around the world.

I hope that by reading this book, people everywhere will emulate his mission and his model to take action to create a more just world for all.

—Bobby Seale
Co-Founder and Former Chairman
The Black Panther Party
Author, *A Lonely Rage*
and
Power to the People: The World of the Black Panthers

FOREWORD #2 BY DAVID WALSH

I first met Elmer Dixon when we both attended a SIETAR Ireland (Society for Intercultural Education, Training and Research) conference in Dublin in 2018. Before that, I had read a lot about this "subversive troublemaker" from the United States whose uniform had been a leather coat and black beret, so I was well aware of his background and history.

As an Irish police officer who had undertaken research on policing pluralism in a changing Ireland and had gone on to drive the establishment of the first Irish police unit to manage and build understanding of diversity and pluralism, I had read and researched as much as possible about experiences in other parts of the world that might help to inform our approach in Ireland.

That research brought me into contact with infamous incidents such as the Rodney King beating and subsequent Los Angeles riots 1992, and the Saint Petersburg, Florida riots in 1996. I realized these were just the latest manifestations in the long passage of racial injustice, tension and violence in the history of the United States. Closer to home, I only had to look across the water to the United Kingdom to events such as the murder of Black teenager Stephen Lawrence in 1993, the Toxteth riots in 1981, the Handsworth riots and the Brixton riots, both in 1985, for further examples of police and community failures within marginalized communities.

Each of these incidents reinforced my awareness as a police officer that policing race, ethnicity and culture can be deeply divided, contentious and politicized issues, and that posters and platitudes were never going to help create the trust and relationships needed to engage with diverse communities, particularly in a country like Ireland that had very little history of inward migration until the late 1990s.

And so through this work, I found myself in the company of this tall, imposing, gregarious ex-Black Panther whom the system had deemed a "terrorist." Every piece of police DNA in my being was warning me:

"Be careful. He is one of them. Mind yourself."

That evening in Dublin, Elmer and I crossed the metaphorical bridge and met in the middle where conversations begin. I was face-to-face with living history.

No longer was he simply words to be read on a page, research in an academic paper, or images on some YouTube video. Here was the real deal, a Black Panther sitting with me, talking about policing difference and prepared to share everything he could to help me.

Elmer graciously provided me with the safe space to ask questions such as why the Black Lives Matter movement was becoming increasingly high profile after the George Floyd murder, and why wasn't the Movement about the fact that *all* lives mattered?

Elmer looked at me, paused briefly, reflected and said, "Dave, of course all lives matter, but to understand the BLM Movement, you have to understand the context of race and colour in the United States. It's all about context."

And of course, he was right. Context is everything and we can never really understand "the other" until we are prepared to examine, understand and empathize with the context of others. It wasn't that I didn't know that, but I remember the particular impact of Elmer saying it to me that night; all human interactions are based upon a context and until we take the time to be aware of our own context, then try to understand the context of those who have been "othered," we will misjudge, misperceive, and misinterpret each other. Elmer's life to date has been about helping others to explore and understand the context of others.

Elmer Dixon and I are really from the opposite ends of many spectrums. He is Black; I am white. He fought the police and the system; I was part of maintaining the system.

He proposed what some perceived as violence—but what I later learned was self defense—to bring about change; I took an oath to stop people like Elmer and help incarcerate them.

Elmer reacted to his environment and situation with resistance, protest and defense, while my career choices meant that I was often on the other side of similar types of protest, resistance and defense. I had sworn to uphold the law, be impartial and afford equal respect to all people, but that can be difficult when we don't experience the world through the eyes, perceptions and history of others and we unquestioningly rely on stereotypes and generalizations to decide who or what "the other" is.

Truly, Elmer Dixon and I should have nothing in common, and yet we have everything in common—a shared interest in the human condition and other human beings, how we are shaped, defined, and categorized by the societies and the environments we find ourselves born into.

We had both been rebels, he with the Black Panthers, while I had become an outsider in an organization that was a male hegemony where talk about understanding differences, diversity and inclusion meant stepping outside of the mainstream of policing. Although I was in the organization, I knew the path I had followed wasn't at the frontline of policing and it could be a lonely space.

Elmer and I share a yearning for social justice and the creation of spaces where diversity and inclusion consciousness are the norm. We are both acutely aware that influencing this type of change—whether it be in societies, communities, organizations, schools, police stations or any other place of human interaction—takes energy, ongoing commitment and a multi-layered approach.

For me, Elmer's experiences, actions and thought processes in his earlier years were the building blocks that have shaped the person we know today. Every event, every experience, every challenge, every knockback, every put down, every discrimination, every hurt, every wound, and every loss, were part of the tapestry that was being woven quietly in the background to shape the Elmer Dixon who delivered a powerful guest lecture to the Black Studies programme in Trinity College Dublin in 2022 as part of the inaugural Black History Month at that institution. As I listened to him that evening, it struck me how the most powerful weapons in Elmer's arsenal today are his words, his insights and his wisdom, and all of that comes from his activism and earlier life contexts.

Elmer journeyed through those earlier life experiences and took the learning into the various chapters of his life. He has shaped and used his knowledge not just to influence change and social justice, but to enable others like me to develop a deeper world view, to explore new paradigms and to always look for context.

For that, Elmer, I am deeply indebted to you and those who in one way or another shaped you and your life.

In any other life, we shouldn't have met. And if we had, we would have been at opposing ends of the dispute.

So, the message to anyone reading this book is that if Elmer and I can find this common space, then anyone can, whether you're in business, services, the community, or any other sector. You can find a sacred space, a middle ground, where human, one-on-one connections can form foundations for profound understanding that inspires change for individuals and the collective.

That can only happen with trust and a willingness to go there. I hope that this book inspires you to do just that.

—David Walsh
Former Police Sergeant
Dublin, Ireland

INTRODUCTION

I was 17, staring into the coffin of a young Black man killed by police—55 years ago—when I committed my life to defending and liberating our people.

"I'd rather die on my feet, than live on my knees," I thought, quoting the Mexican revolutionary, Emiliano Zapata Salazar.

That became the rallying cry for many of my Comrades who became members of the Black Panther Party in April of 1968. Two weeks later, we became the first chapter of the Black Panther Party formed outside of the state of California. This would begin the launch of our revolutionary movement across America.

At the time, we had no idea that—more than half a century later—the image of a cop's knee on a Black man's neck would become one of the most horrifying images of our time, and the global rallying cry for liberation and justice around the world today.

In the wake of the brutal details of George Floyd's killing in police custody, replayed in the courtroom and on news reports during the trial of Minneapolis police officer Derek Chauvin, I continue to be haunted and outraged by the reality that Black people are still dying by the hands, knees, and gunfire of police. The actions of racist reactionaries gunning down Black people in a supermarket and in Black churches brings back the reality of the terrorism inflicted by the Ku Klux Klan on Black communities following Reconstruction, a clear and present danger.

At the same time, while I was encouraged that two award-winning films, *Judas and the Black Messiah* and *The Trial of the Chicago 7*, brought to light some of the realities of the Black Panther Party, they were still inaccurate and didn't tell the full story that we were under siege by a campaign to destroy us after notorious FBI Director J. Edgar Hoover declared us "the greatest threat to the internal security of the country."

On the contrary, our driving truth was that the brutal oppression of our community, including the beatings and killings by police, the socioeconomic disparities that disenfranchised Black people with poverty, hunger, unemployment, substandard healthcare, unfair imprisonment, and despair, were the greatest threat to our survival.

So, we took action, living by the Black Panther Party Code, to die for the people, guided by The Black Panther Party for Self-Defense Ten-Point Platform and Program that Founders Bobby Seale and Huey P. Newton wrote in 1966.

"We want an immediate end to POLICE BRUTALITY and MURDER of Black people," read point number seven in our program that I adopted when Black Panther Party Chairman Bobby Seale came to my hometown of Seattle, Washington, to help my older brother Aaron Dixon, myself, and several others start our chapter.

This happened within weeks of Little Bobby Hutton's funeral in Oakland, California, which was packed with 1,500 Black Panther Party members and supporters, such as movie star Marlon Brando, a staunch supporter of the BPP, who spoke at a televised rally after the service.

Lil' Bobby was the first Panther to be gunned down by police, not the last. He was killed in police custody on the streets of west Oakland. His young body was riddled with police bullets just two days after Dr. Martin Luther King, Jr. was assassinated on April 4th, 1968.

As I paid my respects to this strong Comrade who would be buried in his Panther uniform—a beret, a leather jacket, and a "Free Huey" button—I realized:

Lil' Bobby was 17 years old.

I'm 17 years old.

That could be me lying there.

At that moment, I knew I would die for the revolution.

For the next 16 years, our mission as Party members was to serve the community and stimulate revolution by, among other things, patrolling the streets of Seattle. Our Police Alert Patrol sent teams of Panthers into the streets, armed with guns and law books, intervening in traffic stops and other police interactions where we believed Black lives were in danger.

When state lawmakers attempted to restrict our second constitutional right to bear arms, we protested, and the photograph of me and my Comrades standing on the steps of the capitol building in Olympia, Washington became one of the most iconic images of the Black Power Movement of the 1960s and 1970s.

All the while, we worked to protect, nourish, and educate our community. We opened the Children's Free Breakfast Program, feeding thousands of children every morning in cities across America. We opened health clinics that provided free healthcare and some of the first testing for sickle cell anemia. We distributed free groceries to families in need, and provided free clothing and free shoe programs, community pest control, and free legal aid, among others of what we called community survival programs pending revolution.

Our free busing-to-prison program helped families visit loved ones, and included tutoring for inmates to get their GEDs. We created the Summer Youth Institute, the Summer Liberation

School for children, and a fully-accredited school called the Oakland Community Learning Center in Oakland.

Today, our original mission to defend and liberate our community remains relevant. That's why I'm sharing my story, which mirrors that of so many of my Comrades. It showcases our objective, with the hopes that it can serve as a blueprint for young activists and people everywhere to learn and continue to demand freedom from oppression.

With my memoir, *Die Standing: From Black Panther Revolutionary to Global Diversity Advocate,* my goal is to share my true-life account as a Black Panther Party leader, and to set the record straight about who we were, what we did, and why.

During the earliest of my 16 years with the Party, which included serving 14 months in prison after my police informant bodyguard set me up, we were constantly under threat of violence and death. I was called before the House Un-American Activities Committee to testify in Congress. I, like many of my Comrades, survived many violent encounters, and we never wavered in our commitment to risk our lives for the cause.

Our cause aimed to liberate oppressed people worldwide, as we had chapters and contacts from Vietnam to the Congo to Algeria to England, Denmark, Sweden, Germany, France, New Zealand, Australia, and more.

Similarly, a new version of the Black Panther Party's rainbow coalition, an interracial movement for liberty and justice, was roused once again in 2020 during global protests after the police killings of George Floyd, Breonna Taylor, and so many others.

Sadly, during my time as a Panther, we believe police and government agencies killed 20 or more Panthers, including Fred Hampton, chairman of the Illinois chapter of the Black Panther Party. At the same time, Black people across America continued to die in police custody, and institutional racism succeeded at oppressing our people in every way.

After the Black Panther Party disbanded, I continued my mission for freedom and justice, first running a Boys and Girls Club in a low-income community in Tacoma, Washington, then as an EEO officer focused on preventing sexual harassment and racial discrimination in the workplace.

In 1988, I was recruited by two women who founded Executive Diversity Services, becoming then lead trainer, and eventually president in 2010. During that time, in 1990, I served on the cabinet of Seattle's first Black Mayor, Norman Rice.

Our company has provided Diversity, Equity, and Inclusion trainings for many organizations, including Fortune 100 companies such as Microsoft, United Airlines, and PepsiCo, which includes training more than 600,000 people. Requests for our services have tripled since the 2020 protests for social justice.

Sadly, as one trial after another for cops and citizens accused of killing Black people retraumatize us with new details of those murders, we are reminded of the gross inequities and injustices in our community by the fact that Black women still today die at a rate of 10 times that of white women from medical issues related to child birthing. When, in fact, our first free medical clinic in Seattle was a well-baby clinic focusing on the needs of young, pregnant, Black women, and we're back today dealing with the same crisis.

So, we must all demand freedom from oppression, equity, and justice.

I hope that my story, and the true telling of the Black Panther Party's mission that remains urgently relevant today, can help to advance the American promise of "liberty and justice for all."

—Elmer Dixon
Founding Member
Seattle Chapter Black Panther Party
President
Executive Diversity Services

CHAPTER 1

An Era for Revolution - Early Life Influences

When I was born and the doctor slapped breath into my lungs, I bit his finger. With only my gums as weapons, this became the first of many defiant and rebellious acts that would characterize the militant nature of my life that began on May 22nd, 1950 on the South Side of Chicago at Cook County Hospital, the designated hospital for Colored people.

Black folks were barred from white hospitals, so the doctor and staff who delivered me were most likely Black. When I came into the world, I was unusually long—22 inches—and about eight and a half pounds. It was springtime, and the azaleas were blooming.

I became my parents' fourth child, although my sister Karen had died prematurely at birth. According to the Chinese zodiac calendar, I was born in the Year of the Tiger, and tigers have stubborn personalities, confidence, and strong judgment, all making them proficient leaders who can handle any issue.

"What you are is where you were when," said sociologist Morris Massey, who researched generational values and concluded that a person's values are the result of the events occurring at the time of their blossoming.

So that act of rebellion during the first moments of life foreshadowed my future distrust of authority that would evolve during the 1960s and characterize the Boomer generation and racially oppressive era into which I was born.

At the time, Chicago was heavily segregated. The American version of apartheid was known as redlining, and Black people in Chicago were largely confined to the South and West sides of the city, while whites enjoyed the suburban areas around Chicago that included the North Side and the Deep South Side.

Chicago's version of Jim Crow meant Blacks couldn't eat at the finest restaurants or stay in the grandest hotels, such as The Drake or The Palmer House where jazz greats Duke Ellington, Count Basie, Billie Holiday, and others would sing in the classy Emerald Room, but were not allowed to stay in the hotel.

World War II had ended five years earlier in 1945, and the Korean War had just begun. Throughout my life, I would experience a series of wars—some declared, some not. However, the biggest war that lay ahead for me and America at large was a war against brutal oppression. That war was destined to be part of my life.

ROOTED IN POWER AND FAMILY PRIDE

During World War, my father, Elmer Jr., served in the U.S. Army as part of the infamous Fighting 54th Infantry, the first all-Black infantry that dates back to the Civil War and was featured in *Glory*, the 1989 film starring Denzel Washington, Morgan Freeman, and Matthew Broderick.

My father survived his stint in the South Pacific, where so many others had perished while fighting for both victory at home and abroad—what African Americans called "the Double V" campaign.

"Elmer and Madison are coming home!" exclaimed my mother's best friend Elaine, about the boys that she had grown up with. After

Elaine introduced my mother to my father, they soon began dancing amidst the glow of party lights; a life-long romance blossomed.

"It was a very beautiful spring," my mother recalls fondly. At the time, she was attending Chicago's Teachers College, and my father enrolled in the Art Institute of Chicago. While waiting for admittance later that fall, he registered to the junior college next door to my mother's teaching college.

Whether by fate or my dad's preemptive strategy to be near her, they fell in love. They would walk home together each day with their half dozen friends, chatting away and stopping at the bakery or the record stores along the way. Completely enamored with one another, my parents married soon thereafter.

My father was born in Henderson, Kentucky in 1924 to hard-working parents who were deeply rooted in a strong family foundation. His father, Elmer J. Dixon, Sr., was born in Kentucky around 1898.

Little information remains about his life, except that his extended family was quite large and included dozens of aunts, uncles, cousins, and siblings, many of whom resided in the same house. Our cousin, Clara, whom we regarded as "Sister," shared stories about their childhood and how they often slept four or five to a bed, since there simply weren't enough to accommodate everyone. Cousin Clara grew fond of those times because they created close family bonds and fun while growing up together.

My relatives exemplified the social collective that characterizes many Southern Black families, which often take unconventional forms and include people living together and relying on each other, though they are not blood kin. This included Ms. Jones, who lived down the street and bore no biological connection to everyone else.

My grandfather married Mildred Brooks, who was born in Brookstown, Kentucky, a name bestowed upon the town by her grandmother, Amanda Brooks.

Mildred's grandfather and uncle had both fought in the Civil War and, upon receiving their pay of "forty acres and a mule," purchased the land that would become Brookstown. Despite General William Sherman's failure to deliver on this promise to most Black people who were freed from slavery, my great-great-grandfather and his brother were among the relatively few African Americans to claim their hard-earned prize, due in great part to their war service. With the land, they established their own town, which included a school, livery, stable, church, general store, blacksmith shop, and suppliers of nearly all of the staples people needed during the late 1800s.

Mildred, whom we knew as Grandma Dee Dee, was born in 1898 in Kentucky. In her early years, her entire life experience was within the family's town, which instilled in her a strong family ethic. Residents were either a cousin, an aunt, an uncle, or someone who enjoyed a direct link to the Brooks. Everyone's survival depended upon each other; this cultivated deep relationships and strong family pride that my grandmother carried for the rest of her life.

Grandma Dee Dee often told us stories that were passed down from her mother—tales of life on plantations or indentured farms, where slaves or former slaves worked for the landowner. One story was about a cousin who was so tired of eating the scraps that the master threw at them, that one morning our cousin stole a chicken. For her supposed crime, they chopped off her finger!

My grandfather's experiences mirrored Grandma Dee Dee's and Cousin Clara's. We learned that, while his father had mysteriously deserted the family when my grandfather was about 12 years old, his close-knit extended family instilled a deep pride and belonging.

When my great-grandfather left his family, rumors spread that he had moved to another state, presumably Louisiana, and started a whole new family. While my grandfather never saw or heard from his father again, other family members moved in with his mother to fill the emotional and financial void. His father's absence made him self-reliant and very independent at a young age.

My mother's family was from Mississippi. Her mother, Josephine, was born in Durant, a small town of 1,700 people. She bore a very light complexion and could pass for white. This was typical of many Black people in the South whose mothers had either been raped by their slave owners or were the offspring of a hidden interracial love affair.

Josephine's mother, Ella, died when she was five years old and she was raised by her grandmother, my great-great-grandmother, Emma Ely. Emma Ely was born around 1860 and passed on stories to Josephine about how, after President Abraham Lincoln's assassination, people gathered in their house, crying earnest tears, as if a close family member had died. Though Emma Ely was only three or four years old, she never forgot the pain of that moment, primarily because most Black people always regarded Lincoln as "The Great Liberator" of slaves, when in truth, Black people's emancipation was a direct product of their having fought for centuries to be free.

My great-grandfather, Cyrus Sledge, was a Blacksmith in Durant, Mississippi, where he was born and where he met my grandmother.

Emma lived past her 100th birthday, dying in 1963, the same year Martin Luther King, Jr. organized the March on Washington for jobs and freedom, where he delivered his "I Have a Dream" speech. As kids, we enjoyed her stories, which provided us with a tangible connection to a time long since passed, when there were no cars, only horse-drawn buggies and Rough Riders on the Range, the first United States Volunteer Cavalry fighting the Spanish American War.

One can only imagine the changes that she saw over the course of her life—including the invention of commercial airplanes which she never experienced—from the early 1860s into the 1960s.

Emma Ely's daughter, Ella, grew up at a time in the South when Blacks and whites were deeply segregated, yet it was not unusual for some Black people to appear white because of the history of rape and abuse. Ella was a very beautiful young woman when she fell in love with a white European man and became pregnant. Interracial marriage was illegal. Fearing for his life, the man was forced to leave town and eventually left the country. Ella was so heartbroken that she never fully recovered, later dying when Josephine was six years old. Growing up as a white-looking Black girl in the Black community of Durant, Mississippi made Josephine a strong-willed and resilient woman, as was Emma Ely, who raised her.

Josephine met my grandfather, Roy Sledge, around 1920, during the Roaring Twenties, Prohibition and the reign of gangster Al Capone. The popular dance was the Charleston; Josephine loved it. Roy had a very dark complexion, and photographs of them together captured their contrast. Their skin color provoked comments rooted in colorism—favoring light skin over dark skin—within the Black community. Curtis Mayfield captured this sentiment in his song, "We People Who Are Darker Than Blue."

Josephine and Roy met in college. Roy attended the historical Black college, Fisk University, and Josephine attended a nearby university. They married around 1922, and my mother, Frances, was born in 1925.

At the time, many Black families were migrating to the North for a better quality of life. The Great Migration that began at the turn of the twentieth century made Chicago, Illinois a primary destination. My mother's parents sought this opportunity to leave the South and Mississippi to head to Chicago around the same time that my dad's parents were leaving Kentucky for the same reason.

As an only child, my mother became a very independent woman. Josephine would send her off to the store near their apartment when she was only five years old to pick up a gallon of milk, a pound of butter, or a bag of flour. On one trip when she was on her way to the store, a drunken man cornered her in the vestibule of their apartment and attempted to coerce her and offered her money. Luckily, she was smart enough to escape that situation. She recalls those experiences today as dangerous, but she was never a fearful girl. She had street-smarts at a very young age and always knew how to handle herself.

Josephine and Roy were struggling during this era, the Great Depression. The lives of Black folks were impacted significantly more than whites; Black people suffered the greatest unemployment rates and were often the first to be laid off—"last hired, first fired." The government launched public assistance programs that were often denied to Black people or provided substantially less aid. Many families were forced into poverty after the collapse of the stock market in 1927. There were long soup lines as people struggled to find food to eat.

One advantage they enjoyed as a Black couple was that my grandfather was one of the first Black cooks on the famous Great Northern Railway, also known as "The Empire Builder." The work was consistent, as the railroad was the nation's main transportation. So, while food, jobs, and everything else was scarce, and companies and businesses were going under, my Grandpa Roy maintained a steady job with a railroad company.

Roy worked the leg between Chicago and Seattle on The Empire Builder, along the same route we would later travel during my childhood when we lived in Seattle and visited relatives back in Chicago. When Roy was riding the train, the cars were segregated. The route carried him from Chicago through the majestic landscapes of the Midwest, where he became acquainted with the Minnesota skyline, spectacular views of the

Mississippi River, the wilderness of the North Dakota plains, the Big Sky country of Montana, past the Glacier National Park into Spokane, Washington, then finally into Seattle, where my family currently maintains connections.

Once he had arrived in Seattle and finished his shift, he sped to the Black jazz clubs, where a good time was all but guaranteed. Afterwards, he trekked back to Chicago, only to repeat the same trip over and over again.

My Grandpa Roy was a loving, quick-witted man, but he also had a temper and wouldn't take guff from anyone. One particular evening, he had served dinner and was emerging from the dining car, heading back towards the kitchen, when suddenly a white girl of about 12 years old stood in front of him.

"Nigger!" she yelled.

He slapped her. Before the racist onlookers could exact retribution, his work buddies quickly escorted him from the train. He was spared the worst type of retribution, since many Black men met their fate at the hands of lynch mobs for seemingly more innocuous acts. Surprisingly, he also maintained his job on the railroad, and he continued to work through the end of that leg on another train.

Hearing the N-word was not an uncommon occurrence in the South. However, he was not one to just lie down and take it or turn the other cheek. According to my mother, when he was a young boy in Mississippi, his family was often forced to send him to visit relatives in the North, out of fear that he would be lynched for these everyday forms of racial protest. But that was his nature, and he refused the type of racial subordination white southerners expected from most Black people. He refused to be disrespected. None of us kids ever witnessed that side of him, because by the time we were born, much of his feistiness had dissipated. He was much calmer now that he had rediscovered his Bible and his Chicago White Sox.

During the Depression, my grandmother, Josephine, relied upon her light complexion to secure work at one of Chicago's finest downtown restaurants, where wealthy white businessmen, doctors, and lawyers who came for lunch every day simply assumed that she was white, too. They tipped her extremely well, matching nearly dollar for dollar the tips my grandfather earned in tips on the train. Though it must have been a huge stretch for them to save during the 1930s, they were resourceful; spending their regular income on the basics, they placed their tips in a big jar to save for their first home.

Despite the hardships of the Depression, by the 1940s, Chicago's Black community was booming. Specifically, the city's South Side bustled with businesses of all kinds, many of them Black. By the 1950s, this large industrial town morphed into the second largest city in the United States, due in great part to the large concentration of Blacks who migrated from the South. Englewood, where my grandparents lived, was also a lively neighborhood of businesses that included meat markets, clothing stores, bakeries, nightclubs, barber shops, florists, beauty parlors, and jook joints. Today, a huge Black population remains on the West Side and South Side of Chicago, although many of those businesses are long gone.

My pops attended Englewood High School, where he met some of his lifelong buddies. They formed a group, calling themselves the Four Feathers, a name they borrowed from the Four Horsemen of Notre Dame football players, who attended the university during the 1920s. They made a commitment to each other to stick together through thick and thin and to always observe some honor code that they established. They designed a symbol with the number four and a feather over it, and rocked varsity-like sweaters with this emblem emblazoned on the front. This was their way of being initiated into the group and committing to each other. When the Japanese bombed Pearl

Harbor in 1941, they all rushed down to the Army recruitment center and signed up together, unlike many men who waited to be drafted. As with the many African American men and women who fought in America's wars, they were eager to fight for their country and defend democracy.

Upon receiving his assignment for boot camp, my father misread the state abbreviation "MS" for Missouri. When he later realized he was bound for Mississippi instead, his heart sank. At the time, Mississippi's brutal racism manifested in segregation, the KKK's reign of terror, and the lynching of Black men.

The Army assigned him to an all-Black regiment, The Fighting 54th, which was not unusual, since Army units had yet to be desegregated. Upon completing basic training, he learned that he would be deployed to the South Pacific, but before then, his regiment was afforded the opportunity to march through a Mississippi town to be cheered off to war.

Instead of flying banners and lightly tossing confetti towards their troop, the crowd jeered at them, spat on them, and even threw feces at them.

"You're cowards!" they shouted.

"You niggers will never fight!"

My father never allowed virulent racism to make him hate white people. He viewed the world through a lens of right and wrong, not Black and White. Once, while his division was advancing through the Philippines, they came across a white regiment that had just overrun a village.

A white soldier had sliced off a woman's breast and held it up on his bayonet. Lifting his gun and aiming it directly at the man, my father demanded that he cease his nefarious activities. It is likely that my dad would have been court martialed for killing another soldier, if it were not for his friends who ushered him away.

While serving overseas, my father fell in love with a Japanese woman named Mioko. He spent time with her family, but returned to his base to avoid going A.W.O.L., before returning to the States. He shared this experience with many American soldiers who relieved the isolation and lack of familiarity in a distant, foreign land by dating and oftentimes marrying someone who reminded them of home and the kindness that still existed in the world.

The relationship between my father and Mioko was brief, as fate had other plans for my dad and my mother. Shortly after returning to Chicago in 1944, my father was immediately swept off his feet, and my mother soon became the love of his life. A very beautiful woman with long flowing hair and soft brown eyes, she could have been the next Dorothea Towles or Sarah Lou Harris, two of the most popular African American models in the 1940s and 1950s. On several occasions, one of her friends did photograph her for some publications, but her modeling career stopped there. Despite this, when we discovered the photos of her as young children, we were certain that our mother was a supermodel.

YOUNG FAMILY LIFE

Soon after my parents married, their first child, Karen, died from a premature birth. After my parents recovered from the trauma of losing their firstborn, my mother gave birth to Joanne in 1947. At the time, my parents lived in Chicago with my mother's parents because they were both still in school and couldn't afford their own place. After becoming pregnant with my brother, Aaron, it was time to find a place of their own.

Living with my mother's parents was difficult for both of them, as my grandmother could be very controlling, and she wasn't sure if she liked my father, anyway. By the time I came along, my father had finally graduated from the Art Institute of Chicago, which meant the possibility of gaining work as a draftsman in Champaign County, Illinois, at the Chanute Air Force Base, where the first all-Black fighter squadron, and the first unit of the Tuskegee Airmen, was activated in 1941. Finally, my parents could afford their own home.

While my dad worked, my mom remained at home, which, in many ways, was a luxury for Black couples attempting to make ends meet for a family of five. They were just barely scraping by when my mother became pregnant with my younger brother, Michael. My parents sent me to Chicago to stay with Grandma Josephine, whom we simply called "Ma," while our grandfather was "Bop-bop," until my younger brother was born. Three children were overwhelming, so Ma offered to take me because I was the youngest and the easiest to handle. I was only two or three, but I recall being spoiled by my maternal grandparents as if I were an only child. Having had only one child herself, she heaped her adoring praises on this little grandchild living in her home.

Ma was much older, and she didn't look at all like my mother, whom I missed so terribly. I was searching for someone who could be like her. I found her in my grandmother's next-door neighbor, Marge Lewis. My mother was so beautiful that I must have responded with adoration when I first encountered Marge's pretty face. She had high cheekbones, long flowing hair, and soft brown eyes like my mother. She immediately felt familiar and reminded me of my mother. Years later, my grandmother revealed how I often peered through the chain-link fence at Marge as she dug in her garden and snipped at flowers.

"When I grow up, I'm going to marry you," I naively declared to her. I imagine that, much like my father, I was set upon marrying the most beautiful woman in the world. It was almost as if I was in search of my future mate in that early stage of my life.

When I returned home, I met my younger brother for the first time. Bubbly and round, Michael now replaced me as the youngest. He was often the object of our teasing, but only in a playful way. Custom demanded that we taunt the newest sibling. My mother said I had tantrums because I was no longer the center of attention.

Once, we were playing boogeyman, and it was Michael's turn to be the monster. He had a blanket over his head and Aaron and I snuck down the concrete stairs as Michael was coming after us. At the time, we lived in a housing project called Birch Village, which contained endless rows of brick-faced buildings, fortified internally by concrete that threatened the arms, knees, and heads of children who were aggressively at play.

"Raaahhhhh!" Michael yelled while creeping around the corner, unaware that he was dangerously close to the stairwell.

Plop! He bounced and rolled all the way down to the bottom, as Aaron and I imagined the worst.

"Waaahhhhhh!" he shrieked at the top of his lungs. I was sure that he lay dying, and we both panicked at the thought of the whooping we most certainly would endure after we informed our parents that our brother was dead. Fortunately, Michael's screams were more of a performance than anything. Rushing to the bottom of the stairwell, we immediately tugged at his shirt and trousers, trying to determine the extent of his injuries. He was completely fine. *Whew!* We never told our parents that they almost had one less mouth to feed, but we later joked that the stairs had a chip in it from his hard head.

My mother probably doesn't recall us ever living in a so-called housing project, but that's how it looked to us kids. The three-bedroom apartment was in a public housing complex, where middle-class Blacks lived. At the time, it worked for our expanding family.

Like their parents and grandparents before them, my parents were all about family, and they made sure that we had a strong foundation. For example, at dinnertime, it was important that we all ate together at the same table. My father or mother would always grace the table and we all had to say a small verse or blessing.

Each kid had to say a verse before we could eat.

"Dear Jesus," I sometimes said, "as we bow our heads before our food, we thank you now. Amen."

I often rebelled against the vegetables that seemed to mock me from my plate. I refused to eat brussels sprouts, okra, or rutabaga. Since my parents insisted that I not waste even a crumb, given how hard they worked to provide for us, I often sat at the table for what seemed like hours after dinner was over, refusing to eat my vegetables. It may have actually been only minutes, but it seemed like a lifetime.

After school on Fridays, we frequently headed to the drive-in movies. That was always a special treat for us. My mother prepared pot pies or some other dinner that we then devoured in between our favorite movies. Oh, how I loved the Swanson's TV dinners! In those days, it was actually real food on the metal trays, and the taste of a Swanson's chicken pot pie is something that lingers in my memory decades later.

After church on Sundays, we typically visited a large park that had a maze of tall hedges where we played hide-and-seek. In the summers, we gathered for picnics, delighting in the taste of fried chicken, potato salad, and lemonade. Holidays also represented a special time in our house. My father especially loved the fall and winter holidays. On Thanksgiving, the family took the two-hour drive back to Chicago, where we spent time with my father's parents, Gratdada and Grandma Dee Dee. My other grandparents usually joined us, along with other extended family members. We spent Christmases at home in Champaign, where we eagerly anticipated the colorful giftboxes arriving from Chicago, along with the assortment of presents our parents handed to us. On Easter, we accompanied my mom downtown to buy special clothes for the occasion, including shiny new suits and dresses, which made us feel like were on display to the world.

When I was five, our mother returned to work and left us

at a preschool called "The Tot Lot." Around this time, I was hospitalized with pneumonia, probably from playing outside without a coat. Winters in Chicago and Champaign were hard. Sometimes snowstorms left snow piled up so high that when we walked through the neighborhood, we couldn't see over the top of the snow drifts. Other times I felt as if my tiny fingers would freeze off.

"I had to sneak into the hospital check on you," my mother recalls. "I couldn't let you see me, because if you caught even a glimpse of me or your father, you were despondent."

Hospital felt so much like jail, with the bars flanking the crib as if I were in prison. I just knew that I didn't like the joint, and I wanted to escape. The second time I went to the hospital, I had an operation for a double hernia. I remember going under with the ether after the nurse put the cup over my mouth and nose.

"Just blow to keep that large plastic ball from falling too close to your lips," she said. I eventually passed out. Again, it felt like I was in a little prison. Of course, at five years old, I didn't know what a prison felt like, but I just knew that I couldn't escape.

After graduating from preschool, I started first grade at Lawhead Elementary, feeling like I belonged with the bigger kids, who included my sister Joanne and brother Aaron. Michael was still the little guy at home, or in Tot Lot. I found several new friends in class and enjoyed the new classroom environment as learning felt more fun. But there were still those times when I was defiant and on one of those occasions, I remember doing something at home that got me in trouble with my mom.

"I'm going to tell your dad when he gets home," she said. That was alarming because our dad didn't take any nonsense. When we got in trouble, we paid the price. On this particular occasion, I wasn't waiting around for him to come home and get me with the belt, so I stuffed my pants with books and paper, anything I could, because I knew the belt would be coming. When he got home and saw that my little pants were stuffed with books and paper, he laughed so hard that he couldn't spank me and just told me not to do that ever again. This was the beginning of a long run of experiences with me testing the limits and boundaries.

At the same time, our father often played with us as if he were directing a military drill. Poppy, as we called him, lined us up in the kitchen and gave us each a broom or mop. Then he conducted a drill as if we were in the Army. This was part of his military training from World War II. He did this in a playful way, but it was always in preparation for us to do domestic work. We had our part in keeping the house clean, doing the dishes, and pitching in.

He lined up me, Aaron, and Michael in the small kitchen.

"Alright, here's your rifle," he said, handing me a broom.

"Here's your rifle," he announced, giving a mop to Aaron, and something small to Michael.

"Attention!" he said. "Stand straight. Rest your gun on your shoulder. And get your feet right," he added, demonstrating a military stance as we looked down at our own feet to imitate him.

Also holding a broom as a gun, he spun it around like a rifle and rested it on his shoulder.

"Attention!"

It was fun and serious all at once, and he clearly enjoyed passing on his military training and discipline to his three sons. (When our father died in 1985, my brothers and I stood in line, at attention, and saluted him at his graveside service, the same way he taught us in the kitchen when we were small boys.) After we mastered our complete rifle drill, which included flipping it, we marched upstairs with our little rifles.

"Alright troops," our father, the pretend sergeant, said, "it's time to make the beds! Here's the proper way a soldier makes a bed."

He demonstrated. "Those sheets have to be tight. Make the blankets tight with no wrinkles. Don't be sloppy."

Then he pulled a quarter from his pocket. "Now, Private, it's inspection time."

He tested our skills by trying to bounce a quarter off the bed; if the blanket was not taut enough, the coin would not bounce. We perfected the military style of making beds that I continue to this day.

My last recollection of Champaign was an oncoming tornado. One day while we were playing out in the front yard, the garbage can lids suddenly began flying around. My mother came running outside and exclaimed, "A tornado is coming!" We looked off into the distance; twisters were forming. We needed to get inside. Fortunately, the housing project apartments were made of concrete and served as a natural storm shelter from tornadoes. This made those old housing projects seem much more sturdy and sound, and being with my sister, brothers, and mother made me feel all the more safe.

Even though Michael and I were younger than Aaron, he easily made friends with a bunch of older, tough kids who also lived in Birch Village. Aaron showed me around, educating me about the neighborhood code and about places that were fair game to venture, and others that, for a number of reasons, may have proven dangerous. In particular, the playground area contained a series of round, concrete sewer piping. Apparently, these seemingly medieval devices were there for kids to play. "Why does it smell like pee in here?" I wondered, referring to the scent of urine and calling attention to the disparities that plagued many Black neighborhoods and children who desired the same resources as many of their white counterparts. Obviously, kids were doing stuff in there that they shouldn't have been, but it was a totally new environment to me, so we just held our noses and played games inside the pipings.

We also loved to play near the railroad tracks behind the complex, another place that remained off limits as far as our parents were concerned. But we didn't know any better! One afternoon, we were out playing near the tracks, and I found a dead kitten. Excited, I carried it home to my mom and held it out to her. "Look, I found a kitty!" She was as unimpressed as she was unbothered. But those were normal things we kids did back then—make mud pies and eat them, and bring home dead kitties.

This was a deadly world for Black males, I learned, when a 14-year-old boy from our neighborhood named Emmett Till traveled to Money, Mississippi, and was brutally tortured and murdered for allegedly smiling at a white woman. The white men who killed him on August 24th, 1955, tossed his body into the Tallahatchie River. They were acquitted by an all-white jury. Emmett's murder made global headlines after his mother kept his casket open at his funeral in Chicago for all the world to see how those men had disfigured his face.

My father, who grew up in that neighborhood, wrote a poem about the murder. It was published in the local Black newspaper and I saw it years later.

The Poem My Father Wrote After Emmett Till's Murder

Deep in the heart of Dixie
Where the cotton blooms in June
An old black man tills the field
Humming a sad tune.

His heart was heavy, his eyes were full
His body aching and sore
I wish I was dead, I wish I was dead
My heart can't take no more.

They took a little Negro boy
And chopped and smashed his eye
They tormented, teased, and cut him up
Just to make him die.

They tore off an ear, when he shed a tear
And they beat him in the face
Each mark and scar was symbolic of suffering
By the Negro race.

They threw him in the river
His hands and legs all bound.
Hoping that his body
Never would be found.

The river current surged and splashed
To free its mangled prey
But it didn't matter anymore
For it was Emmett's Judgment Day.

The two White men who did these things
Are free to lynch and kill
Now my God I pray to you
Avenge poor Emmett Till.

The hate and evil in this world
Is something sad to see
Why Oh Lord do they hate us so
Why can't we all be free?

The children played on the courtroom floor
The grownups drank cold beer
They laughed and joked, and enjoyed themselves,
Like they had no God to fear.

I'll never forget you, Emmett Till
And how you horribly died
I'll never forget the smiling jurors
And how the lawyers lied.

Well Emmett's gone, ain't nothing to do
But push this White man's plow
I guess little Emmett's made his peace
'Cause he's with his father now.

— Elmer Dixon, Jr.

The murder of Emmett Till galvanized Black people and anti-racist activists nationwide to protest inequality and injustice, segregation, and oppression. This gave rise to the Civil Rights Movement led by Dr. Martin Luther King, Jr.

CHAPTER 2

The Move West–The Fantastic Journey

In 1957, the Little Rock Nine—students seeking a better education in segregated Arkansas—enrolled at Little Rock Central High School, whose student population had been entirely white until then. Three years earlier, the U.S. Supreme Court decision *Brown v. the Board of Education of Topeka, Kansas* had ruled segregated public schooling unconstitutional.

But that decision was not honored by the mob of white people who shouted, threw stones, and threatened to kill the Little Rock Nine as they entered Central High School.

This was the backdrop in America as we were leaving Champaign, and the state of Illinois altogether, when I was seven years old. I had just completed the first grade when my parents decided we would move across the country to Seattle, Washington. Poppy was always looking for a better job than Illinois could offer, and he was secretly looking for an excuse to escape his mother-in-law. So, when a job opportunity came for him to work for Boeing in Seattle, he took it. It was a good job opportunity, one that was bringing many Black families to the Pacific Northwest.

He had considered taking a job back in Hawaii, where he had been stationed for a time during his Army service, but Hawaii was too far for my mother. So instead, we were off to the Pacific Northwest, the "Evergreen State," to the far-away city of Seattle. And so began the next chapter of my life of fun; I call it The Fantastic Journey. This move was exciting for us children. We had never been outside of Illinois, not even Champaign except to visit Chicago, which was enormous and seemed to stretch on forever.

As we packed all our belongings into our 1952 Dodge and a Mayflower moving van, my father beamed with excitement. He had always wanted to travel the globe, and this move felt like leaving the edge of the earth—and all things familiar—into a great, uncharted frontier.

Before heading west, we drove to Chicago to say goodbye to the family, grandparents, and cousins.

Poppy had mapped out the journey across the country, and what may have been a two- or three-day drive became two weeks. He was so excited to be on the road, he wanted to stop and see everything along the way. We took the "Great Road West," which was I-90, up through Milwaukee, then over to Minnesota as we passed by the Twin Cities.

"I had so much fun visiting here as a girl," our mother said, sharing stories that included the high school prom. "I had to become very independent, out of necessity, and I made a lot of decisions on my own, like picking my own prom dress and getting there without any help. That just made me stronger and all the more self-reliant."

We drove through long stretches of highways while listening to Top 40 hits on rural radio stations. The lull of "Tammy" by Debbie Reynolds laid the foundation of my lifelong musical odyssey, as songs and music genres began to characterize every phase of my life.

Picnic stops, motels, and fast food highlighted our trip. We were eating BIG. One place in South Dakota had giant hamburgers. I swear, as a kid, they were as big as my head. We washed them down with giant fries and milkshakes. I had just left the first grade, so the excitement of this adventure and the unknown helped me forget that I was leaving friends—especially my closest buddy, Eric—behind in Champaign. Aaron had a harder time leaving friendships that he had developed over two years in school together and on the playgrounds.

I was convinced we were in the scene of a Western movie when we stopped in the South Dakota Badlands, a vast wilderness in the middle of the Dakotas. One can look out on the sprawling jagged hills and mountains and envision Cochise or Geronimo evading the U.S. Military. Geronimo was a great Apache warrior and hero to his people, who fought over a 30-year period and attacked the U.S. military at every turn, frustrating them to no end.

We drove on to Keystone to see the Mount Rushmore National Memorial. Presidents Washington, Jefferson, Roosevelt, and Lincoln were in a much more raw state, carved into the granite face of the mountain. In 1957, the park was not commercialized and built up; it stood alone as a monument in its raw majesty. The only thing missing was Chief Crazy Horse, who is now among those carved into the mountains of South Dakota. Leaving the granite faces, the highway cut through the rock mountain near Mount Rushmore. For children who had never left Illinois, the splendor and vastness of the United States was magical.

When we reached Montana, we marveled at the openness and the path that laid before us as we climbed up through the Rocky Mountains. This was scary for my mother, but thrilling for my brothers and me. We had never seen mountains before, not like these. Unfortunately, the old Dodge couldn't take the climbs, and broke down. We had to stay in a small Montana town for several days while repairs were done.

One afternoon, Poppy walked downtown to get a drink at a bar, and we followed him. But what he found wasn't a bar, it was a saloon! We hung out outside as he entered the swinging doors for a drink. We kept peeking underneath the doors to see what happens in a saloon. It, again, was a real novelty and felt like we were in a Western movie. Poppy had only been in there a little while but was then challenged by some guy, likely because he was Black, and by this man's estimation, did not belong in that saloon.

In my childhood imagination, it was like in the 1953 Western movie, *Shane*, where the kid is looking into the saloon as Shane gets into a gun fight; I watched as if I expected my father to have a Colt .45 on his hip, but whoop the dude with his fist like Shane did. The guy eventually backed off, Poppy came out, and that was it. We had some similar encounters as we passed through the Midwest, but nothing dampened our spirits on our adventure as explorers across the country.

We finally emerged from Montana and Idaho into the state of Washington. The first town in the eastern part of the state was Spokane, which had no large buildings and featured the Spokane River flowing through it. Little did I know, as we stopped and ate our typical fare of hamburgers, fries, and milkshakes, that I was in the hometown of my future wife.

The next phase of our great western adventure took us into the desert, where rolling tumbleweeds ignited my imagination, as did the petrified forest, filled with hardened, dark, dead trees. I envisioned riding horseback with my brothers, either chasing bad guys or escaping from a bank robbery. We passed through Ellensburg, Washington, home of the Ellensburg rodeo, then headed up to Snoqualmie Pass, where the mountains were beautiful. As we emerged on the other side, we saw a huge mountain—bigger than any mountain we had ever seen. It was Mount Rainier. My father named it Sugar Lump, a name that would stick with us kids for the rest of our lives.

When we rolled into Seattle during the summer of 1957, this "city" with lots of hills and no tall buildings seemed silly from my childhood perception. Chicago, with its skyscrapers and endless streets, was a city. But Seattle had only one tall building—The Smith Tower building standing alone on the horizon amongst five- to ten-story buildings. (The Space Needle was not yet built.)

Still, I felt excited to explore.

CHAPTER 3

Settling In

We had no place to stay in Seattle. Having just left the segregated reality of Chicago and needing to find a safe place to stay in a Black neighborhood, Poppy asked some Black folks he met for guidance on where to live.

"There's a couple down on Hiawatha Place who have an apartment downstairs in their home that they could rent to you temporarily," they told my father.

We went there with the intention of staying only a few nights until we found a permanent place. But that first night, we realized we weren't alone in the place: it had roaches.

"We're getting out of here," my mother said. We moved to a motel on Highway 99, then found an apartment on Hiawatha Place down the street from the nasty old house, which was just behind Rainier Avenue. My parents rented this apartment from a Japanese landlord, who was a bit of a slumlord because the building was pretty run down. But as kids, we didn't notice. All we knew was that our family was together and we had food on the table every day. We didn't think of ourselves as poor.

Hiawatha Place was on the border of the Central District, the community where most of the Black population had migrated. Seattle's population was about 10 percent Black; we lived in a mostly Black and Asian area with very few whites.

After WWII, Black people were moving further west and north in search of new jobs. Because so many came from the South, people kept asking my mother:

"What part of the South are you from?" She found that funny, as she had grown up in Chicago and had no southern accent.

When migrating to Seattle, Blacks didn't face blatant discrimination, but were not given the same job opportunities and were often led away from buying homes in white neighborhoods. We didn't know it at the time, but this was redlining, a deliberate segregating of Black and other people of color away from white communities. These practices shaped why Seattle's Central District was home to almost 80 percent of the city's Black population.

Behind our apartment building was a big alleyway, and on the other side were businesses that faced Rainier Avenue. These included a little restaurant and a small corner store selling simple groceries. We quickly found our way around.

We could walk to Coleman Elementary School, where I met my first best friend in Seattle. Eddie Leon was one of the tougher kids in second grade.

"Don't mess with the older kids," Eddie warned, "and stay with the students in your grade." Our friendship grew quickly and we became very close. Eddie helped me identify the bullies; on the playground, I could rely on him if I got into a pinch.

Across the street was Coleman Park—a big, dirt playfield surrounded by trees and bushes all the way around the block. We used to pretend that was our little jungle hideout.

We played marbles on the playground, where we could get down on the ground and draw a big circle in the dirt, and put our marbles in the middle of the pot. Everybody had their best marbles that we named. The best shooters were the Bowlies and Steelies; they could knock an opponent's marbles out of the circle. The Cat Eyes and Pearlies were the most prized. Every marble was described by its look, like Beach Ball, Devil Eye, Red Devils, or Pearlies. I guarded my Bowlies with care, because those are your biggest marbles. If you rolled it into the pot, it could knock five or six marbles out at once. Anything you knocked out of the big circle, you got to keep, because we played "keepsies." But if your Bowlie got stuck in the pot, and knocked out by another larger Bowlie, you would lose your best weapon. Playing keepsies meant they could keep your marbles and you would lose. But there was always the opportunity to trade at the end. The games we played were a sort of rite of passage, allowing us to understand the rules of this new neighborhood and be accepted as one of the group.

While in second grade, I had a crush on a Japanese girl in my class, Susan Nakamura. As it turned out, we attended the same high school years later. Of course, she didn't pay me any attention and she didn't know my name from Adam, but I thought she was cute. It was the first time I'd ever liked a girl other than my mother or Mrs. Lewis in Chicago. She wouldn't talk to us, probably because we were boys and she was more concerned with her girlfriends and her studies. Girls were sweet; I told myself, "Man, I never want to make a girl cry."

When we were walking home on the last day of school, I had been conspiring with Eddie to try to kiss Susan on the cheek. We took the same route home, so when I had my chance, I eased up behind her and prepared to launch my kiss. Before I knew it, someone pushed me from behind and I bumped her. She fell and started crying. She was the first girl I was sweet on, and I ended up making her cry. That made me feel bad about the whole plan and decided girls were too much trouble at this point.

We had our first Christmas in Seattle on Hiawatha Place, and while it may have been in that old creaky apartment, it was home and it didn't matter to us because we were with our family. We reminisced about our time in Champaign, especially visiting the park, and I longed for those outings.

We started meeting people in our small, diverse neighborhood known as Hiawatha Place. The Ashuk family was Russian, and their daughter, Toma, attended school with my sister Joanne and they became good friends. Toma and her mother spoke very little English because they were probably recent immigrants. As her mother spoke to her in this strange-sounding language, I wondered what she was saying, and was enthralled hearing it for the first time. Across the street were the Liggetts, a large Black family who had recently come from the South. Down the block were Fred and Mary Mayo, who would become my parents' lifelong friends. They had three sons, Duke, Raphael, and Junior.

We played after school at a little community center called the Atlantic Street Center, which was run by Ike Ikeda, who welcomed kids from all over the neighborhood. There, we learned how to get along with kids from different backgrounds. Years later, it would become the site of one of the Party's first Children's Free Breakfast Programs.

During our first summer in Seattle, in 1958, my aunt, Doris, my father's sister, came out to visit us from Chicago. She brought our cousins, Mark and Keith.

"You need to get out of this apartment," she told my father.

We moved 10 blocks to the east, up to 24th Avenue and Charles Street; our home was a four-block walk to school. Living on 24th Avenue for the next two years, I made lifelong friends, including Ronald Bolton, known as Bonnie, and his older brother and sister, Cornelius and Shirley. Cornelius was the oldest, several years older than us, and Shirley was the same age as Joanne.

Bonnie was Michael's age, a couple years younger than me. I was eight; he was five or six. I became good friends with his siblings, and our parents struck up a great relationship with one another. To this day, Bonnie and I celebrate a close friendship spanning more than 60 years.

Next door to the Boltons' house lived Mr. Santos. His son was a famous baseball player for the Chicago Cubs. Being from Chicago, we of course knew who Ron Santos was! It was pretty cool to have Ron Santos' dad living across the street. He grew tomatoes in his backyard and his was one of the yards that we respected in the neighborhood. We didn't go messing with his tomatoes! Although, the other yards in the neighborhood didn't get the same respect.

We helped ourselves to luscious peaches in the trees one guy had in his yard. Several homes on that block had huge cherry trees. During the summer, we crept around in the middle of the night, plucking those cherries and filling our bags. Our neighborhood was largely Black, with a few Asians here and there.

Rather than walking six blocks to the park, we played football in the middle of the street. We played with a kid around the corner on Norman Street named Eric, who was friends with my older brother, Aaron, and Bonnie's older brother, Cornelius. One day, I was doing my impersonation of Gale Sayers, a famous Chicago Bears player, and when I tried to juke this guy, he tackled me face down with my arms pinned around me. I landed on my face and chipped my tooth. Furious, I ran into the house crying. I found my father's hammer, ran back into the street, and chased this dude all the way home. He was a much bigger, but I was going to get him with that hammer for breaking my tooth!

When it came to eating, if you walked in the door with a candy bar that you didn't want to share, you would have to proclaim, "Ban bites!" before someone could ask for a bite. As long as you said, "Ban bites" first, then nobody could get any. In our family if you saw something on someone's plate and it looked like they weren't going to eat it, and nobody said "ban bites," then it was fair game to snatch it! We learned this rule from the neighborhood, and Michael was a master at it. If we each had a piece of pie, we would gobble ours down while Michael saved his for later. Then while we were watching TV and craving something sweet, he'd be over in his little chair eating his pie one bite at a time, after warning, "Ban bites!"

One Sunday evening, my mother prepared pork chops for dinner. We gobbled ours up and Michael saved his pork chops. It was okay with my parents if you saved your dinner to eat later that evening, but not overnight. Michael tucked his pork chop sandwich under his pillow that night and the next day he had brought it downstairs, nibbling on it, teasing me and Aaron by saying, "Ban bites!" But when he set his sandwich on the counter in the TV room and looked away, Aaron took a few bites. I was about to take a bite, but I didn't have enough time, so I just got a quick nibble. Michael was furious!

"They ate my food!" he told our parents.

"You shouldn't have that thing anyway," they said.

Sure enough, later that day at school, Michael and Aaron were vomiting with food poisoning. They were sent home. During the four-block walk to our house, Michael was so sick that he passed out on the street curb and a stranger ended up carrying him all the way up to our house. Later, I felt so lucky that I didn't get a full bite of that pork chop sandwich.

RACISM IN THE JOB MARKET

When we first moved to Seattle, my mother stayed home with us. After we got settled, she started looking for employment.

"I'm calling to see if the job advertised in the newspaper is still available," she told the person who answered the phone at a company that said it was hiring.

"Yes, we are," they said.

My mother went to the company to apply for the job.

"What do you want?" the receptionist asked.

"I'm here to apply for the job I saw in the newspaper," she said.

"That job has been filled," the receptionist said.

My mother left, went to a phone booth, and called again, saying, "Hello, I'd like to know if the job listed in the newspaper is still available."

"Yes, come down and apply," the same receptionist said.

My mother returned.

"What are you doing here?" the clerk asked.

"You can't tell me that the job is not available because I just called for a second time, and you told me that it was still open," my mother said.

She was hired. The bottom line was that she sounded white over the phone, and they did not want to hire a Black person. Yes, we were in the North, which had no Jim Crow laws. But racism festered even in the progressive city of Seattle.

CHAPTER 4

Return to the Windy City

By the summer of 1959, we were ready to head back to Chicago for a long-anticipated visit. It didn't seem like two years since we last saw our grandparents, but indeed two years was far too long. So, the trip was planned as a cross-country adventure by train. My father would not come for the first part of this trip due to his job, so my mother was going to have to manage the four of us kids by herself. Everyone was excited to see the family. For me, that not only included my grandparents, and in particular, Ma, my mother's mother, but also my cousins, Mark and Keith.

We were so excited to take our first train trip for this 2,000-mile, cross-country journey. Poppy helped us get our bags on the train and while he was saying goodbye and giving final instructions or advice to my mother, we scouted out the rest of the train, including upstairs in the Dome Car. These seats were first-come, first-served, so we staked out our luxury view seats. They really weren't luxury seats, but to us as kids, they were luxurious compared to the 1952 car.

The train finally started moving and we settled in our seats, then eagerly made our way to the dining car, which was something to behold. In those days, it was like being in a restaurant. My mother discovered upon entering the car that one of her college buddies, perhaps a boyfriend or close acquaintance, was working in the dining car. This was a huge bonus for us kids because whether or not he was trying to impress my mother, his offer to let us eat just about anything we wanted made a huge impression. We often snuck into the dining car to find "Gordie."

"Can we have a snack or a treat?" we asked.

"Try this!" he said, holding out plates of Empire Builder pancakes—named for our route—and they were as big as a plate, thick and moist, all covered with whipped cream and syrup. I was in seventh heaven.

As we traveled along the tracks up in the Dome Car, it was like being in a fantasy world. It had a glass encapsulated ceiling that offered unobstructed views of the sky, the countryside, the mountains, and lakes. When nightfall came, we waited until everything settled down, Mommy was asleep and the Porter had made his last rounds. Then we would sneak up into the Dome Car to watch the world pass by under the stars. You are not supposed to sleep in the Dome Car, but we snuck our blankets up, curled up in the seats, and fell asleep under the moonlit sky. The sky, at first, was dark blue, but as we rolled away from the city lights, the night lit up with a million stars. It was like being out in the galaxy traveling through space.

By the time we arrived in Chicago, we had been traveling for more than two days. When we got off the train, our legs were vibrating as if we were still moving across the tracks. That sensation lasted a whole day. Ma and Bop-bop picked us up from the train station. My mother had always called our grandmother Ma, but Joanne, as the first grandchild, had anointed my grandfather with the name Bop-bop. I couldn't wait to get reacquainted with their home—a large house, grand in style, and spotless.

Ma laid down the house rules as we explored every nook and cranny. But one room was off-limits: the living room, or parlor. The furniture was very neat and tidy and covered in fitted plastic covers to prevent anyone from spilling anything on them, something popular during the 1950s and '60s. Near the living room, I was fascinated by my grandfather's mahogany wood desk that was in perfect, shiny condition. It had a fold-down top and served as a curio cabinet. My grandfather lowered the desktop and let me sit in his chair. He showed me where he kept his fountain pen and the inkwell along with his stationery and envelopes for writing letters; it was all so perfect.

The next room, directly behind the living room, was the dining room, which contained his TV set and his easy chair where he watched his favorite team, the Chicago White Sox. In the back of the house was a sunroom, which served as a breakfast nook. It contained a daybed where my grandfather slept. We didn't think much of the fact that he slept in a separate area; we just thought that was where he was supposed to sleep.

Upstairs, we finally got to see where we and our mother would sleep: in the huge front bedroom that contained several beds. The next bedroom over was occupied by a boarder, Mr. Mason. It wasn't unusual for homeowners to take in boarders back then to help pay for the mortgage. Mr. Mason was a nice man who was neat and clean, which of course was a requirement for my grandmother for him to live in her home. In the hallway closet was a small refrigerator where Mr. Mason kept his own items, including bottles of Coca-Cola. It came in small, green bottles that were ice cold. If you drank it too fast, it fizzed up your nose, causing a freezing sensation. We, of course, were not allowed to go into the refrigerator and touch his things.

"Can we please have a Coke?" we often asked.

He always obliged. We liked Mr. Mason.

In the back bedroom was where my grandmother slept with our great-great-grandmother, Grandma Ely. Everyone called her Grandma, including my mother. She was a very strong-willed woman who had survived four husbands. She had six children, one of whom was my grandmother Ma's mother, Ella.

She came from a large family. Her sister had 12 children, most of whom lived well into their nineties and into their hundreds. She was a laundress for most of her life and ran it as her own business. Many Black women at the time not only survived, but thrived, owning their own businesses doing other people's laundry.

Many days, she sat in her rocking chair on the front porch, as all of us great-great-grandkids sat at her feet, listening to her stories.

"When I was 15," she said, "American Indians kidnapped me out of a covered wagon. They returned me, though."

Here was where we heard the story about President Lincoln getting shot, in the context of her being born into slavery in 1860.

"I remember my family weeping like he was a relative," she told us.

Her living history lessons made her life seem surreal and fascinating to us. Someone who had survived slavery and the Civil War as a child, lived through the Mexican-American War in the early 20th century, World Wars I and II, and saw the transition from horse and buggy and covered wagons to the first automobile, the *Titanic*, and eventually the first airplane (which she never flew on), and the start of the Civil Rights Movement.

"She refers to herself as Black," our mother told us. "Not Negro, not Colored, but Black." This was something that would not become popular again until the Black Power Movement of the 1960s.

Outliving four husbands, and having eight children, she knew the power of the mind.

"I had cancer in the late 1940s," she told us. "I started the treatment but then I said, 'I don't need this.' I walked away from those treatments and the cancer went away."

My father's parents lived around the corner from Ma and Bop-bop, and we had a ball running out of Ma's house to Grandma Dee Dee's stately house. It had a formal entryway and you had to pass through a second door to enter the grand foyer. To the right was the parlor or living room, and while we could not run willy-nilly through the house, this was a much less formal atmosphere. We could enter the living room at our leisure as long as we didn't touch anything. The graceful furniture was also covered in plastic, which was commonplace in most Black homes during that era.

A crystal chandelier hung in the dining room behind the foyer. And nearby was Gratdada's desk, which held an old clock that chimed through the house. We later learned that the clock dated back to the mid-1800s. Gratdada had worked as a handyman in the Gold Coast district, north of downtown Chicago, during the Great Depression and had brought this beautiful chandelier among other things back to his home as a gift from one of his employers. The curio cabinet they had in the dining room and the one in the living room parlor were filled with crystal glasses and other fine dinnerware. Among the collection were my grandmother's teapots. They had come from an assortment of mansions along the Gold Coast and were prized possessions.

The kitchen had a large pantry full of delightful, aromatic spices that made it smell like a professional kitchen. A large sun porch led to a spacious backyard where Gratdada's BBQ grill sat. There, he cooked up the finest barbecued mutton, complete with his brand of Kentucky BBQ sauce.

This is where we got together with our cousins for the first time since seeing them in Seattle the year before. They were my Aunt Doris' and Uncle Gables' two sons. Mark was the oldest and was the same age as me, and Keith was the same age as Michael. They lived in another part of the South Side, but came to Gratdada and Dee Dee's house daily during the summer. Our days were always full of playful activities or other planned events that were organized by our grandparents.

One of our favorite activities was going over to State Street, which is chronicled in the song "Chicago." I can still hear Ma singing, "State Street, that Great Street, what a wonderful place." State Street was full of vegetable stalls and free markets. There was even a row of meat markets, so one could go up to State Street and buy everything they needed for their grocery shopping: farm-fresh vegetables and fruits, dairy, and meat. It was an amazing sight because it was several blocks long on both sides of what had become the Dan Ryan Freeway, which is a large stretch of highway that ran straight down through the South Side, and that many thought was a blight on the neighborhood. It had unusually dangerous freeway entrances and exits that crisscrossed each other, and Gratdada had nicknamed it the "Damn Ryan."

The South Side of Chicago was a community full of pride and respect, full of Black-owned businesses, from barber shops, beauty salons and boutiques, law and doctor's offices, grocery stores, bars, and restaurants. Sadly, years later, economic apartheid would destroy most of the businesses and surrounding communities. Economic apartheid is the result of years of the discriminatory practice of redlining. Initially, redlining restricted Black and other people of color from buying homes in areas reserved for whites, isolating Black communities. This also led to depriving the community of money and resources to allow them to grow their businesses and keep their homes up, ultimately leading to the destruction of businesses, communities, and families.

Both sets of grandparents planned activities that enabled them to show us off to the rest of the family. One of these outings was the 50th anniversary of my mother's Aunt Marie and

Uncle Milt. She had spent a lot of time with them when she was a little girl, and shared fond memories of her time out on 95th Street when she was a little girl.

In the 1930s, Aunt Mary and Uncle Milt ran a bustling business from their home. On their large property, they had a basement ice cream parlor complete with a soda jerk fountain and high stools for people to sit on to enjoy their homemade ice cream.

Their children were Mabel, Marva, and Milt, Jr. Mabel and Marva were like my mother's big sisters, whom she never had. They dressed up in nice clothes and went to church and the movies together. They played the piano, which she was learning while growing up, as well. When the girls were 16 and 17, Mabel had been hit in the stomach while playing basketball and developed a rare tuberculosis of the stomach. She became bedridden and eventually passed away. My mother often visited her while she was in her tent-covered bed, and became very close to her. That was a very sad time that my mother would often recall.

So, on this warm sunny afternoon, we were going to Aunt Marie and Uncle Milt's 50th Anniversary and it was a large gathering of people, family, and food, and I remember thinking, "Fifty years together seems like an eternity, but somehow they're still happy and enjoying life together."

On another occasion, Ma took us to meet cousins on that same side of the family. We went to my mother's cousin Joanna's house for a birthday party. We had to get cleaned and spotless and shiny before we went over to the house. When we arrived, four little girls in pretty white dresses stood on the other side of the room.

"She's cute," I whispered to Aaron and Michael.

"We're all going to get a girlfriend," Aaron said.

However, we soon learned that they were our cousins and none of that was going to happen, so we were resigned to the fact that they were our cute cousins and that was the end of that discussion.

Ma also used to take us to the movies. This was a big outing, because she fixed sandwiches, cookies, and potato chips, to avoid buying theatre concessions. We carried the food in shopping bags as if we'd been shopping; perhaps that was why the theater owner never bothered us when we saw movies like *Darby O'Gill and the Little People.* The wicked witch made it a little scary, but also fun. Here's where I grew to like scary movies such as *Frankenstein, The Werewolf, The Mummy,* and of course, *Count Dracula.*

When we returned to Seattle to begin another school year, I was becoming more aware of music.

"I want to play the guitar," I had told Ma.

She promptly sent one to Seattle. Poppy and Mommy loved jazz. They played the likes of Duke Ellington and Count Basie, and Poppy's favorite was Ella Fitzgerald. The first R&B song I ever heard was "Quarter to Three" by Gary U.S. Bonds. I started taking guitar lessons, sitting in the house for long hours trying to get used to the guitar that seemed oversized to me. This, while my brothers were out playing football in the streets. I thought, "This guitar will have to wait. Football comes first." So, I eventually lost interest in the guitar.

That year in 1959, we became members of Grace United Methodist Church. It was walking distance from the house, which meant that our parents would stay behind while we walked to Sunday School (which would give them a break from us) and they would later join us for Sunday Service. The pastor was Rev. Harris, and the assistant pastor was Rev. Bob Vahey. They were two white men who really cared a lot about the Black families who were part of the church. A lot of Black families came to this church: the Johnsons, the Dineshes, the Gardenhires, the Crosses, and the Bigbys, all of whom contributed to a strong sense of community.

Every now and then, our parents enjoyed a Sunday away

from the kids by sending us to church by ourselves. They made us breakfast, gave us money for the offering, and sent us off to Sunday School. One Sunday, we had our pocket change, a couple quarters, to put in the offering and we decided to go to Jackson and get some Hostess Snowballs instead.

"I'm gonna tell Mom and Dad," our sister threatened. As the oldest, she typically got her way, so we diverted from the store and wandered to a Baptist church a few blocks down from our church. We were curious to see what happened inside the Baptist church. The preacher's fire and brimstone sermon was nothing like our quiet little Methodist Church.

"If you paint your lips, and if you suck on those cigarettes and party on Saturday night, you ain't nothing but a hypocrite," he preached.

We had never seen anything like that before. Then the music started, and it was bumping and people were up and clapping their hands. Others jumped to their feet and shouted out to the Holy Ghost! The drums were rolling and the tambourine was shaking! We were in shock. This atmosphere was drastically different from our church; it was alive. We never told our parents about that. We decided not to return to that Baptist church; we liked the music, but not the fire and brimstone being thrown out from the pulpit.

At our church, we were in the Methodist Youth Association, or MYA. The pastor organized football games and sometimes he took us out on his boat to teach us how to water ski. There was always some activity going on around the MYA, and the families that we met back then became lifelong friends.

Most of the families were large, with at least five or six kids. The Dinesh family had five brothers and four sisters, and they had lost both of their parents around the time we started attending the church. The older siblings had to take care of the younger siblings, and this created a strong family bond and made them a more cohesive family because they were on their own. Donald Dinesh was my age and we got to know each other a bit while hanging out. He later changed his name to Umeme Upesi, a name of African origins. His three older brothers, Dominic, Ronald, and David, were excellent athletes and played football at Franklin High School. David and my sister were secret sweethearts. Joanne saved all of his newspaper clippings because he was quite a prolific athlete.

The Johnsons were another large family, having four boys and three girls, and Gregory, who was also my age and became a lifelong friend as well. The MYA provided the perfect opportunity for us to interact with all of these families and develop friendships that would last a lifetime.

CHAPTER 5

Home

In 1960, our parents found their forever home. It was Poppy's dream to purchase a home for our mother that, together, they could raise his family in and call their own.

Our home was in the Madrona neighborhood, a working-class community that had previously been a white and Jewish community. As true to what happens in many urban settings when Black families began to move in, white families moved out, causing what became known as "white flight" to the newly created suburbs. In their wake, their old neighborhood became mixed, and Madrona was the epitome of the American melting pot.

It was the year that President John F. Kennedy was elected as the first Catholic president of the United States. Kennedy was also the first president that many in the Black community believed would give Black people some measure of civil rights.

My parents had been supporters of Adlai Stevenson when he was running for office in 1952 and 1956 against Dwight Eisenhower. When Kennedy ran for office, there was a very different feel for what people believed he could accomplish under the backdrop of Camelot. The Civil Rights Movement was still brewing heavily in the South.

The house was located directly across the street from Madrona playfield, the neighborhood gathering place for kids to challenge each other's budding manhood or womanhood. For the next several years, that became the place where I learned how to fend for myself with the art of fighting without throwing a punch. We called it "woofing," but one had to be ready in case it came to blows, which it seldom did. On Madrona playfield, I developed more lifelong friendships.

Our large, four-bedroom home had a grand front porch, and balconies in the front and back of the house. This provided excellent opportunities for sneaking out after our parents had gone to bed. While the boys' bedrooms had doors to the balcony in the back of the house, there were no railings. Jumping off the balcony became a "do or dare" game to see who had the balls to jump free-hand without hanging from the gutters. At first, I hung off the gutters to jump when we wanted to get out after dark. Later, I developed the courage to take a flying leap. It was a miracle that none of us broke a leg.

We met up with friends on the weekends to hang out or get into mischief before sneaking back in the house—through the back door that we had left unlocked. We had to be careful to not wake our parents, but that wasn't the biggest challenge; they were tired from a long week of work or from partying with friends. No, the biggest challenge was not waking up Joanne, because she would always threaten to tell on us. We were more afraid of her than our parents.

We also brought along our trusted dog, Pal. He caught the attention of all the kids on the playground, who wanted to challenge Pal to a chase.

"What kind of dog is he?" they asked.

"A mix of some Doberman and Dalmation," we answered.

Everyone feared Pal, and they quickly learned how fast he was. We let him go and the children would see if they could get to the fence before Pal caught them. Most kids needed a considerable head start, three quarters of the way of the field, to get to the fence before Pal caught them. He quickly gained the reputation as a dog not to mess with. It made us feel good, since we had one of the baddest dogs in the neighborhood.

Madrona playfield had two tennis courts where we learned to play tennis. The neighborhood school was Madrona Elementary, which was one block away from the house.

"I want to finish fifth grade at Coleman Elementary," I told my parents. "I can start Madrona next year."

I had the best and favorite teacher in the school, Mrs. Greene. So, I walked two miles across the Central District to Coleman. Mrs. Greene was a Black teacher and she really cared about her students. She was strict, but she was good and everybody wanted her as their teacher because she was the best.

Though the walk was long, on the way back from school, I stopped at our favorite bakery, The Good Bakery, on 27th and Jackson. It had the best homemade baked pies and small tart pies called turnovers. Back then, Hostess pies were popular and good, but they couldn't beat the homemade taste of The Good Bakery. They had homemade strawberry and apple tart pies for 25 cents, and most days I ate one on the way home from school.

The fall of the following year, I enrolled at Madrona Elementary, where I was assigned to another Black teacher, Mrs. Beverly. She too was considered one of the best teachers at the school and everybody loved her. Until then, my friends were my classmates at Coleman. By transferring to Madrona, for the first time I actually built friendships with kids in my neighborhood. One of those friends was a white kid named Mark Sprague. Mark lived a couple blocks from us. Unbeknownst to us at the time, our homes were separated by an invisible redline border.

Mark and his brother, Paul, were the products of a divorced family. Their father, Dave Sprague, was the State Representative for the 37th District, where we lived. They even had a housekeeper named Hazel. Ironically, there was a television show around that time called *Hazel*, about a housekeeper that took care of a family. Mark's family represented the all-American white family and Mark became one of my closest friends.

Across the street from Mark was David Booth. David's family was more of a working-class family, even though they lived in the nicer part of the neighborhood. Like Mark, his parents were divorced. He had an older brother, Tom, and an older sister, Vicky, and like me, he was the third child. Both David and Mark became my two closest friends. They competed with one another to see who would be my best friend.

Mark was a child-actor who performed in the local theater. Right in our neighborhood, on the corner of 34th and Union, was a hub with a little theater called the Cirque Theater. Mark's regular performances there included a play with a well-known actor, Sterling Holloway, as well as the stage version of *West Side Story*. He introduced me to it, and for months, we anticipated the release of the film in 1961. We attended one of the first showings, and I fell in love with the movie. Score one point for Mark, as we had something in common that David did not share.

We acted out scenes from the movie in his family room downstairs. Mark of course played Riff, the leader of the white gang, the Jets, while I played Bernardo, the leader of the Puerto Rican gang, the Sharks. Our favorite scene to act out was the fighting scene where Bernardo accidentally stabbed Riff in the gut, killing him. We became so good at it, we performed it for his father, brother, and Hazel.

In 1963, Mark also introduced me to the Rolling Stones, which became one of my favorite groups. David was the opposite of Mark. David was very outgoing, but also incredibly rebellious. In fact, David's rebelliousness was probably why we were such good friends. I had a rebellious spirit myself, and David's influence confirmed my belief in who I was, and I knew I belonged.

CHAPTER 6

Hot Fun in The Summertime

In the summer of 1962, the group Booker T. & M.G.'s released "Green Onions" and it became the theme song for many of our adventures that year. My sister had introduced us to James Brown and the Famous Flames because she had the album *Live At the Apollo.* Still, the Booker T. song seemed a little more universal.

Next door, an old white woman sang "Old Black Joe" as her piano player boomed the melody behind her. We loved hearing her stories about our house.

"Lake Washington used to come up the 34th Avenue," she told us, "which was a block from our home. Now it was eight blocks to the lake. Somehow when the Ballard Locks over in the Ballard Community were cut in the early 1900s, it drained the lake." She also said that two kids had died in the bedroom in the front of our house, upstairs adjacent to my parents' bedroom (which was now Joanne's bedroom) so we knew that our house was haunted. She died later that year and a Black family moved in and I could hear them play an organ, which replaced the piano player. The dude's name was Coleman Brown and he was playing “Green Onions.” It was like we had a rhythm and blues band that had moved right next door.

Later that summer, the Seattle World’s Fair opened with a popular exposé called Century 21, whose inauguration drew President John F. Kennedy—a ray of hope for the Black community—and his beautiful wife, Jacqueline. It was also the summer that our cousins, Mark and Keith, along with Aunt Doris, visited. Our last trip to Chicago had been in ’59, so it was their turn to visit Seattle in the summer of ’62. We enjoyed long days, picnics, water fights, summer nights, and trips to the World’s Fair, which apparently was a big deal. My parents told us about the 1938 Chicago World’s Fair, which they had enjoyed as kids.

Many of the exhibits still existed at the Chicago Museum of Science and Industry when we visited. One highlight was a German submarine that had been captured during World War II, and other amazing feasts for the eye, including a mine shaft that had gone into a makeshift mine, and other science wonders looking into the late 20th century.

The Seattle World’s Fair also featured a glimpse into the future. The Space Needle was built as an eye in the sky to illustrate how future buildings would look. The monorail looked nothing like the el-trains of the big city, but something more sleek and futuristic at transportation, gliding on an elevated system, taking passengers from downtown Seattle to the fairgrounds. The Science Center’s maze of futuristic possibilities and architecture featured the Coliseum. This drew President Kennedy and Mrs. Kennedy to the Seattle World’s Fair to inaugurate the event, complete with limousines, Secret Service agents, and bodyguards. The lines to events were very long, especially ones to the futuristic rides in the kids’ activity center. We enjoyed afternoons on this space-age adventure while eating cotton candy and other treats. When Mark and Keith went home, we planned for our next Chicago adventure together in two years.

CHAPTER 7

The Madrona Playground–Where Legends Were Made

David was the second biggest daredevil I knew, with Mike Rossetti being the biggest, although the stuff he dared was not physically dangerous. David, on the other hand, was fearless. One afternoon, as we were roving the neighborhood finding trees to climb, we saw something in a tree that looked like a frisbee. David climbed up to retrieve it. The branch broke and he fell. Without stopping to cry, he ran home. Later, we found out that he had a broken shoulder. He must have run with some serious pain, and it didn't stop him.

Mark, being the opposite of David, had no real lust for danger, other than acting out the knife fight between Bernardo and Riff with plastic knives. And while his favorite group was the Rolling Stones, who played edgy music, David's favorite group was the Beatles, who played a more genteel style of music. And of course, he had a Beatles haircut. So, David, Mark, and I had this ongoing competition about which artist was better and who had better music.

"It's the Beatles!" one would argue.

"No, it's the Rolling Stones," another countered.

I played the cat in the middle, since my favorite music was R&B, anyway. That meant I favored the Stones. Mick Jagger had patterned his dance moves off the living legend, the Godfather of Soul, James Brown, even though he was a far cry from moving like James Brown. Much later, a documentary by Eric Burdon of The Animals explained how he and other British bands were influenced by Black cats from the U.S. He said that Little Richard and Chuck Berry were on tour in the U.K. and were playing a gig in Liverpool when, afterwards, they held a jam session with local musicians, including the Beatles, the Stones, the Animals, and others.

In a 2006 interview on NPR with David Dye called, "Animal No More, Eric Burdon Goes to the Blues,"[9] Eric Burdon talked about how Rhythm and Blues defined soulful music that inspired white musicians. For example, he said that Mick Jagger's dance style mimicked that of James Brown. And he emphasized that the magic of R&B music came from the soulful sounds of Black artists.

I realized then that the influence of soul music was the reason those groups had so much meaning in my life as I was growing up.

My introduction to soul music began in the early 1960s. In the backdrop of the Rolling Stones and the Beatles was Motown, with the Four Tops, Smokey Robinson and the Miracles, and The Temptations. At the time, Motown really exploded on the scene with groups like The Marvelettes, Mary Wells, Marvin Gaye, and Tammi Terrell. Meanwhile, the most influential music came from my parents, who played a lot of jazz. We learned how to appreciate Duke Ellington, Count Basie, Charlie Byrd, Dave Brubeck, and Paul Desmond, Billie Holliday, Dinah Washington, and Ella Fitzgerald.

My parents exposed us to a variety of music, including on some Saturdays, when Poppy gathered my brothers and me to wax the floors. The house's hardwood floors, especially in the living room, dining room, and hallway, needed to be shined on a regular basis. We moved the furniture out of the rooms, waxed these floors on our hands and knees, then buffed them with a portable electric buffer. While we cleaned the floors, he played his favorite opera soundtracks: *La Bohème, Madame Butterfly,* and *The Tales of Hoffman and Carmen.* As he sang along, we became indoctrinated to opera and loved it. He also loved classic musicals, including *South Pacific,* because it reminded him of his time there, and Jeanette MacDonald and Nelson Eddy were his favorite vocalists. This exposure to a variety of music included every style except polka and country.

We later learned the reason for frequently polishing the floors. Our parents had about 25 Swedish and Norwegian friends who visited our home each month on a Friday night. They rolled back the rugs, moved the furniture, and did Norwegian or Swedish dancing. Their heels clacking loudly on the floors messed up our shiny floors.

This multicultural experience was teaching us through my parent's actions the philosophy of Dr. Martin Luther King, Jr. They took us to march with Dr. King in Seattle in 1961. And they lived his message to not judge a person by the color of their skin, but by the content of their character.

Our parents' friends included Jewish families such as the Sussmans and the Castles, who taught us to celebrate Hanukkah and Passover, along with our Christian holidays, Christmas and Easter. I enjoyed my first matzo ball as a 12-year-old celebrating Passover in the Sussmans' home and relished that flavor whenever we went to their house. While joining them for Hannukah, I also learned about their beliefs as Communists.

Sadly, the outside world did not reflect this harmony. This was an era of assassinations, including: President Kennedy in 1963; civil rights lawyer Medgar Evers and Malcolm X in 1965; and Dr. King in 1968. Though we had marched with the Prince of

Peace, our generation was not prepared to turn the other cheek. I was always followed what Malcolm X said—if someone slaps you on the cheek, slap them back.

This did not stop our parents from visiting their friends' homes and going to see their favorite jazz artists at a little joint called the Poop Deck, where they saw the likes of Wes Montgomery and Charlie Parker. Once, the place lucked up and found a new singer. They didn't know much about her except that her name was Aretha Franklin, who would become the beloved mega-star known as the Queen of Soul.

"I was sitting so close to Aretha that I could reach out and touch her," my mother recalled.

On those nights when our parents were away, our sister Joanne was in charge, ruling the house and us boys with what felt like an iron fist. Older and smarter, she was "Joanne in Charge." When we acted up, she threatened us with a broom, vowing to tell on us when our parents got home. She usually came out on top, so we learned to respect her rule. She also had backup: two of her best friends, Thane Hellmuth, and another sister whom we called Big Joanne. Thane was from a wealthy white family who lived in Denny Blaine, an upper-crust area of Madrona. An artist and a visionary, she was a unique soul who died at age 21. Big Joanne was from a large Black working-class family, and together they were not to be messed with.

Madrona was a collage of races and ethnicities. The playing field was a mini United Nations, so I quickly had a core group of friends who ranged the full spectrum. But not everyone celebrated our melting pot. A few neighborhood gangs whose members were older than us were the Inkwells and the Chain Gang. The Chain Gang was led by the Bell Brothers, three tough dudes who lived in the neighborhood and had already established their reps. The Inkwells were led by a dude by the name of Butch Gill, who had a reputation for being a solid fighter. He was sweet on our sister, Joanne, which meant that we enjoyed Butch's protection.

Other tough guys in the neighborhood included a family of light-skinned, green-eyed siblings. The Chapmans were feared and respected. The girls were stunningly beautiful, but their brothers were Rough and Tumble, so we didn't even go near them. Another dude my age was Dwayne Howard, an up-and-coming tough guy with an established rep. His older brother was gay and sometimes the kids made fun of him, only at the risk of being beat down by Dwayne. Perhaps that made him tough, standing up for his older brother. It was an odd irony, a reversal of roles.

My buddies included a white dude named Kevin, whose father was a championship boxer, and Hugo Karose, part of a large Japanese family with two brothers and two sisters. His mother, Acke, was like the neighborhood mom of many kids. Hugo's dad was a jiu-jitsu expert and showed us moves on his front lawn. He taught us how to defend ourselves, while Kevin's father instructed us on how to box.

When we first moved on the block, a Filipino family with older kids lived next door on the opposite side of the old white woman. Beside them lived a Black family, the Scotts, whose twins were younger than us. Next to them was another Black family. I didn't know them very well because the kids were all younger, and the only one I met was Richard, the oldest, but still younger than me.

Their next-door neighbor was a young white girl, Bonnie. Her mother was known in the neighborhood as Auntie Barbara. We didn't know it at the time that she was a Madam, although we had heard rumors that she ran an escort service. We didn't know what that meant. All we knew was there were always pretty women coming in and out of her house, and I supposed it was because she had a dog grooming service for poodles:

French poodles, large poodles, toy poodles, poodles of different sizes. We suspected that the company was a front for her prostitution business.

Next to them lived the Melansons, who had eight kids: one girl, Wanda, who was the oldest, and seven boys, Wayne, Gary, Marlow, Erroll, Euwel, and later, Robert, who attended St. Theresa Catholic School a few blocks away. Another large Black family lived on the corner.

At our house, competition was always brewing between me and Aaron, to see who would have a girlfriend first. Would it be Bonnie or Wanda? Of course, Wanda had seven brothers we would have to go through first, not to mention her mom and dad. With no visible father figure, Bonnie seemingly had no obstacles, but Auntie Barbara was enough of a deterrent, so we could only dream.

I don't think anybody ever became their boyfriends, but they were the cute girls on the block that we could at least flirt with. We all talked about Bonnie and Wanda. Bonnie's cousin, Mike Rosetti, lived in Magnolia with two sisters and often stayed with Auntie Barbara. Like many of my white friends, his parents were divorced, and he was rebellious, and a little crazy and wild, acting out and pushing limits.

His dad came to town every now and then to visit his kids while they were in Madrona with Auntie Barbara. Mike's dad was an Alcoa aluminum salesman. In the 1960s, aluminum siding became popular as an exterior for homes. It was durable and lasted for many years. The men who sold aluminum siding made very good money and became known as The Tin Men. In fact, our parents had our house covered with aluminum siding as well.

Mike's dad came rolling into the neighborhood one Saturday in a big, white-on-candy-apple-red, drop-top Cadillac, complete with a white leather interior. The long tail fins were so big, it looked like a spaceship, and he would put all the kids, Mike, and his sisters, in the car to show them the town for the day. When he came to our neighborhood, he loaded all three or four of us Black kids, and Mike, in the car and took us down to the Guild 45th, a burger joint off Broadway. We rolled up in the Cadillac like superstars, and he later dropped us off at the movie theater.

Without parents or chaperones, Mike ran up and down the aisles, tipping over people's popcorn or snatching a bag of popcorn, then dashing to the balcony to throw popcorn at people sitting below until we got kicked out of the theatre. Mike tried to teach me to steal, because I wasn't good at it and didn't want to do it.

"Stick that in your pocket!" he'd say. "No one's going to notice."

So, I'd slip a candy bar or something in my pocket, but I always felt so guilty and nervous that I never made a very good thief, while Mike was a natural.

"Let's go steal some candy bars," Mike said one afternoon. I was nervous, because I hadn't really stolen anything before. In fact, someone could look at me and see that I was about to steal something because I was that nervous and looked like I was about to do something stupid. Standing there with my knees shaking, I was having visions of getting a whooping before going off to youth prison.

Mike had already done the deed and was standing with a devilish grin outside Joe's Market, a Mom-and-Pop grocery store a few blocks from our house on Union between 33rd and 34th Avenues. A larger grocery store, the Madrona IGA, was across the street, but folks in the neighborhood went to Joe's for fresh-cut meats from his butcher shop. Joe was Chinese American, and with his wife Mei, their store was a favorite for kids to get candy, knick-knacks, and our favorite Chinese goodies—sour balls and ingamores.

When I left with a candy bar in my pocket, Mei caught me and said, "You bad boy!" She made me put it back, sweep the floor, and take out garbage for what seemed like weeks. "You bad boy," she said every time I entered the store for years. I never stole from there again. Mischievous Mike persisted, taking me to small neighborhood stores, but it wouldn't work. Instead, I committed to getting a job so my pockets would never be empty. Ironically, Mike's dad always gave him money. He didn't have to steal. Still, I liked him. He was always making jokes, having fun, and living on the edge. I also wanted to be more of an adventurous risk-taker.

CHAPTER 8

War Games and Reps

Friday and Saturday nights were reserved for our favorite horror shows and movies. Among them were *Frankenstein, Frankenstein Meets the Wolfman,* and of course, *The Wolfman* series, which led to *Count Dracula.* Before the movie started, we went down to Joe's with a little bit of money and got our Wham Whams and Zuzus. Our movie snacks included my favorites: a Hollywood Bar, a Fifth Avenue, or a Hershey's bar with almonds. We also had: a bag of barbecue potato chips; a package of Hostess snowballs or Twinkies; and either an orange Crush soda or a grape Crush. The total price was a dollar because everything was 10 cents.

At home, Saturday mornings featured cartoons and pancakes before chores. We had to make our beds, clean our rooms, and do anything else that our parents had lined up for us. But our biggest activity was going out into the neighborhood and playing "war" games.

"War" was an elaborate game staged throughout the neighborhood. Years later, a brother told me on a Facebook post that he remembered watching us carrying our play guns and equipment through the neighborhood as if he were watching a war movie. Thanks to Christmas gifts, we had an arsenal of plastic toy guns of every size and make, pistols, sub machine guns, .50-caliber carbine rifles, and even plastic grenades. The action started at Mark and Paul's house because they had the most weapons, including a bazooka and plastic grenades.

I could only imagine if we had grown up in the 2000s; we would have been shot dead by the police if we were playing with these weapons out in the street, like Tamir Rice, a 12-year-old boy killed by police in 2014 as he played with a toy gun on a playground in Cleveland, Ohio.

Our war games included 10 to 20 kids on a Saturday. Sometimes we built a bunker with a tent housing two people, and we had to attack the bunker and blow it up by lobbing our grenades in the small slits of the tents. Whoever was attacking the bunker had to devise a plan of attack to avoid exposure; if you were exposed, you got shot. Then you would have to play dead until the next round or until somebody else rolled a grenade into the bunker and blew it up.

We got ideas for this stuff from one of our favorite TV shows, *Combat*—about World War II, following a combat troop that was fighting in Germany. In our war games, we were always fighting against the Nazis, but that meant someone had to play the Nazis and we always had to draw straws to see who would be the bad guys. Kids playing German soldiers got the German Luger.

When battling the Germans, we referred to the enemy as "Krouts"—the slang term for German soldiers we heard on TV. However, we never referred to the enemy as Japs, the other US enemy during WWII, because we had Japanese friends. We had roving bands of kids playing this game because we were fighting on multiple fronts, including a wooded area down the street from Mark's house.

This wooded area was on the edge of a kid named Matey's

house, so the woods were known as Matey's Woods. Inside, a little treehouse became one of our home bases and a Prisoner of War (or POW) camp. One goal was to capture the other team's home base and free the POWs. Playing in and out of the woods and up and down the streets, we laid it out as if we were having real wargames that lasted all day.

We also played football, baseball, and basketball on the playground across the street from our house. Football was my favorite. I pretended to be NFL quarterbacks Johnny Unitas, Bill Wade, or Y.A. Tittle. I wouldn't dare pretend to be Bart Star, the quarterback for the hated Green Bay Packers—longtime rivals of the Chicago Bears. We watched Bears games with Poppy and he schooled us on Bears history and the rivalries with the Packers.

While we rotated playing quarterback, that was most often my designated position because I could throw. The mostly dirt and rock field was a good place to get bruises, knicks, and bumps when we played tackle football, but we loved it. My favorite football players were Gale Sayers, who played for the Chicago Bears, and Jim Brown. The Seattle Seahawks didn't exist until I was an adult, so we grew up staunch Bears fans. As kids, we related to their rough and rugged leather helmet era, so we played tackle football without pads; this made us tough.

But that didn't mean I knew how to fight. Learning how was not a priority for me, even though I had always had the confidence to stand up for myself or my brothers. I witnessed my first fight on the playground behind Coleman school, between this kid Clifford and another dude who was "woofing"—talking shit but not doing anything to back it up. They were pushing and shoving when Clifford swung fast and hit the guy in his temple. His face swelled up really big and fast.

Oh shit, I thought, remembering what my buddy Eddie Leon taught me:

"If you're going to get in a fight, get in the first punch and don't wait to be hit. Don't just stand there 'woofing.'"

But I didn't pay much attention to it because I just didn't consider myself a fighter. Years later, as I was walking home one afternoon with my friends from Meany Junior High, I was woofing with one of my friends about some mess at school. Jim was a quiet kid who wore glasses and one would never think that he would swing on you. Before I knew it, we were tussling. He caught me off-guard and I ended up on the ground with him on top of me pounding me in the back as I took a curl-up, defensive position. His mother came out of the house and broke up the fight. When I got up, I was more embarrassed than anything else because I let this cat get the best of me.

I was determined to never let that happen again and to always fight standing up and not waste time woofing, but to swing first. Two or three weeks later on the Madrona playground, however, the field was loaded with kids, shooting the breeze and huffin' and puffin'. We were all 12 or 13 years old, hormones flying and testing our manhood. A Black kid named Richard, whom I wasn't really good friends with, challenged me.

"I saw Jim whoopin' your ass!" he said. "You can't fight!"

"If you think that," I said in my fighting stance as the crowd of kids taunted us, "then throw your best shot."

He backed down.

"I didn't think so," I said. Winning this small victory earned me some respect.

NEW MUSIC AND THE CIVIL RIGHTS MOVEMENT MOTIVATE ME

In 1962, a new artist came on the scene—Little Stevie Wonder. They called him the "12-year-old genius" and we were the same age. I really related to this dude and his new song, *Fingertips*, because here was this blind cat who could sing and dance, and had overcome adversity.

He hit puberty, dropped the "little," and I fell in love with the song, "I Was Made To Love Her," about a girl named Susie, which made me realize that I would be looking for Susie for the rest of my childhood, and maybe longer, until I found that special one.

In '63, the British invasion began with the Beatles and the Rolling Stones, followed by all the groups that had learned from Chuck Berry and Little Richard. Soul music was beginning to have much more of an influence on me. My sister Joanne had purchased an album called *James Brown, Live at the Apollo*, recorded in 1963, and we listened to his songs over and over again. She was older and played all the hits, including songs from the girl groups: the Marvelettes, The Shirelles, and Martha Reeves and the Vandellas. Oh, how I loved "My Baby Loves Me," "Will You Still Love Me Tomorrow," and "Mister Postman," all with rhythms that would tease my ability to dance, making me more soulful and drawing out my inner Rhythm and Blues.

Around this time, when Motown was exploding, soul music became popularized on Seattle's first Black radio station, KYAC. We also watched these groups on *The Ed Sullivan Show*. This was the only way we could actually get to see them perform. I loved watching the Temptations sing "My Girl," the Four Tops singing "Bernadette," and The Supremes performing "Stop In The Name of Love." It was a family gathering to watch that show together.

Also unfolding before our eyes on that little black and white TV set was the Civil Rights Movement. Our parents made sure that we saw the brutality in the South as people fought for their rights with Dr. King. We saw Bloody Sunday and the battle at Pettus Bridge with peaceful demonstrators being beaten by police, bitten by police dogs, and hosed by firefighters simply because they wanted the right to be treated as human beings. We heard the cries of the parents of the four little Black girls who were murdered in the Sixteenth Street Baptist Church that was blown up by racists while the children were preparing for communion; this left an indelible imprint on my psyche. It probably was the dawn of my deep desire to stand up against injustice and to champion the cause of anyone who was bullied or oppressed. I didn't know it at the time, but it would come forth years later. It began to emerge in me stronger and stronger, that I would rather die on my feet than live on my knees.

CHAPTER 9

The Last Summer Trip to Chicago

As the summer of '64 approached, we were excited for our semi-annual trip to Chicago. Poppy had purchased a green station wagon for the journey. He wanted to test the car before we left, so early one Sunday morning, we drove to the recently constructed I-520 bridge. The Evergreen Point Bridge was just the second bridge to the east side to Bellevue and beyond, and it had a toll booth on its East End.

"Hold on, boys," Poppy said, entering the on-ramp from Seattle heading east. "This is our test!"

He put the pedal to the metal and sped across the bridge at what seemed like 100 miles an hour as we watched the speedometer. He suddenly slowed before the toll booth, did a U-turn, and went back across the bridge. Mission accomplished! The car passed the test; now the green monster would take us to Chicago.

A few days before our trip, Poppy popped an Achilles tendon while playing basketball or soccer with his buddies after work. Our spirits dropped. Would this cancel our trip? No! Mommy drove while Poppy dealt with the pain and healed. On departure day, Joanne rousted us from bed, packed the cooler with our sandwiches, cookies, and cold drinks, and made sure we were standing at attention, ready to journey cross-country to the tunes of "Dancing in the Streets" by Martha Reeves and the Vandellas, "Keep on Pushing" by The Impressions, and "Under the Boardwalk" by The Drifters. Dionne Warwick had another hit with "Walk On By," The Supremes with "Where Did Our Love Go" and "Baby Love," while the Righteous Brothers had "You've Lost That Loving Feeling."

Both sets of my grandparents lived on the Southside. My mother's parents lived on 69th and Prairie, and around the corner on 70th and Calumet, my father's parents lived. We stayed with Ma and Bop-bop, my mother's parents, and ran around the corner every day to visit Gratdada and Dee Dee, my father's parents. Each set of grandparents had their own unique style. For example, Ma and Bop-bop did everything in tandem. In the mornings, they came downstairs and fixed breakfast together for us. A true partnership. Bop-bop meticulously fried the bacon, laying each strip on napkins before placing them in the oven to keep warm, while Ma squeezed the orange juice and prepared the eggs. She simultaneously prepared his breakfast while Bop-bop went into the basement to prepare for work.

The freshly painted basement was cleaner than other people's houses! He had a shoe tree attached to a post, and shined his shoes and ironed his white shirt. My grandfather was meticulous about everything, including how he would dress and present himself. After he put on a suit to walk to work, the brothers in the neighborhood—his peers—said my grandfather looked like a Wall Street businessman with his pressed suit, tie, and his shirt, a paper under his arm, and his briefcase.

Grandpa Bop-bop had left the railroad and now worked at the local post office. When he got to the post office, he would change into another white shirt and pants with his post office apron to finish it off. The point is, he was going to be sharp whatever he was doing. Even in his work clothes, he remained looking clean and sharp at work, again, being proud in his presentation. When he finished his shift, he took that uniform off, donned his "businessman" suit, and walked home. No one would have a clue that he worked at the post office. He was so conscious of the way that he dressed, from his crisp white shirts down to his socks and high polished shoes, even to the way that he laced his shoelaces. My mother used to say he tied his shoes so tight, it caused abrasions on the instep of his foot. Polished shoes, he and Ma told us, was an indication of a man being clean and sharp.

"Never leave the house without your shoes being polished to a bright shine," my grandfather often said.

I can only imagine how different his life was, compared to the early part of their marriage, when he struggled with alcoholism, yet we never saw that part of him. We only saw them as very strong and proud. Ma and Bop-bop and everything in their house was always spit-shine clean, which stayed with us kids when we would go back home as we were being taught by our parents to keep the house clean. The other influences in our lives at that early age were Gratdada and Dee Dee; they were much more laid-back in their lifestyle. And while their house was also clean and orderly, they were much less meticulous about how things looked. I'm not saying that my mother's parents were rigid, but they were just . . . different.

Grandma Dee Dee was also very conscious of her surroundings. She played bridge up until she was 100 years old, and lived to 102. She belonged to a bridge club that rotated to different homes. When they came over to her house, it was always tidy and clean. Everything was precise on bridge day. They served tiny sandwiches and tea. Dee Dee was very attentive to detail in how she hosted. When Grandma Dee Dee wasn't entertaining, she was more laid-back and relaxed, at least most of the time, it seemed.

Gratdada, on the other hand, was consistently laid back. He had worked most of his life as a handyman for wealthy people on the North Side of Chicago in an area known as the Gold Coast. There lived wealthy white folks who had large mansions, and he was able to go freely in and out of their homes. He was well-paid, and sometimes was even given food to take home to the family. By the time we were born, and now visiting back to Chicago, he would sometimes have treats for us. He had a real laidback style.

"Just leave the dishes till later," he would tell Grandma Dee Dee. "Come sit down and relax."

His favorite pastime was sipping a little whiskey and smoking a cigar. It seemed like he always had a cigar in his hand because he smoked them slowly, and one cigar could last the whole evening. He had a light sense of humor. Watching him and Poppy interact was always an interesting side study. The fragrance of his Kentucky-style BBQ smoking on the grill was unmatched. However, adjusting to the different rules and expectations between the two households could sometimes be challenging as we traversed back and forth between the two homes.

Playtime was an interesting time for us in Chicago. It was the first opportunity we got to hang out with my cousins as older kids in this South Side Black community, because we moved to Champagne at such an early age, and left there to move directly to Seattle when I was seven years old. And on our first trip back, I was still just nine years old, so hanging out with my cousins now was a totally new adventure.

My cousins and I would find all kinds of daredevil things to do—from jumping off garage rooftops to running through alleyways while dodging dogs and other obstacles. We were always finding exciting things that could keep us occupied during the day. We would meet up with their friends from the neighborhood, like Dolphy, Ron Benson, and Bobby La Chapelle. On one such afternoon, a block up from Gratdada and Dee Dee's house, on 71st Street and Calumet, was a funeral home.

71st Street had been given an honorary street name after Emmett Till, because this was the same neighborhood that he had lived in, although I would not learn this until years later.

Standing in front of this large, ominous building, we were curious and wanted to see what was inside. I had never been in a funeral home and we wanted to see what a dead person looked like. As we peered inside, we saw a posted sign for an upcoming funeral service for a Mrs. Pitts. Down the long aisle, the casket was open. We slowly tiptoed down the aisle, careful not to make a sound, and looked inside the casket, and there inside laid a light-skinned woman with bright orange-red lipstick. Her makeup looked as natural as possible and she was eerily beautiful with her freckles gleaming as if sleeping. She didn't look too different from a live person.

"What do you think she feels like?" one guy asked.

"I dare you to touch her!" someone else said.

I would never back down from a dare, so I reached in and touched her face. Her skin was ice cold.

"Aaaahhhhh!" someone shrieked.

We ran out of the funeral home, laughing and shrieking. For many nights to come, as we told ghost stories to scare each other, one of us would bring up Mrs. Pitts and how cold she felt.

"She's walking among us trying to touch our faces," someone taunted. "Just like we touched hers!"

After we had met up in the morning for our run through the neighborhood, we had strict rules to promptly report back to Ma and Bop-bop's house to have lunch at noon. First, we had to strip down and take a bath in concrete laundry tubs located in the basement. Ma's basement was cleaner than most people's upstairs bathrooms.

In her home, nothing was out of place and you couldn't find a single spot of dirt. So we bathed in the concrete tubs and didn't complain about it, because we wouldn't get lunch if we didn't.

Following lunch, we had to take a nap. We weren't really down for that, but we had to do as we were told. At two o'clock, before going back out, we would have to put on clean-pressed shorts and t-shirts.

"Don't get dirty again!" our grandmother ordered before we left the house.

Our cousins teased us for being so clean and getting dirty again was just a matter of time.

Summers in Chicago were hot; kids don't feel the heat. On warm summer nights in Chicago, lightning bugs floated everywhere. So, we would play a game to see who could fill up a jar with the most lightning bugs. When the jars were full, it was like having your own lamp. We would make rings out of the tails by stringing them together.

Chicago was full of fun and adventure. We often visited my cousins' home or went to the theater. Finally, we went to Riverview, the largest amusement park in the world, and it had been around since my father was a kid, when he paid five cents per ride. He told us stories about how he rode on all the fantastic rides and saw all the circus acts. He and his friends dared each other to ride the most treacherous ride of all—the Bobs—fashioned like a bobsled race in the Olympics.

"When I came here," Mark recalled, "we had 25-cent days when every ride was a quarter."

Riverview's 1,000-plus rides were all sizes and shapes and for every age. We laughed when we passed by the kiddie section because we were big boys, and we weren't going to have anything to do with that section. We walked by the roller coaster ride billed as the tallest in the world. We marveled at the Bullet—the fastest roller coaster in the world going up to speeds of 100 miles an hour.

We walked into a circus tent to behold the fattest woman in the world. She was sitting on a sofa—filling its entire length! Near her was the world's thinnest man who would pass his skinny body through a narrow wooden barrel.

We were amazed, but nothing could prepare us for the Bobs. My younger brother Michael and Mark's younger brother Keith were too small to ride, but Mark, Aaron, Dolphy, and I said our last prayers as we boarded the sled and became a four-man bobsled team.

As the sled took off, it wound along the bottom area of the ride and passed by several bobsled cars that were wrecked or damaged, that looked as if they had flown off the track and crashed. When the bobsled crawled by them, we said,

"Wow, look at that there, we're in for it now!"

The bobsled climbed the long track up, then hurtled down through the curves, just like my father described, swinging left then swinging right, then swinging left again. We felt like we would fly out of the car!

Still, we couldn't wait to be scared to death as the ride reached its peak. We screamed into the daylight as the sled hurled with ferocious speeds—screaming as the force slammed us from left to right—sure we would die, but not caring because we were together having fun. Better yet, we survived the Bobs and earned bragging rights for it.

Meanwhile, the first girl I fell madly in love with was Karen. She lived next door to Gratdada and Dee Dee. I used to sit on the porch waiting for her to come outside so I could utter some words to her. It always seemed like she was supervised by a parent or aunt or whomever she was living with at the time. My brother Aaron and my cousin Mark also had eyes for her. Aaron, however, always seemed to get the girls, and every girl I liked, he liked, too. Unfortunately, every time I was interested in a girl, she would end up liking my brother, and I was like the odd man out. Perhaps I began to develop some insecurities about my looks when it came to girls, as they always seemed to think that Aaron was cute, and never paid much attention to me.

I had it in my mind that Karen would be my girlfriend, but of course she ended up liking my brother. Years later, I found out that she died of an enlarged heart and never made it past her thirteenth birthday. Such a tragic ending for my first would-be girlfriend.

This summer trip to Chicago ended with a treat: we visited Champagne. In the old neighborhood, the brick and concrete housing complex of Birch Village, we stayed with an old family friend and visited our previous neighbor, Mrs. Naylor. She was a nice, old woman and genuinely glad to see us. That night, we ignored the heat and humidity and talked long into the night.

The next day, we drove to Danville, a small town in Southern Illinois, where I met some cousins for the first time in a rural part of town. Their son, who was about our age, took us out into the fields.

"See those quicksand patches?" he said. "Steer away from the quicksand! We also got snakes. Blue racers. Watch out. They're fast and they'll get you unless you run zigzag through the weeds."

I was deathly afraid of snakes and wasn't going to have anything of it. At one point, we heard some rustling in the reeds.

"They're over there!" he shouted.

We all started running zigzag, just in case he was telling us the truth. That was enough for me, and the last time I ever wanted to visit Danville.

Our next stop was Henderson, Kentucky, the birthplace of my father and his parents. Brookstown was long gone by then, but the legend still existed. We listened to the old folks talk about the old days and all of the changes in life that had occurred since way back when my great-great-grandfather and uncles purchased that land. We spent the warm summer nights chasing lightning bugs and eating my grandmother's buttermilk pie or chess pie; it was the best of times. Then we headed back to Chicago.

While spending the night across the street from Gratdada and Dee Dee's, at Bobby La Chappelle's house, a young dude and his girlfriend were sitting on the steps of the porch next door. We were watching them to see what kind of moves this guy had and what would happen. Eventually, they went upstairs to the bedroom adjacent to the bedroom that we were sleeping in. Under the cover of night, we silently stared wide-eyed out the window as they came out of their clothes and did "the act." It was my first time seeing what sex actually looked like.

A few days later, we began the long journey back to Seattle, in a car equipped to make the journey. We had no breakdowns, as there were during our first drive out to Seattle in 1957, but still an adventure all the same.

CHAPTER 10

Becoming A Teenager

By the fall of 1963, I was maturing into a young teenager—and somewhat of a rebel. I was noticing girls more, and music was influencing my life.

I had no agenda, but things were brewing inside me as the Civil Rights Movement evolved. Most notably that summer, Medgar Evers—the Field Secretary for the NAACP in Mississippi—was assassinated in his driveway by southern racists who opposed the group's fight against segregationists and injustice. At the same time, my subconscious was scorched by images of Black people being bitten by police dogs, hosed by firefighters, and beaten by those who were sworn to protect and serve the people.

Then in the fall of 1963, the country was jolted by the assassination of President John F. Kennedy. This was a shocking setback for many civil rights workers and a nation that had seen the slim hope of ending segregation and the Apartheid atmosphere in the South.

We were sent home from school, and all day the next day, on a Friday, we were watching TV. Reports showed Jack Ruby—live in black and white—murder Lee Harvey Oswald, the man accused of assassinating the president. It was almost surreal to see these events happening in rapid succession. We watched Kennedy's state funeral the next day as the whole nation was in mourning. It was a period where it seemed as if the hopes and dreams that Black people had about freedom—especially given that the March on Washington had happened three months earlier where Dr. King had delivered his famous "I Have a Dream" speech—were all lost. The president's assassination left many Black people feeling like they had lost someone who was a champion for civil rights.

Just as Stevie Wonder had influenced the idea of me finding Susie, Eric Burdon and The Animals with their song "It's My Life and I'll Do What I Want," and The Rolling Stones and Mick Jagger's defiance of American pop culture, went hand-in-hand with my defiance of authority or someone trying to tell me what I should be doing. This, coupled with my anger and frustration over the way Black people were being treated, would eventually lead me on a path to becoming a revolutionary.

My exposure to different cultures was also an integral part of my growth and struggle to find my identity. Living around and being exposed to people from many different backgrounds brought to life what our parents taught us about not judging others by the color of their skin. It wasn't anything they said, but it was literally how we and they lived.

Our parents hung out with an interesting variety of friends. Two of their best friends were Frank and Austerie Richardson, who lived across the street when we lived back on 24th Avenue. Austerie had three children from a previous marriage: Cornelius, Shirley, and the youngest, Ronald Bolton. We would often spend holidays at each family's house, or just a Saturday night get together. Frank was famous for his fried chicken and biscuits inspired by his Louisiana background. They came over on

Saturday nights, staying up late listening to the jazz sounds of Duke Ellington, Count Basie, or my dad's favorite, Ella Fitzgerald.

We would sit at the top of the stairs, watching them dance and enjoy cocktails. One Sunday morning after a long night of partying, I snuck downstairs before anybody else was awake and surveyed the damage in the living room. On the coffee table were several empty cans of beer. I picked one up, swirled it around, and noticed some beer in the bottom.

"I'm going to find out what this beer tastes like," I said.

As I turned the can up to my lips, I saw too late that cigarette ashes and butts were going into my mouth. I gagged and spit them out. This removed any desire to ever smoke cigarettes! It also killed my taste for beer for the rest of my life.

We also interacted with the Sussmans and the Castles. They were Jewish and lived nearby in Madison Valley. In their homes, we celebrated Hanukkah and Passover. My first taste of a matzo ball was like heaven. The Sussmans had purchased some property on Cyprus Island, one of the San Juan Islands in the Puget Sound, where they eventually planned to build a summer home.

In the summer of '64, Mr. Sussman asked Aaron and me if we would like to work on his boat, making repairs in order to get it ready for a trip up to Cypress Island, to help build the summer home. It sounded like it could be another exciting adventure. But first, we had to work on the boat, starting with it being in dry dock. We had to scrape the barnacles off the hull, so we could prep it for painting. Once that was done, we got it back in the water to the docking area on Lake Union. We then began the tedious process of removing old paint and varnish off the inside and outside of the boat.

The work was long and challenging, especially while it was docked in the sloop. Working in the galley or on the inside of the boat was particularly challenging because it would rock back and forth, giving me fits of dizziness. Still, after the work was completed, the reward was to journey over to the islands.

This classic, old wooden boat was called The Puffin. Aaron and I drove up to Bellingham where we met Mr. Sussman at the boat dock and loaded equipment and supplies on board. The lumber for the cabin was already on the island. We finally set sail off to the San Juan Islands with our supplies on the boat. The island was remote and had no dock. It had no visible evidence of inhabitants—only trees and beaches.

We loaded all the supplies and equipment aboard the dinghy, rowing to shore one load at a time. Then we set up camp on the beach. We had no tents, so Aaron and I found a good spot for our sleeping bags on the beach away from the tide, under the stars. It was probably the safest place to sleep, since creatures were probably lurking in the woods above.

The next morning, we hiked up into the woods to the construction site on a point overlooking the ocean and Puget Sound. Mr. Sussman had set up a rig with a pulley, and long ropes going down to the beach where we had stacked the lumber. We had to pull the lumber all the way up from the beach to the cliff, but with a double pulley system, the weight was manageable. Working alongside Mr. Sussman, building the cabin was quite an adventure, and we worked most of the day, then relaxed on the beach in the evening.

A typical day began by harvesting oysters. Oyster beds near our camping site on the beach made it easy to pick fresh oysters right off the sea bottom while the tide was out. Each morning, we baked the oysters in a rock oven that we had built, just long enough until they popped open; then we put garlic butter on them. They were a delectable new treat as a first-time experience.

We also discovered the joy of onion pancakes—a pancake with a slice of onion in the middle. Mrs. Sussman would slice the onion, put it on the grill, pour the batter on top of it, and then flip it over when ready. The perfect nautical breakfast—a pancake with sweet onions in the center, and fresh baked oysters enhancing this culinary adventure.

After breakfast, we hiked up into the woods, pulled lumber up, and worked with Mr. Sussman building the cabin. With a glorious view of Puget Sound, and the San Juans straight out into the ocean, we sometimes ate dinner or lunch up there or on the beach. One evening, I found myself alone at the cabin while working on a particular project for Mr. Sussman, after everybody had finished their chores and left. The sun was beginning its long, warm stretch over the island, heading towards sunset.

The dinner bell ring signaled it was time for dinner. I had two ways down to the beach: the long trek back through the woods and trails; or the oceanfront path down a series of large rock ledges forming a natural staircase.

"Don't use that route," Mr. Sussman had said, "unless you absolutely need to get down to the beach fast."

It seemed like such an easy opportunity to get down there quickly. So, I started down the rocks, hopping down from one plateau to the next, hurrying because whatever we were having that day for dinner would get eaten up by Aaron if I didn't get down there in time.

About halfway down, I stopped in my tracks.

My heart pounded with terror.

On several of the rock plateaus going forward were five or six snakes that were sunning in the late afternoon sun. I turned around slowly to head back up to the safety of the trail, but a half-dozen snakes were on the plateau I had just come from.

Should I creep back up the rocks passing the snakes again or run past the snakes in front of me?

I took off, down, running past the snakes and making it to

the beach. That was the last time I took that route! Every night after that, I made sure no snakes were in my sleeping bag.

GRANDFATHER VISITS SEATTLE

Later that summer, Poppy's dad, Gratdada, made his only trip to Seattle. He always had a big smile on his face and would always laugh and tell us stories about growing up. The afternoons were warm and sunny that year and we had learned to play tennis, since we lived across the street from the courts. While Mommy and Poppy were at work, we would get up and go out and hit a few strokes on the court before taking a break to hunt for food. One afternoon around lunchtime, Gratdada, who had been up for some time, asked:

"Boy, where's the liquor store?"

"I know right where the liquor store is," I declared, "because I've been there with my dad."

"Show me," he said.

We had no car, so we walked two miles down to 12th and Jackson. The liquor store was next door to a little take-out restaurant, which had some of the city's best Chinese food. Poppy always went in there on paycheck days after buying his whiskey shot for the weekend. Then he would buy Chinese food for dinner for all of us at the house.

Now, Gratdada bought me a little Chinese food for taking him down to the liquor store and then we began the long trek home. Once in the house, I watched him take his collection of alcohol out of the bag: two quarts of beer, a fifth of vodka, and a pint of Old Grand-Dad, a popular whiskey of the time. Gratdada was from Kentucky—known as the "Bourbon State." Most folks from that part of the country knew how to drink and could hold their liquor; my grandfather was no different.

As I ate my egg foo young, I watched him prepare his first drink.

"Can I have a glass?" he asked. "And do you know where the

eggs are?"

"Yep." I opened the refrigerator and pulled out a carton. He took a couple of eggs and sat down. He cracked an egg into his beer mug, filled it with beer, and chugged it down.

I watched with amazement, guessing that the egg would help coat his stomach or something like that. I finished my food and headed on back out to the playground. When I came in later after my parents had come home from work, both bottles of beer were empty, the pint of Old Grand-Dad was gone, and he was starting on his fifth of Vodka. I never saw the man drunk or tipsy, but he knew how to put it away and could handle it.

"I found some chocolate popcorn," he told my father. "It sure was good."

My father looked at him with a strange expression. "Chocolate popcorn?"

"Yeah, that bag right over there."

We all chuckled. The bag was dog food—Gravy Train!—big chunks of hard dog food. He had popped them in his mouth and chewed them up like popcorn. We all had a great, big laugh.

Those were always the best of times, when the old folks from Chicago visited, shared stories, and made us feel connected to the family, since we had no family in Seattle.

My other grandfather, Bop-bop, also visited during the summer with a suitcase full of gifts. Kind and gentle, he delighted us with stories. I could listen to his smooth, velvet voice for hours. Proud and well-respected in his community, he spoke like a philosopher about his days in Mississippi, where he fell in love with our grandmother, Josephine, while in college at Fisk University.

"You have to get a good education," he said. "Go to a good college."

He had grown up during difficult times in the South, and moved to the North to find better work, but the only opportunities were menial jobs, even though he had a college education. But fortune favored him; he found work on the railroad, which he maintained through the Great Depression, until the little girl called him a nigger.

"Josephine and I saved all our tips," he said. "We put those silver dollars in jars. One day, we had enough to buy a home."

This was the last time I would see either of my grandfathers alive.

BACK TO SCHOOL

When the school year began, it was business as usual: trying to find a place to fit in, to discover purpose and identity, and figure out what life was about. Since my desire to be a guitar player had worn off, I was learning to play the trumpet. The public school system introduced students to music and selected the instrument they thought would be best suited for the student. Aaron had been introduced to the violin, but he never really took to it. Michael inherited his violin, but soon became disinterested. He had an inclination to play tennis and chess, and would end up besting Aaron and me. He would later play on the high school tennis team and chess club.

I loved playing the trumpet, probably thanks to the jazz that my parents played. Listening more to Dizzy Gillespie, Miles Davis, and Donald Byrd, plus other jazz greats who played the trumpet, influenced me. Later on, I really dug Hugh Masekela, a South African trumpeter who had arrived on the scene playing a unique style. I attended his Seattle concert, and adapted my style to his Afro-jazz style. His hit, "Grazing in the Grass," is still very popular today.

Now entering my last year of junior high school, ninth grade meant that my buddies and I stood at the top of the Heap; we were Kings of the mountain because we were the oldest kids in the school. One of David's and my biggest challenges was identifying which girls were easy pickin's—girls we could flirt with, pull pranks on, and get away with it.

One of those girls was Lori Iszler; she was popular and, like everyone else, was out of our league. One afternoon, David dared me to kiss her in the hallway. When the bell rang for the sixth period, students poured out into the hallways, anxious to leave at the end of the school day.

I knew where Lori would be, so I rushed to that part of the school, ran up beside her, and gave her a big kiss on the cheek. Then I dashed down the hallway. Did she even see who kissed her?

"You won the challenge!" David exclaimed after witnessing the kiss.

THE DIXON BROTHERS: NEIGHBORHOOD CRIME STOPPERS

During the holiday season, our family traditionally went gift shopping. Usually, our parents gave us change or an allowance. This year, I had my own money, thanks to odd jobs. Meanwhile, Poppy bought all his gifts on Christmas Eve, arriving home after we were asleep. He started to unload the gifts from the trunk, but stopped for a holiday drink on the couch, where he took a nap.

When he went outside, the trunk was empty. He was devastated and distraught over losing a telescope for Aaron and an erector set for me, as well as a beautiful black and white cocktail dress for our mother.

When we heard the news, we immediately went out into the neighborhood and put the word out that someone had ripped us off and there would be hell to pay. Later that day, all the gifts showed up on our porch! I guess those thieves thought that we would find out and end up sicking Pal—the most feared dog in the neighborhood—on them after we found out their identities.

EARTHQUAKE SCARE

In the spring of 1965, I was in school when the big earthquake hit during lunchtime. Kids were running and screaming. Desks were bouncing up and down off the floors in the classrooms, as the whole building shook back and forth. I was trying to navigate my way through the hallway, trying to be cool because I was a ninth grader. My plan was to find a desk to get under as we had been taught in the earthquake drills.

My algebra teacher was standing in a doorway with her arms folded, watching the chaos. She waved me over with her finger, and said, "Get under the desk." She was just as calm as could be. It was the first time I had experienced a rumbling earthquake. We later learned that the earthquake had followed a much larger, destructive one in Anchorage, Alaska.

COMPETITION PLAYS OUT WITH CAMPING

David was winning our best friend battle. He beat me at outdoor stuff, and hoped to triumph in our unspoken competition thanks to my classmate, Rocky, a white dude who had parents who liked to do outdoor activities, and hike in the woods. He invited me to join him and his family on a weekend excursion to hike into the Cascade Mountains to a high lake where we fished and enjoyed the quiet peace of the outdoors. While I didn't enjoy the mosquitoes nipping on my arms, the adventure of being high up on the mountain trails—sometimes so narrow that only one person could pass—made me want more.

David and I had always talked about going on camping trips, but we lacked the necessary gear. So, along with Aaron, we went to the Army Surplus store on 1st Avenue to buy a large army tent, heaters, and sleeping bags. We started going to Mount Si, located east of Seattle at the foot of the Cascade Mountains, just before Snoqualmie Pass. On one of our first trips, David's mom dropped me, him, and a few other friends on the summit—a popular camping site with running streams, open forest, and wilderness. We loved it!

We set up camp and began exploring the other side of the creek. That's when we saw a medium-sized black bear entering our camp, searching for food. We had brought slingshots that had an arm brace to provide greater velocity, so we fired rocks at the bear to chase him out of our camp. We were just dumb enough not to realize that if we agitated the bear too much, we were dead meat, but at 14 years old, you don't think about such things.

Fortunately, the bear got bored when he couldn't locate our food. After swatting away a few pebbles that we had tossed his way, he went off into the woods. The next day, it rained. Our gear got wet and we were soaked to the bone.

"We've had enough!" the guys declared. "We're going to hike down to a phone to call David's mom."

David and I, however, decided to stick around for the entire weekend. We cooked a chicken on the barbecue grill while drying our clothes next to the fire. Just when we were ready to have our Mountain Man meal, David's mother pulled up in her car.

"It's time to get off the mountain," she ordered.

We rode back to Seattle with our lips poked out, because we were Mountain Men and we were going to stick it out.

Over that same winter, we took another stab at Mount Si. Aaron came with us, along with a couple of other older dudes. We also brought a .22 caliber target rifle and a starter pistol that we had modified to shoot bullets. David's father had been an avid hunter and had all the tools for loading his own shotgun shells and replacing spent cartridges and shotgun shells. We learned this skill in David's basement, along with how to handle weapons for the first time.

For our trip, David's mother, again, was the driver, but thanks to heavy snow, she could only make it about halfway up the mountain.

"This is it!" she said.

We hopped out, took our gear, and said, "We'll see you in a couple of days." Right then and there, we dug out a big patch of snow where we set up the huge Army tent that could hold five to seven men. We had plenty of food in our cooler, along with soda pop, which we stuck in the snow, and comic books. Then we took a short hike into the woods to see what was in the area. It was a winter wonderland for sure, a quiet forest covered in snow.

We took target practice with the rifles, observing the safety rules that David's father had taught us. It was my first time firing a weapon. That night in the tent, we told spooky ghost stories and read comic books while eating our dinner. We were free from our parents and any authority, and no one could tell us what to do. It was utter bliss!

About that time when we were feeling full of ourselves, we heard a bear outside messing around with our cooler where we had stored most of our food, but the bear wasn't finding any satisfaction.

"Let's throw out a big hunk of meat," Aaron suggested. "Maybe that will appease him."

So, we zipped open the tent door and threw out the meat. The bear chased it. Apparently happy, it left.

The next day, it snowed, completely covering the road. We packed up and started hiking to find a lower altitude campsite. But David's mother came early. Again, we wanted to stick it out, but we realized it was time to go home. We had fended off a bear, survived nights in deep snow in the woods, and considered it a success. At home, we discovered that our gear—including our sleeping bags—were full of snow worms. Fortunately, none of us had gotten sick.

CANDY HEIST INSPIRES LESSON

One night, Aaron invited me to join him on a candy heist down on Madrona Beach. He and his older friends, members of a Filipino family who lived around the block on 34th Avenue, had ventured down to the closed-for-the-winter snack bar, which contained a stash of candy bars.

"We'll go in through the roof and make off with the candy," they said.

I was down for the fun. We used our Escape Route—jumping off of the back balcony, after unlocking the back door in the kitchen, so we could sneak back in later. We met up with Aaron's friend and headed down the familiar path through the Madrona Woods. At the edge of the woods, we waited for a scout to go ahead and make sure it was all clear across the street to the snack bar.

We climbed trees to access the roof, where we pried open the skylight and lowered ourselves into the room. It was actually like being a kid inside a candy store! We helped ourselves to our favorite candy bars and assorted snacks. Then we escaped back up through the roof and headed back to the neighborhood.

Was this the right thing to do? Guilt seeped through me. So, I played it off as just another adventure. Besides, we were like bandits in the night, a sort of Robin Hood. *What harm could a couple of hundred candy bars cost?*

We divided up the spoils, each of us having 20 or 30 candy bars to stick under our beds for late-night snacks. Later that year, I heard that the police had raided the Filipino family's home; it turns out, they were involved in much more than just candy bar snatching in the middle of the night.

Gossip had it that the older boys were getting time in the Green Hill juvie prison for a series of burglaries and larcenies. My brief life of crime ended right then; I found less dangerous mischief to get involved in. Besides, what would my parents think if I got caught? And what about the community mothers who were like hawkeyed scouts watching us?A new family had moved next door, the Hardings, and Mrs. Harding was someone not to mess with. Plus, down the block were Auntie Barbara and Mrs. Melanson. Nearby were the Conallys, the Pellums, and the

Ellises. We had the proverbial village, and we knew not to cross any of those mothers.

FEBRUARY 1965—A TUMULTUOUS TIME FOR CIVIL RIGHTS

The backdrop to our teenaged hijinks was the ongoing Voting Rights Movement. Bloody Sunday had occurred with Alabama State Representative Bull Connor's troops beating the demonstrators on the Pettus Bridge. The 1965 Voting Rights Act was pushed through Congress by President Johnson.

And while Dr. King was still advocating non-violent protests, a new leader had emerged from Harlem and prison, becoming the spokesperson for the Nation of Islam. I had heard very little about Malcolm X and knew nothing about what he stood for, until the day he was assassinated—February 21st, 1965. Then, I learned that Malcolm X had a different approach to the race problem in the United States. Rather than turn the other cheek when one was slapped, he suggested slapping the assailant back. It was the same rule that I had learned at the Madrona playground: let yourself get slapped and you would be bullied forever till you hit back. Still, I remained oblivious to the impact that he and his philosophy would ultimately have on my life as a revolutionary.

ADVENTURE BECKONS IN OREGON

By the time summer rolled around, David and I were all set for our next big adventure. His family was headed down to the Oregon coast, and they invited me along for the trip. David and I were inseparable. And as skateboard aficionados, we took our skateboards.

One stop along the way was Crater Lake, the deepest lake in the United States, and the second deepest lake in the world. Driving up the winding, switchback road, this beautiful, prehistoric volcano came into focus. At the summit, we were on a ridge outside the visitor's center, peering down into the crystal-blue lake.

"The crater was formed by an old volcano," an attendant said, "and because it was so deep, it was ice cold—glacier cold—up on a mountain. The water is so frigid, it's usually unswimmable, but a group called the Polar Bear Club comes to the lake every year and takes their annual rite-of-passage-dip in the frigid waters."

David and I loved the idea!

"Let's do it!" I challenged. "Let's join the Polar Bear Club and make the dip ourselves!"

"Yeah!" David exclaimed.

"No!" David's mom said. "It's time to leave, to get to the campsite in time for dinner."

As everyone loaded into the station wagon, David and I told his mother that we would meet her down the mountain a ways. We rode our skateboards down a newly paved road that was very smooth and circular. It was perfect for skateboarding. We came across three little brown bear cubs that were playing alongside the road. David and I had had enough encounters with bears at various campsites before to know to stay away from bear cubs, because within 10 or 20 yards, there would always be a mama bear. We saw some people who were stopping to look at them and trying to get out of the car.

"You don't want to do that!" we shouted, whizzing past on our skateboards. Sure enough, mama bear bolted out of the woods. She probably chased the onlookers. But David and I had made another great escape!

While driving toward the Oregon coast, we encountered a mountain lion crossing in front of our car.

"Let's get out and follow it!" David exclaimed.

"No!" his mom said.

We arrived at the coast, where David and I pitched the tent while his mom, Vicky, and brother, Tom, prepared the campsite for dinner. David and I couldn't wait to jump into the river running alongside the campsite. On the ridge, we looked down at people in the water.

Several snakes were swimming downstream! No swimming for me!

The next day, we drove up to the Sea Lion Caves, a series of century-old seacoast caves with huge formations inside hanging from the ceilings. Then, we saw sand dunes stretching for miles along the coast. Beachgoers were zipping around in rented dune buggies as if they were on a roller coaster. This idyllic scene let my thoughts run loose, away from the troubling times gripping Black communities across the country.

BACK TO SCHOOL

In the fall, it was time to head to Garfield High—"The Big House" as it was called—and being a young kid who played war in the streets with plastic guns and toy grenades was now in the past. We all seemed to change overnight.

Becoming a high school student meant that you were supposed to be more mature and into teenage stuff, but I wasn't sure what that actually meant. It was a time of new discovery, identity search, and finding out where I would fit in with the juniors and seniors.

But that didn't stop our thirst for adventure or mischief; it only meant that we had graduated to a higher level of devilment. What it really meant was that the games became more elaborate. On the first snow day of that sophomore year, we were let out of school early, because the snow was falling so heavily, piling up high and fast.

David and I went home and found the perfect spot for our next caper. On his street was St. Teresa Catholic School. Classes had been dismissed earlier and the quiet streets were growing dark. On one end, near the school's entrance and gymnasium, we built a snow barrier that was three or four feet high, leaving a gap for cars to drive through on their way to the other end. At the other end of the street, we built a similar barrier, with a small gap so that it appeared the cars could get through. The plan was that once a car entered the street, our snare, we would roll a huge snowball—the size of the bottom of a snowman—into the first gap. As they moved slowly up the street, we would signal our accomplices to roll a snowball the same size into the other end, trapping the car.

Around five o'clock, a car tried to get down the street. We rolled the first giant snowball into the gap. We gave a signal to our operatives as he approached the other end; they rolled the other giant snowball into the gap, trapping the car. He was now in our snare. So, we pelted the car with snowballs from our stack of 30 or 40 snowballs that we had prepared in advance.

When a Volkswagen Beetle entered the snare and tried to plow over the snow wall, it got trapped atop it. So we gave them an extra pummeling for trying to prematurely escape. We had elevated our fun from playing war in the streets to lobbing snowballs at cars.

During that same snowstorm, as things began to thaw out, we went around the corner to the local hardware store and snatched several cans of snow spray paint that were sitting outside. Then we went through the neighborhood, spraying car windows with snow paint, so the car owners couldn't see out of either the driver side or the passenger side. We were having a ball! Until we turned the corner and saw a cop car. We were cold busted! Spray cans dangled from our hands as the cop approached.

"I've been watching you guys for the last few hours," he said, "and here's what we're going to do. Take these window scrapers and clean off all the windows you painted. Then go to the hardware store and settle up with the owner."

The hardware owner admonished us, told us to be good

kids, and let us go. What a whooping I would have gotten had he taken us to our parents' houses!

I'm sure David had the same thoughts, but we loved living on the edge. At the time, we didn't know the word that would later become a popular term for the times: antidisestablishmentarianism. Whatever the status quo was, or the establishment represented, I wanted to be the opposite of it.

That's why David and I dressed differently than the rest of our classmates. One day, I arrived late to school wearing a typical outfit: jeans with no socks, penny loafers with a penny in each shoe, and a jean jacket. I had sewn iron crosses on both sides of my jean jacket on the pockets. They were small pewter replicas of what German officers wore on their uniforms in World War I. As I came up the front stairs of the school with my books, two seniors were standing in front of me.

"You dress like a freak!" they taunted.

"Look, he's not wearing socks!"

I just put my books down and said, "Hey. I'll kick both of your asses at the same time!"

They just looked at me like I was crazy, shook their heads, and went into the school. They probably would have kicked my ass thoroughly, but I didn't care. I had a defiant edge to rebel against anyone who hinted at taking advantage of me. I wasn't going to be punked.

Like most 15-year-olds, I was struggling to discover who I was and where I fit in. As for my future, I had always known that I wanted to become a physician.

"You're going to become a doctor," my grandmother, Ma, had drilled into my head, explaining that she had worked as a waitress during the Great Depression in a downtown Chicago restaurant, passing for white, while serving wealthy white doctors and lawyers. This provided the tips to help her and Bop-bop buy their first home. She was impressed with the fact that they always had what they needed, and she wanted her grandkids to be self-sufficient.

So, she planted in my head that I was going to be a doctor, and that's what I wanted to be all that time. I was confident that I would be a doctor someday, but I was still searching for meaning.

"What are you about?" Poppy always asked us. "Whatever you do in life, know what you stand for, and who you are."

I was trying to figure that out. I had studied French for five years and was very proficient in math, which would be a good prerequisite for getting into college. Thanks to the Madrona Park playground, I could throw an accurate pass pretty far, so I tried out for the football team as a sophomore.

I made the squad as a backup quarterback. I hadn't played organized football and didn't have years of coaching behind me that these other cats had who played in the PeeWee leagues through Gill Doby, the level before entering junior high. Once in practice, the head coach, John Boitano, and the assistant coach, Mr. DiAmbry, said it was my turn to run the play from scrimmage.

We were playing against the top defense, and they called a run play out to the left. It was a simple dive play. The defense was lined up to stop the run, so when the ball was snapped, I faked the handoff to the running back, pulled it out, and ran a naked bootleg around the other end, running for about 20 yards down the field before I was tackled.

The coaches liked that, but there weren't enough opportunities for me to show what I could do on the field. Still, I wanted to be a football player. One of Grandma Dee Dee's brothers had been an all-city quarterback in high school, but, tragically, he was killed in a car crash on his graduation day in the early 1920s. I needed to complete his unfulfilled dream of playing football.

But music was taking a front seat in my life. Having come from playing in the orchestra at Meany Junior High, I was now put in the concert band, which meant I would be in the marching band. So, between playing football and studying, I had to learn how to simultaneously march and play the trumpet, and learn the formations for halftime at varsity football games. Mommy became my personal taxi service, running me to my trumpet lessons, football games, and other activities, while doing the same for Michael and Aaron.

As Halloween rolled around, David and I concocted our next scheme. White kids from across the city would all go down to the wealthy area in Madison Park and gather in a huge crowd down on Madison Street near the Waterfront. I decided I was going to dress up as a mummy, so I found gauze bandages that I rolled around my body from head to toe.

I had one of the starter guns that David and I had been playing with; we had bored it out, so they could actually fire a .22-round caliber bullet. We didn't know what we would do with these pistols, but we decided to carry one just because we thought we were bad asses. As we made our way through the neighborhood streets, picking up expensive candy bars along the way from the rich folks, we got down to the Madison Park area where there were hundreds of white teens packing the streets. Some were drinking, some were smoking, and eventually, the cop cars came to disperse the crowd.

"I have a car," said one of the dudes we were hanging out with.

Six of us piled into his car, and almost immediately got pulled over.

"What do we do with the pistols?" David panicked.

"Give me yours!" I said, tucking it inside the small of my back inside of my pants before I got out of the car.

As the cops frisked everyone looking for alcohol, cigarettes, drugs, or who knows what, one of the cops came to me and said, "Okay, you're okay. You stand over here."

My mummy costume saved the day! It was the last time that

I would be the only Black guy pulled over out of a group and not frisked and searched. It was hilarious.

Later that fall, the Rolling Stones were scheduled to play in Seattle. Mark and I had missed them when they first rolled through with the British Invasion in 1964, but this time, we bought tickets early. The show included a group called Paul Revere and the Raiders, and they wore bluecoat uniforms from the Revolutionary War. The other group was Patti LaBelle and the Bluebells. This was my first big concert unaccompanied by my brothers.

BLACK POWER RISES

By the summer of 1966, the Civil Rights Movement was taking another turn. James Meredith was leading his March Against Fear in June, intending to walk from Memphis, Tennessee, to Jackson, Mississippi, on his own to advocate for Black voter registration. His trek ended on the second day when he was shot.

Jackson, Mississippi, was near our grandfather Bop-bop's original home. Because he had no intentions of being called a nigger and standing idly by, his family got him out of the South as quickly as possible. He was definitely a stand-and-fight person, rather than one to live on his knees.

Meredith survived the assassination attempt, and the march continued, led by Dr. King and Stokely Carmichael. This also marked the first time that Stokely Carmichael introduced the need for and the rise of Black Power, sparking a new era in the Civil Rights Movement. Prior to that, Malcolm X had been firing up the Muslim faith, but he had not yet become fully recognized as a civil rights leader until his death.

This was also the peak of Muhammad Ali's career. He had knocked out Joe Frazier in 1964 and changed his name first to Cassius X, then to Muhammad Ali. Then he fought Floyd Patterson, who had held the title before Frazier. Patterson, who had publicly criticized Muhammad Ali for changing his name, and refused to call Ali by that name, was set for a punishing by Ali.

"What's my name?" Ali demanded while punching Patterson repeatedly.

This power play sparked a realization about justice and victory, bringing the era into sharper focus.

That summer, I was determined to get in football shape to compete for a starting position. David and I were working out hard, running long distances, aiming toward the fall to get a shot at unseating the starting quarterback. Davon Smith was popular with the coaches and had good skills, but I was ready to take him on. My sister was dating this dude named Curtis Harris. He was three years older than me and played basketball at Highline Community College. I was in his car bragging about my ability to play football.

"Show me what you can do," he said in the backyard.

I got down into a three-point stance and was ready to knock him down. As I charged him, he sidestepped and threw me to the side. I landed awkwardly on my shoulder—breaking my collarbone! That eliminated my chances of making the varsity football team and challenging Davon Smith.

Before the injury, I had purchased a ticket for another Stones concert.

"Are you sure you want to go?" my mother asked.

I was going to that concert, broken shoulder or not. She dropped me off. Wearing a sling, I sat near the front, mindful that any sudden movement would give me serious, sharp pain on my broken collarbone. So, my calm exterior did not reveal the excitement within during my last time seeing the Rolling Stones.

*My stylish paternal grandparents,
Gratdada and Grandma Dee Dee, (Elmer Dixon, Sr. and Mildred "Dee Dee"
Dixon) are the couple in the center, around 1920
in Chicago, with friends.*

*My grandparents holding my
mother, Frances Sledge, in 1925
in Chicago.*

*My mother, Frances Sledge,
in Chicago.*

My great-great-grandmother Emma Ely, my mother's great-grandmother, in back of my grandmother's house in Chicago. Born around 1860, she remembered hearing stories of people crying when President Abraham Lincoln was shot.

My father, Elmer Dixon, Jr., with a buddy in the U.S. Army.

Dad with college friends.

Frances Sledge, my grandfather Roy Sledge's mother. My mother was named after her.

Aunt Doris, my father's sister, in Chicago.

My parents walking downtown Chicago during the mid-1940s.

My grandfather, Bop-bop, in his "yard clothes." He was so sharp, he even dressed up to do yard work.

My mother, Frances Sledge, walking downtown Chicago, probably on her way to college classes.

My well-dressed Dad, Elmer Dixon, Jr., ready to step out on the town.

Gratdada with baby Joanne, my sister, in 1947.

The Dixon brothers (from left) Michael, Elmer and Aaron.

The Dixon family. From left: Michael, me, Aaron, Joanne and "Poppy," our father.

My grandmother, Josephine Sledge, Bop-bop's wife, in Chicago.

My childhood crush, Marge Lewis, who lived next door to my grandparents.

My great-great grandmother Emma Ely (far left) with her nieces and nephews, my great cousins. Most lived into their hundreds. This photo was probably taken during the 1930s or 1940s.

The Dixon kids with cousin Keith in the front and cousin Mark in the back. I'm behind Joanne with Aaron and Michael, during one of our summer trips to Chicago. The girl in front is another cousin.

My Grandma Dee Dee, Mildred Dixon, my father's mother, at 100.

My parents (center) celebrating our first New Year's Eve in Seattle in the late 1950s with their friends, Fred and Betty Mayo (left), the first family that we met and socialized with.

Ella Ely, my great-grandmother, who was Emma Ely's daughter and Josephine's mother. She died when Josephine was only 6 years old.

My paternal grandmother, Mildred "Dee Dee" Dixon, wife of Elmer, Sr., on their front porch in Chicago.

The Dixon kids at home in Seattle. From left: Aaron, me, Michael and Joanne.

My childhood friend, David Booth.

This is my grandmother Dee Dee's brother. He was an All-American quarterback at Western Kentucky and died in a car accident on his way to graduation.

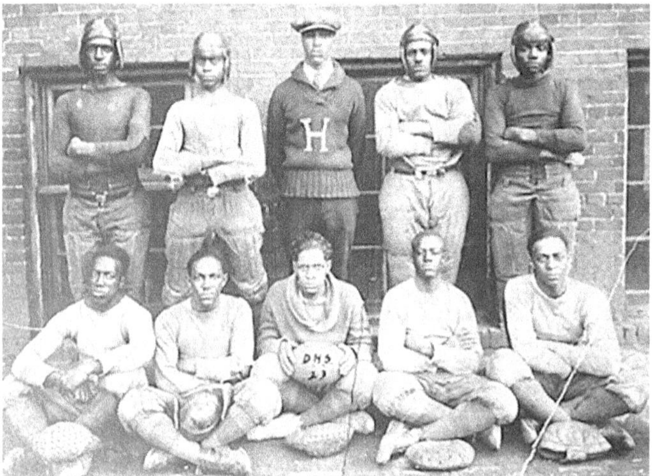

CHAPTER 11

Death of Innocence

My junior year in high school marked a transition for two of my closest friendships. Mark was following his ambition to be an actor by getting involved with the drama club. He'd been acting in productions since he was a small child and his entire focus was on the arts, music, and drama.

Both our ambitions were creative, in different directions. I was honing my skills as a trumpeter. I was now playing in the Jazz Band or Stage Band and was getting involved in The Regents, an R&B band formed by my bandmate, Gary Hammond.

The drummer was Ralph Brooks, and the organ player was Dennis Blackmond, whose older brother, Ronny, played with the hit group War. Our guitar player was a sophomore, Biggie Lewis, a little dude with a lot of soul who played like Wes Montgomery. Our bass player was Freddie Eaves, who lived around the corner. He had a fine sister named LaTonya. Another sophomore, Leanard Rhodes, occasionally sat in with us on some sets, and later in life would become known as Doc Rhodes because of his musical prowess. There wasn't an instrument that he couldn't play, and he was at the top of his game. A couple of dudes sang with the group. Paul Allen was our main singer, and occasionally we let a young cat, Michael Cook, do some guest vocals. They needed a trumpet player, so Gary invited me to join the band, which provided an additional sense of belonging and inspired me to up my game.

Around the same time, unbeknownst to me, two cats in Oakland, California—Huey P. Newton and Bobby Seale—were forming the Black Panther Party for Self-Defense. I didn't know it at the time, but it was probably the most significant event that would change my life forever.

I was busy getting into my music and hanging out with the band, practicing and doing gigs every weekend. Our band manager, Garvin Terry, would book whatever gigs he could find for us. Sometimes they were little joints way out in the boonies; other times we played at the Pink Pussycat, an after-hours joint down on 1st Avenue. The owners had to sneak us in through the alley and back door, because we were underage—15 and 16 years old. Once inside, we would play long into the night, till 3 a.m., when they let us back out the back door. One of the more popular venues that we played was the Saturday night cabarets at the Chamber of Commerce in downtown Seattle.

During junior year, I changed the friends that I hung out with. David and I had gotten in more mischief, and it probably led to us hanging out less together. Mark's family had grown; his father had been divorced for several years, and he met a new love and married. She brought with her three sons who were all older than Mark and me. Two of the sons were twins and were regarded as being very intelligent, in the genius category with high IQs. The other brother, Tombo, was a year or so older than us, but we still let him hang out with us.

They came from an elite family. One of the twins had an expensive coin collection. David and I thought they were snooty and uppity, so one afternoon when we knew that the house was going to be empty, we snuck in through a way that we had known for years, went up into their bedroom, and took the whole coin collection. As we sorted through it back in our den, we noticed that all the coins were in mint condition and brand new; we started feeling bad about our crime. So, we decided to take the coins back to the house, confess, and return everything. As we sat in front of Mark's dad and his new stepmother, they admonished us for taking the coins in the first place and praised us at the same time for having the courage to confess and bring everything back.

Soon after that, I began hanging out with a couple of dudes whom I knew from school and the neighborhood. One was a Filipino guy who lived around the corner. Jesse Parrot had a passion for cars and had purchased a '65 Corvette, which he and his brothers had refurbished. It was dynamite. I liked riding home with him in that car.

I had always been somewhat of a self-driven individual and had taken my first job as a paperboy at age 12. My paper route ran through the wealthy neighborhood on the other side of the red line, and I would get large tips when I went to collect for the paper delivery. This money allowed me to purchase my own food, to the envy of my friends who had no money. Later on, while doing side work at the Madrona Café, I purchased a moped, and by the time I started my junior year, I had purchased a Honda motorcycle, but it was nothing like riding in that Corvette. I vowed to work enough odd jobs to one day own a car.

The other cat I started hanging out with was Michael Dean—a long, lanky dude who also lived on that same block with Jesse. He was a sharp dresser, like Aaron, and he used to hang out with this other cat named Leroy Fair. Leroy had all the girls chasing after him because he looked so good in his dapper clothes and a cologne called By George. I hadn't yet learned how to dress in nice clothes and felt awkward doing so, but I was learning by hanging out with these cats.

THE WORLD AROUND ME

As 1967 rolled around, I took a more serious look at what was going on around us and the broader world. The Vietnam War was taking center stage, and being that I was about to turn 17, I would be eligible for the draft the next year. Young men my age could not escape thinking about it.

The world was shifting fast in front of our very eyes! Even though I still had the idea of becoming a doctor, going to the University of Hawaii, and being around fine Hawaiian women, those were just distant dreams clouded by the reality of the '60s.

Besides, I hadn't had much luck with girls. That year, I was persuaded to go to the Tolo, a midwinter ball. I asked my cute friend, Hideko Baise:

"Will you go with me?"

"Yes," she said, much to my surprise.

So, I bought her the obligatory corsage and took her to the dance. While dropping her off at home, I wondered, *Am I supposed to kiss her?* I didn't feel like it.

"Good night," I said, and left.

I was always somewhat of a serious guy—some would say even moody, but the country's mood was serious and it was affecting me. Late that spring, Dr. King gave his now-famous speech on the Vietnam War at Riverside Church in New York. His tone had changed, as he questioned the validity of the nonviolent approach that he had encouraged for so long.

IGNITING THE "I'M BLACK AND I'M PROUD" MOVEMENT

Both Aaron and I became increasingly interested in the Civil Rights Movement. We began to explore what was happening in our community and around the country. We had marched with Dr. King in '61 with our parents, and were well aware of the Movement and its harsh realities.

Yet things were taking a different turn. Black youths were speaking out, and people were fighting back.

"This heavy cat named Stokely Carmichael is coming to Garfield," Aaron told me. "You need to hear his message."

It was the spring of 1967. I was 16, about to turn 17. At the time, Stokely was the head of the Student Nonviolent Coordinating Committee, SNCC. His predecessor, H. Rap Brown, had gained notoriety during the rebellions in Detroit. A notorious poster of him holding a lit match said, "Burn, Baby, Burn." That was the only thing I had heard about. I didn't know much more about who they were or what they stood for, so I couldn't wait until Monday to go check this cat out at Garfield.

The crowd was overflowing. We couldn't even get into the auditorium, so we listened to his message blaring over loudspeakers as we stood outside amongst hundreds of people.

He said the reason Black people were in such deep trouble was that we didn't love ourselves or the color of our skin.

That's B.S., I thought. *My two best friends are white. That has nothing to do with me.*

Stokely Carmichael said we had been programmed to think that Black was dirty, that Black was wrong, and that everything associated with Black was bad. He gave examples of the hidden messages and negative connotations around being Black. He said:

"So why is it that when you go to the theater to see a movie, the good knight's dressed in white, shiny armor and riding on a white horse, and the bad knight is on a black horse and wears dark, dingy armor? And when you go turn on your TV set and watch a western, the good cowboys are all dressed in white? He wears a white, ten-gallon hat and rides a white horse named Trigger, and the bad cowboy's in a dirty, black, dusty outfit, on a black horse, and his name is Dirty Bart?"

He was presenting ideas that I had never considered.

"Why is it that when you go to a restaurant after you finish a meal and you want dessert," he continued, "the angel's food cake is white and the devil's food cake is black? It's because you have been conditioned to think that black is bad. You don't like your natural hair, so you process your hair and you run around with your conks."

My immediate thought was, *I don't have conked hair!* So that didn't ring true to me. I had too many close friends who were white and I didn't understand that he was not just talking about a Black and white thing. It just didn't resonate yet because I wasn't able to separate the two; that if you liked being Black, that meant that you disliked what was white. In fact, on the playground, calling someone Black constituted fighting words.

It wasn't until later that summer when I was at the tennis court that I began to contemplate some of the things that he had said. I thought about my white friends: they lived in larger homes and Mark even had a live-in maid, yet they were only two blocks away. I realized that no Black people lived on their block, except for Eddie Cotton. He was a famous, world-class middleweight champion boxer and was very popular in Seattle. I would later find out that the area had been redlined and Black people weren't allowed to own homes in that area. Eddie must have been an exception.

Similarly, I reflected on the summer that a young white woman who was a graduate student from the University of Washington came to work at the park. Her name was Ms. Sullivan and she taught us the finer points of playing tennis. Black folks had inherited the tennis courts of Madrona, an unexpected benefit from the white flight. And while the tennis courts were left behind for the incoming Black families, it was most likely a prevailing thought that we couldn't or wouldn't play tennis, anyway. Ms. Sullivan changed all of that. We loved her because of her kindness and her genuine interest in us.

That summer, we won all or most of our matches and qualified to play in the City Championship, which was being held at the Seattle Tennis Club. It was not far from our neighborhood in the affluent area known as Madison Park, near the private, gated Broadmoor community. We didn't know at the time that Black people were excluded from this exclusive club, but I'm certain Ms. Sullivan did, though she didn't tell us. When we entered the club, she took us to the cafeteria to await our matches.

Wearing our little white shorts and T-shirts, we were waiting for our opportunity to go out and play, when in walks this tall, lanky brother all dressed in his kitchen whites. He looked at us and said, "You guys better get up and get in the kitchen and get to work," as if we were the summer help in this tennis club where Black people were not allowed.

"We're here to play tennis," we said.

He cast a shocked look at us.

Then we went out on the tennis court, whipped that team, and won the championship! But when it came time for us to get our trophies during an award presentation on the center court, the administration was nowhere to be found. So, Ms. Sullivan presented us with our trophies and we left, without ever receiving recognition from the tennis officials that we had just won the Seattle title. They had most likely cleared the courts for us to play after realizing that little Black kids were coming to play in their lily-white tennis club.

These experiences all came back to me as I reflected on Stokely's comments. Something ignited inside me!

Before I knew it, I joined SNCC, the Student Nonviolent Coordinating Committee, along with a group of students. We started dressing in dark black pants and dark navy-blue jackets with SNCC written on the backs.

I paid closer attention to the news. Earlier that May, a group of Black Panthers led by Bobby Seale and Little Bobby Hutton had descended upon the California State Legislature in Sacramento. Later that summer, Detroit would explode into a rebellion commonly referred to as a "riot" in the white established media across the country. A well-known writer of soul music, Kenny Young, who had written tunes like "Under the Boardwalk" for The Drifters, wrote in an op-ed that Detroit's "insurrection" was a natural response to the conditions that Black people were forced to live in.

STARING DOWN THE BARREL OF A GUN

Over the summer, I had taken a job at the local corner grocery store, the Madrona IGA. It was the most popular grocery store in the neighborhood, and I often got good tips from the wealthy white folks who came up from over the hill to get their groceries. I was a bag boy and was responsible for tidying up the back room and keeping the floors clean.

One evening, as I was sweeping the floors with the large push broom, I came around the corner toward the front of the store. A guy was standing there with a stocking cap over his head holding a gun on the two checkout clerks.

My eyes and his eyes met. As he turned toward me, I was staring down the barrel of the gun. I dropped the broom, which made a large bang as it hit the floor.

For a quick minute, I thought I was dead, but he grabbed the bag of money and ran out the door.

Another brush with death! The money that I made from the store along with the tips were enough to save up to purchase my dad's car. Poppy and I had made a deal; since I was ready to enter my senior season at Garfield, it was a perfect time for me to have my own vehicle. My 1957 Buick special was a big tank of a car, with big fish fins on the back and a monster grill on the front. It was big, heavy, and roomy.

PASSION FOR MUSIC

That fall, music took center stage in my life. I saw Diana Ross and The Supremes in concert, as well as Hugh Masekela, who remained a huge inspiration for my trumpet playing.

"Want to join our band?" asked Michael Mitchell, a popular singer for a rival band called The Majestics. He was a dynamic singer. Always dressed in flashy clothes—a full-length white mink coat—he had processed hair, or as we used to call it "a conk," whose waves flowed like a perfectly coiffed hairdo, with every hair in place. He was like Seattle's own James Brown.

"You and Gary can play your horns for our band," he said. "We've already got two lead guitar players, a rhythm guitar player, a bass guitar player, two saxophone players—including a bass sax—two trumpet players, and two full drummers, along with an organ player."

Gary and I were excited.

"We'll be battling The Night Men on New Year's Eve," Michael said, "and I need two extra horn players. We want to beat The Night Men."

What an electric night!

Women screaming for Michael packed the Seattle Center; this was the biggest audience and venue I'd ever played. Wearing Black tuxedos with white pants, like all The Majestics, Gary and I waited at the back of the crowd with white tuxedo-clad Michael, who was immensely popular with the girls.

"Should we just walk up to the stage?" Michael asked.

"Let's approach the stage at a slow trot," I suggested, "moving through the hordes of screaming women before we get up on the stage to join the band."

Once the battle started, the overflow crowds erupted as we battled back and forth between The Night Men all night long.

The Majestics were declared the winners! It was exciting being a part of that magnificent night. We were showmen and could stand our ground with the best. We would later compete in several battles of the bands playing with our own group, The Regents, and could hold our own, and sometimes win.

Seattle's Black community had a rich tradition of music and bands. Quincy Jones came out of Garfield, as did Jimi Hendrix, later. In our class was this drummer, Wayne Bibbs, who was by far the most advanced a drummer that anyone we had ever seen; this prodigy would go on to play with Quincy's band. In the '60s and '70s, live bands were in, and when people went out on the weekends, they expected to see live music.

I was in the thick of it with my buddies and enjoyed being creative on stage with my horn. I had even purchased a Dizzy Gillespie-style trumpet—which had two horn barrels. I soon got a rep as a good trumpet player as I began to get more serious about my music.

A YOUNG BLACK ACTIVIST TAKES ACTION

My friends and I were not going to take "no" for an answer from our white principal, who was refusing to allow us to form a Black Student Union at Garfield High School.

"No," Mr. Hanawalt said as a half-dozen of us gathered in his office. "You don't need a Black Student Union. You have a Boys Club."

"That's different," I countered. Perhaps the school's willingness to change the name from Boys Club to The Men's Club—at the insistence of its Black president Larry Taylor, because the word "boy" was derogatory—meant the principal would now say yes to a BSU.

But his stern expression conveyed that he wasn't about to concede to our demand right now. Anger welled within me.

"The Men's Club is not the same as a Black Student Union,"

I protested, sporting my newly sprouted afro, black pants, and navy-blue jacket emblazoned with the Student Nonviolent Coordinating Committee logo. "We need a Black Student Union. We need a voice!"

Mr. Hanawalt shook his head and said more forcefully, "No, the Black students don't need their own group."

We had to make him understand and grant our request.

"The reason we need a Black Student Union here at Garfield," I explained, "is that we need to organize around the issues facing Black students. And we need you to put relevant Black History in the curriculum."

"I don't see the need for that," Mr. Hanawalt said flatly.

"We need a Black Student Union!" I declared.

Determination surged through me as my mind flashed over the months leading up to this showdown. Returning to Garfield for my senior year in the fall of 1967 saw a significant shift in my view of life in American society. I could no longer be a passive observer, watching the beatings and murders of innocent Black people. I had seen death close up by now and it was more than some obscure occurrence on TV in some far away city.

For example, one afternoon, after my friend David and I arrived home from school, we were near the park.

Screech! A brother jumped out of his car, screaming, and firing a gun at three men.

A bullet whizzed past David's head.

All three men dropped to the ground, dead and bleeding.

We had never seen such violence close up. We later learned that the shooter was Dewight Harris, a member of a neighborhood family, who had been a victim of ongoing bullying by the three men. They pushed him to a breaking point, and he defended himself. On top of that, one of the Dinish brothers, who was a member of the one of the Black families in our church, had been attacked and brutally murdered just blocks away from our house. Life had gotten serious and real in a short amount of time.

At the same time, across America that summer, deadly racial insurrections had erupted in Detroit, Newark, and Watts. Dr. Martin Luther King, Jr. continued to lead nonviolent protests, two years after the assassination of Nation of Islam Leader Malcolm X, who advocated for change "by any means necessary." All the while, countless Black people were routinely beaten and killed by police, financially oppressed, and doomed to suffer in poverty, poor health, unemployment, and neighborhoods plagued by drugs and crime.

My growing consciousness of Black powerlessness—and several brushes with death of my own—had ignited an urgent need to change the system that was crushing our people. This racist system included public education, and we were going to make change right here, right now.

I remembered the previous spring, when SNCC Chairman Stokely Carmichael had spoken words in this very school that ignited a fire in my spirit to commit to the cause of liberating and uplifting Black people. Remembering him in that moment, as I stared down the principal, I thought:

We can do this! Now!

I felt emboldened and confident as a leader in a national network of student activists who were working to empower the Black community. The Student Nonviolent Coordinating Committee had chosen me as one of the initial co-chairs of its Seattle chapter. SNCC was organized by Ella Baker, who led Dr. King's Southern Christian Leadership Conference to provide a platform for younger Black people to help make change through activism. While SNCC organized voter registration drives in the South, violent opposition to its mission became personified in the KKK murders of three young activists during the Mississippi Freedom Summer of 1964.

For our SNCC chapter in Seattle, we were still trying to

figure out how to strategically organize the community. To what end? For what goals? Most of our organizing mimicked SNCC's voter registration work in the South. But in our town, we saw no local Black candidates to endorse for office outside of established lawmakers like Sam Smith, whom many young people viewed as part of the old guard establishment, and not really representing Black people.

"Where are the Black candidates that we can support to get people to register to vote?" I asked my group, because we really didn't feel like we were going to make a difference. During these same conversations, we focused our urgent quest for change on our school.

"Look, we need a Black Student Union at Garfield," I announced to my friends who were now SNCC members. My brother Aaron was already at the University of Washington, working with Larry Gossett, and they had joined other students to start a Black Student Union.

Around that time, a *Seattle Post-Intelligencer* reporter interviewed me about my opinion on the Vietnam War. As I stood there responding to questions with my afro, dark shades, and my SNCC jacket and dark clothes, I never thought about the fact that I had stepped into a new phase of my life—Black and fearless.

And that was exactly how I felt, staring down our principal as we demanded a Black Student Union.

"No," he said.

I took that as his declaration of war on our mission to start a BSU. So, we fought back at our next pep assembly, when hundreds of students—Black, white, Asian, Indian, and Latino—packed into the bleachers in the school gymnasium.

Here's when I leveraged my popularity and visibility at school sporting events, to protest the school's refusal to give us a BSU.

First, I was the drum major who led the band down the field during halftime shows during our football games. I loved being decked out in a white uniform, a tall band leader hat covered with feathers, and commanding the band with a purple and gold baton.

"Elmer, would you like to be the drum major?" Mr. Putchi, the band director, had asked at the start of the school year. "You're the perfect height and the perfect candidate."

I figured since I wouldn't be on the football field playing quarterback, I might as well be leading the band down the field during halftime shows. I had watched some halftime shows for Black universities, like Texas A&M, Grambling State University, and Southern University; their high-stepping drum majors impressed me so much, I decided to emulate these cats and become a high-stepper myself.

So, on game nights during the halftime show, I'd gather the band at the end of the stadium underneath the goal post, blow my whistle, turn, and high-step it out onto the field.

"Elmer!" girls yelled from the packed stands.

I must be high-stepping in style, I thought, so electrified that with every scream of my name, I invented some new moves, or a new baton-twirl, hoping that I wouldn't fall on my ass.

After the games, the cheerleaders piled into my car and I drove them to the popular eatery, Dick's Burgers on Broadway. Then we cruised to local haunted spots where they screamed like it was Halloween.

On the way, I showed off my spooky storytelling skills that I'd learned from Poppy, who was a master ghost-story teller. By the time we reached our favorite haunted spot—the ritzy community of Madison Park that must have been some sort of sanitarium for wealthy people—the cheerleaders were terrified, perched on the edge of their seats.

"Watch out for people walking around in white clothes," I warned as my car approached the community's long gates that opened automatically for us to enter the grounds. "They're zombies! They might put their hands through the car windows!"

The girls shrieked. And I, who had no girlfriends at the time, was loving the thrill of a car full of cheerleaders on these Friday night adventures. Back at school, the girls were among my many friends and supporters, who of course attended the pep assembly.

Little did anyone know, my Comrades and I were about to begin our protests in the name of forcing the school to give us our BSU.

As the trumpet players in the jazz band, we sat positioned in the front-and-center focal point on the gym floor, flanked by the other seated band members. So, when the pep rally began, so did our protest.

I refused to play "The Star-Spangled Banner" or stand to recite The Pledge of Allegiance. My Comrades in the audience did the same thing.

Everybody saw me. I got kicked out of school.

My dad brought me back.

And our protests continued at the next pep assembly. When the jazz band stood to play the national anthem, I played it while seated.

Again, I was sent to the principal's office and kicked out of school.

"Listen, if you're in the band," the band director said, "you have to play."

At the next pep assembly, I played "The Star-Spangled Banner" while sitting.

"You can't keep doing this," the band director and principal admonished. "As a member of the band, you have to do what everyone is doing."

Instead, at the next pep assembly, we waited until the silent pause after The Pledge of Allegiance and the national anthem.

"Bing, bing!" I shouted, front and center on the gym floor, looking up at the crowd.

"Bing, bing!" yelled my Comrades in the bleachers, including Kathy Jones and other brothers and sisters.

"Bang, bang!" I shouted.

More students joined the chant: "Bang, bang!"

"Ungawa!" I shouted a word rooted in Swahili that means, *listen to me!*

"Ungawa!" most of the students echoed.

"Black power!" I screamed.

"Black power!" the student body thundered along with me, over and over.

Then our chant morphed into ear-splitting applause and cheers.

It was a glorious moment!

But they still denied us a Black Student Union. Instead, I was suspended once again. When my mother returned me to school to get reinstated, the vice principal asked her, "Mrs. Dixon, can't you make him stop?"

She replied, "I can't make him do anything."

She was having no part of making me cow down to the system.

So, we huddled up in our next meeting to talk about our next move. We decided it was time to go to the school district office and confront the superintendent. The group of us included myself, Anthony Ware, and a young sista by the name of Kathy Jones. Kathy came from a strong family of women and she was not to be messed with. When we marched in the office, she got up in the superintendent of public instruction's face and told him that under no uncertain terms would we back down, and that there would be hell to pay if he didn't overrule the principal and give us the BSU.

The superintendent acted as if he was shocked by Kathy's aggressiveness and said it wasn't up to him; it was up to the individual schools to grant a new club. But we had another plan and we were ready to execute.

When we got back to the school the next day, our group marched into the principal's office and said:

"If you don't give us a BSU, we're going to organize a class boycott."

"No one will support you," Mr. Hanawalt said, not believing that the Black students could convince the student body to participate.

Well, he was apparently unaware of the deep allegiances we had formed with the Asian, Latino, and white students, who had been our friends since elementary school. As such, they showed their solidarity by joining our fight when rival Ballard High School students attacked us.

It happened while we—band members and Garfield spectators alike—were at their school for a basketball game. When it ended, the all-white Ballard kids jumped our student body. As the Black kids defended ourselves and fought back, our white, Asian, and Latino classmates from Garfield were fighting right alongside us.

Earlier in the year, Ballard had jumped us twice, and we retaliated by pummeling their school buses with rocks and knocking out all the windows.

The next fight further demonstrated our white schoolmates' solidarity. It happened at the Seattle arena after the city basketball championship. The referees, the worst in the Athletic Association, were known to cheat for the white teams when they played against multiracial Garfield. Sure enough, during that game, the referees heavily favored Ballard.

That, plus the on-going feud between our schools, let everybody know that a post-game brawl was imminent.

"Look what I got," said Dave Shyatt, a white guy who played in the band with me, as he opened his trumpet case to reveal brass knuckles, chains, and a small billy club.

Sure enough, a fight ensued with the Black, white, Latino, and Asian students of Garfield fighting against the Swedes at Ballard. Of course, we always won the fights. And now, when we asked our friends to support our class boycott to force the school to give us a Black Student Union, they were all in.

On the designated day, when the morning eight o'clock bell rang, nobody went to class. Hundreds of students of every race flooded the hallways, packed in like sardines.

And we became the first high school on the West Coast to have a Black Student Union. I was elected president, and we organized events, read books by Black authors, and spoke out against the Vietnam War and other atrocities.

It never dawned on me that my BSU leadership and activism would cause feelings of isolation, distance, and ultimately the loss of my two best friends. They were white, and came from some measure of privilege, perhaps Mark more than David, however, there was a distinct difference between myself and each of them. At the time, I thought that whether I was an activist or a revolutionary, we could still be friends, that we could still dream about our future goals. But life was becoming much more serious for me.

CHAPTER 12

Awoke

I had no idea that I was about to cruise into a riot—or a jail cell—as I headed over to Dag's Drive-In after the basketball game. All I wanted was to enjoy some wholesome Friday night fun, hanging out with my friends in this popular South End gathering spot near Franklin High School. I was looking forward to coasting into the huge parking lot at the intersection of Empire Way and Rainier, to see my classmates who liked to park, listen to music, talk, and laugh.

But that wasn't what I saw.

Black kids were running and screaming.

And white cops were chasing them, wielding billy clubs.

Red and blue lights flashed.

Apparently, a fight had broken out and the cops were dispersing everybody. I glanced around the chaos.

A cop was wrestling a sister to the ground with his knee in her back.

I rushed toward her. I recognized her as my friend, Debbie Rodriguez.

"Are you alright?" I asked, and yelled, "Get off of her!"

Before I knew it, two cops jumped me, wrestled me to the ground, and arrested me.

"You're under arrest for interfering with an officer," they said.

The cops took me to juvie and I was charged with inciting a riot; that was my first time in juvie. When I got before the judge, rather than sentencing me to jail time, he made me write a 500-word essay on why young Black people were organizing. This was my first exposure to mass chaos and it illustrated a need for the Black community to be better organized to respond to cops when they were attacking us in our community.

It was early 1968, and things were growing more intense, in the Movement, in general, and in my own role in particular. My eyes were now wide open, thanks to local and national acts of brutality and murder against Black people.

At the South Carolina State University campus, police had opened fire on students who were protesting segregation at Orangeburg's only bowling alley. Three protesters died and 27 were wounded. The nine officers were tried and then acquitted, while the protest leader was charged and convicted of inciting to riot and served seven months in prison. Little did I know, that I, too, would soon be arrested for the same thing.

I was no longer getting my hair cut, and my natural hair was growing out. The Black Power Movement was in full stride. James Brown had come out with a song, "Say It Loud—I'm Black and I'm Proud," and more people started wearing afros. My parents knew that Aaron and I were organizing in SNCC, and they were aware of it—along with its leaders, Stokely Carmichael and H. Rap Brown—because the organization was very prevalent in the Civil Rights Movement in the South.

As long as my grades were good, they were not going to say much that year to discourage me, because they were also politically aware and supportive of their children becoming politically active.

The mood in the country was changing. Young people—Black, white, Latino, Asian, and Native Americans—were not satisfied with just marching and taking a beating, but were standing up and being counted. They were not asking for their civil rights, but demanding their God-given rights. They were not going to beg; they were going to take them.

Vietnam War protests had spawned groups such as Students for a Democratic Society (SDS), the Peace and Freedom Party, and the more militant wing of SDS, The Weathermen. We weren't quite sure what that meant for us or what was going to happen, but the dynamic of struggling against racist oppression was about to change in Seattle. It was like a pressure cooker was about to blow its top.

Still lingering in our collective Black psyche was the June 1965 police killing of 40-year-old Robert L. Reese. He was shot in the back of the head while fleeing a fight scene by an off-duty cop. King County prosecuting attorney Charles O'Carroll refused to charge the officers, even though the inquest jury had delivered a verdict of reasonable homicide. Instead, the three Black men riding in the car with Reese were charged and convicted of assault after they had responded to racist taunts by the off-duty cops. Now, three years later, the Black community had not forgotten.

Nor had I.

During the last week of March, a group of Black students from Franklin High School invited my brother, Aaron, his fellow University of Washington BSU leaders, Larry Gossett and Carl Miller, me, and a few of my Comrades from Garfield, to meet at their hangout, the Beanery, a small burger joint across the street from their school.

"We heard about your BSU chapters," said Charles Toliver and Trolis Flavors, "and we want to organize a BSU at Franklin. We need your help to deal with some problems we're having."

A few weeks earlier, they told us that a young Black female student had come to school one morning wearing her new afro. She was called to the office.

"Your hair is not becoming of a young woman," the vice principal told her. "You're suspended from school. You can come back to school when you have an appropriate hairdo."

Charles and Trolis then told us that when Black students got into fights with white students over some trivial thing, the white students were sent back to class, while the Black kids were disciplined or kicked out of school. When they asked Franklin's principal to grant them permission to organize the BSU, to help deal with these issues, he refused.

"Let's go!" we said.

The eight of us immediately left the Beanery, marched across the street, and entered the Franklin High School principal's office.

"Get out!" we ordered. "We're running the school," we declared, "until you give in to our demands. We're staying in your office until you give the students a BSU."

The principal, vice principal, the secretary, and counselors quickly exited the building. We barricaded ourselves in for the night and for the long haul, with no intention to leave until our demands were met.

The next morning, the phone rang, and we answered.

"Good morning, this is Franklin High School, can I help you?"

On the other end was the principal and he said, "You know, they can have a BSU, we give up. Please leave our offices."

We briefly celebrated our success and left the school.

A week later—on April 4th, 1968—I was back at Garfield in my geometry class when the phone rang.

"Elmer," said my teacher, Mr. Bob Naramore, "they want you in the office." That was not unusual, as I had been called to the office on multiple occasions.

"Fine," I said. "What did I do now?"

I closed my books and as soon as I stepped outside the classroom, two detectives read me my rights and handcuffed me.

"You're under arrest for unlawful assembly," they said before quietly marching me out of the school and driving me off to juvie.

Unbeknownst to me at the time, one of my BSU brothers, Clifton Wyatt, was also arrested at the school. At the University of Washington, Aaron, Larry Gossett, and Carl Miller, as well as several Franklin students, were being arrested simultaneously.

When I arrived in juvie, TV reports showed riots and burning all across the country. We learned that hours earlier, Dr. King had been assassinated.

This created bitter irony for the timing of our arrest. It was almost as if authorities knew the assassination was going to occur, so they were rounding up the so-called Black Power leaders to get us off the streets before any chaos happened in Seattle. As I sat trapped inside the walls of juvie in a holding room, we crowded around the TV, watching the shocking news as the nation erupted and the streets burned.

Riots were breaking out in Washington, D.C., L.A., Dallas, Chicago, and other cities. James Brown was performing at a concert in Boston and made a plea for Black people to not riot. But they were so distraught, they took their rage and grief to the streets.

Later that evening, when Poppy and Mommy came to get me out of juvie, they were in shock, anger, and disbelief over the death of Dr. King while their two older sons were in jail.

"Are you alright?" they asked.

"I'm fine," I answered.

We drove home in silence as hurt roiled in my parents' eyes. I could sense their dismay, frustration, and pain of losing yet another important leader. NAACP leader Medgar Evers, Malcolm

X, President John F. Kennedy, and now Dr. Martin Luther King, Jr., had all represented so much hope for Blacks. The world was in for some serious shit and my parents' two oldest sons were now a part of this Movement that was evolving and growing, and they couldn't do anything to stop it.

That night, with Aaron and our friends, we left our mark to express outrage over Dr. King's death. We lived on the edge of the red line—though we didn't know the term at the time—that separated the Black neighborhood from wealthy white residential areas. We were only blocks from the ritzy gated community of Broadmoor in Madison Park on Lake Washington. So, carrying a gasoline can, we snuck past the guards on the front gate by entering through the University of Washington arboretum. On the perfectly manicured putting green of the 13th hole, we drizzled gasoline in the shape of a giant B and P. Then we lit it up.

No one ever knew how the giant Black letters for Black Power were emblazoned there.

Meanwhile, Dr. King's death inspired contemplation amongst us BSU leaders about his message, versus that of other Black leaders of the time.

Dr. King had taught that if someone slaps you on the cheek, turn the other cheek. We endorsed the philosophy of Malcolm X, who said that if someone slaps you on the cheek, slap them back. That was the rule on the playground. If somebody punched you, and you didn't fight back, you would get your butt kicked. That was how you stopped bullies. You fought back.

This mindset seemed the only option when I thought about the ongoing killings of Blacks, such as the 1963 KKK bombing of the 16th Street Baptist Church in Birmingham, Alabama. The mothers and fathers of the four little girls who were murdered would never see their babies again. And we were standing up to say, *No, we're not taking this!*

That was the temperature of the country then—boiling over.

White radicals were marching—30,000 to 40,000 people in the streets—demanding the end to the Vietnam War. On the other hand, Black and Latino people were demanding freedom and justice.

And I, as a 17-year-old, was ready to change the world, starting as the leader of our school's BSU. And so, a week after Dr. King's murder, I was excited to travel with my Garfield Comrades, along with Aaron and his college BSU leaders, to California for a pre-scheduled event to attend the West Coast Conference of Black Student Unions at San Francisco State University.

I couldn't leave town, however, without permission from the juvenile judge who was in charge of my case. It was granted. We left early Thursday, stopping in Portland to pick up more students and chill for the night. We stayed in a commune-like setting where people slept wherever they could find an open spot on the floor.

This was the second time I saw two people having sex, but unlike our childhood peeping back in Chicago, this was in full view of whoever cared to pay any attention. *Was anyone else checking it out? Probably not.* I turned my attention to falling asleep, yet the moans of ecstasy were hard to ignore. It was my first exposure to the dawn of a new era, the Free Love Movement, which was now intertwined with the Freedom and Black Power Movements. I was becoming a young adult, now exposed to the realities and freedoms of being grown. My transition was in full swing. The Intruders had just released their hit song "Cowboys to Girls," about how boys would tease girls and pull their hair, until hormones kicked in and the boys wanted to kiss the girls instead.

I was struck by the idea that people in these communes lived in collectives rather than in their own individual homes. I'd never experienced anything like that before, where people lived together and shared their resources.

We arrived at San Francisco State University on Friday. We were all assigned to different communal homes where people invited us to sleep and shower. After a meal, we headed up to the university. The auditorium was packed with Black student leaders from across the country, and several speakers roused the crowd.

But the air seemed to ignite as Black Panther Party Chairman and Co-Founder Bobby Seale took the podium and gave the fieriest speech I would ever hear in my life.

"P!" he declared with a pissed-off tone. "O. W. E. R!"

"Power!" he shouted, wearing a Black leather jacket with a "Free Huey" button. Huey P. Newton—who co-founded the Black Panther Party for Self-Defense with Chairman Bobby in 1966 while they attended Merritt College in Oakland, California—was now in jail, accused of killing a police officer.

Now, Chairman Bobby announced, "Huey said, 'Let's give off a universal definition of power. And then give an adjective to it and define it in terms of Black people.'"

I was mesmerized as Bobby lit up the auditorium, which erupted with claps and shouts that punctuated his unique version of fire and brimstone.

"Power is the ability to define phenomenon and make it act in a desired manner," he said, as two brothers, one on crutches, stood at his side.

"Phenomenon!" Chairman Bobby said. "That social phenomenon is 400 years of racist oppression on the part of this exploitive government of America. That racist oppression is manifested in what? By example. By historical fact. Pointing out in history, from 1890 to 1900, on the average of every three weeks, a Black man was lynched in this country, for a period of 10 years. And not one racist dog, who committed such atrocious acts against Black human beings, was brought to trial by this racist, stinking government." [1]

Anger blazed in my soul as he spoke, overwhelming me with the desire to do whatever possible to dismantle this oppressive system and give power and freedom to Black people.

Chairman Bobby also referenced the Black Panther Party's Ten-Point Platform and Program, which demanded freedom, employment, decent housing and education, exemption for Black men from military service, freedom for all imprisoned Black men, and Black juries for Black people brought to court.

"We want land, bread, housing, education, clothing, justice, and peace!" he said. "We want an immediate end to POLICE BRUTALITY and MURDER of Black people!"

Then, Chairman Bobby told us about a young brother named Little Bobby Hutton, who had been brutally murdered by Oakland cops—shot 30 or 40 times while standing in the middle of the street as he tried to surrender. And he said the brother standing next to him, Eldridge Cleaver, had been in the shootout leading up to death of Little Bobby, who joined the Black Panther Party when he was 16 years old, and was the first member to die.

It happened on April 6th, 1968, two nights after Dr. King's assassination. Unrest continued in cities across America; tensions were high, and Black activists were leading the "Free Huey" movement.

On this night in Oakland, a group of Panthers were returning to central headquarters when a street shootout erupted between them and the cops. When everyone dispersed, Lil' Bobby and Eldridge were cornered in a house surrounded by police. For more than an hour, the police fired barrage after barrage of bullets and tear gas into the building. The cops set fire to the house to smoke them out. In the chaos, Eldridge was hit in the leg with a tear gas canister. Wounded and outnumbered, Eldridge told Lil' Bobby:

"We've got to surrender. Strip down naked. If you go out there with any clothes on, they'll say you have a gun and gun you down."

Lil' Bobby said, "I'll strip down to my waist, but I'm not stripping down all the way."

When they emerged from the house under a white flag, the cops saw Eldridge with his arms in the air, naked, so there was no way that they could say he had a gun. They shoved him out of the way, toward a police car, beating him with their batons and gun butts.

Lil' Bobby, who had stripped down only to his waist, stumbled forward with teargas in his eyes. When the cops pushed him in another direction, one cop yelled, "He's got a gun!"

They all opened fire, hitting him 30 times.

Hearing this story ignited rage within me, and determination to stop the slaughter of Black men at the hands of police.

"We'll fight this revolution until our blood runs in the street!" Chairman Bobby declared. "Give me liberty or give me death!"

I was mesmerized and re-energized because I knew we had a direction, a leader, someone we could follow, a cause that we could get behind. After Chairman Bobby finished, a group of us made a beeline, without hesitation, to where he was standing. It was me, Aaron, and two or three others from our group who were audacious enough to stand and say, "We want to fight alongside you."

You could almost see the line drawn in the sand, as the majority of the students there from BSUs across the country were too scared to step up and join the revolution in that moment. But we were unafraid.

"Chairman Bobby," we said, "we're from Seattle, Washington. We want to start a chapter of the Black Panther Party there."

He nodded. "Come to Little Bobby's funeral tomorrow to see how this organization operates. Then I'll come to Seattle in two weeks to get you organized."

That evening, we went down into the Fillmore district on Divisadero Street to find berets to wear to the funeral to show our support, but all the stores were sold out. The next day, we left the BSU Conference early to drive across the Bay Bridge and into West Oakland. As we exited into West Oakland, we immediately saw large groups of Black people standing along the street, many of whom were lined up in military formation, all wearing afros, leather jackets, and berets.

The streets around Ephesians Church of God in Christ were so packed with cars, people, and TV news camera crews, that Black police officers were directing traffic. We had to park several blocks away, and while walking toward the church, we passed hundreds of leather jacketed men and women who were standing, walking, and—in the field of a park—doing drills in formation.

This looks like a Black Army, I thought. As we entered the church, amidst 1,500 people, the church walls were lined with Panthers dressed in leather jackets and berets.

This is where the revolution begins, I thought. *And we're in it.*

Chairman Bobby was inside, as was the writer, James Baldwin, and a white dude that I recognized as the movie star, Marlon Brando, who was a longtime supporter of the Black Panther Party. (After the funeral, Brando would later speak at an outdoor rally with Chairman Bobby, Kathleen Cleaver, and others, to a mixed crowd of 2,000 people and news crews. "That could have been my son lying there,"[1] Brando told the crowd in remarks televised on KTVU News.)

We were led toward the front of the church, where Chairman Bobby had someone save us seats. With us were several Seattle sisters and one of them was Kathy Jones, who was a member of the Garfield BSU.

"She smells like vinegar," a Black woman quipped.

I later learned that Kathy had spent the night trying to get her new afro to stand up. She was half white and had hair that would not cooperate; the sisters had told her to use vinegar. She reeked of it.

As we sat there, I looked at Lil' Bobby's coffin draped in a Black Panther flag. It was a surreal scene. Here we were in the heart of the revolutionary movement, at the funeral of a fallen Comrade with the flag of the Black Panther Party on the coffin. It was a foreboding sign of what lay ahead.

Mrs. Hutton, Lil' Bobby's mother, wanted to leave his coffin open for the public to see what the police had done to her son. When our turn came to file by the coffin, I looked in, and I saw Lil' Bobby. The mortician had done his best to sew Bobby together. He still looked like a young, strong Comrade, wearing his Panther uniform: a beret, a leather jacket, and a "Free Huey" button. As I stared into the coffin, I thought,

Lil' Bobby was 17 years old.

I'm 17 years old.

That could be me lying there.

At that moment, I knew I would die for the revolution. I became a member in heart, spirit, mind, and body of the Black Panther Party. I knew this was serious. It was not a game. It was not a club. It was not a regular organization. This was a revolutionary body.

Our core group was ready to give our lives the way Lil' Bobby had given his. I knew my life was transitioning into a vastly different reality, unlike anything I could have imagined. But I had no idea what was in store; I only knew that we wanted to be a part of this movement.

As I stood there, staring down at Lil' Bobby Hutton's lifeless body, I was reborn as a revolutionary. My life as a Panther had begun.

And I knew that I would rather die standing than live on my knees.

CHAPTER 13

The Revolution Will Not Be Televised

Two weeks after Lil' Bobby Hutton's funeral in Oakland, Bobby Seale flew to Seattle as he had promised, arriving with the Minister of Education, George Murray.

About 50 recruits who wanted to join the Party convened in our home for the meeting.

When Mommy and Poppy got home from work and walked through the front door, they stepped over all these brothers and sisters sitting on the floor, went back to the kitchen, closed the door, and never said a word.

During this meeting, we started the first chapter of the Black Panther Party outside of the state of California.

"In order to be a member of the BPP," Bobby told us, "you're required to read a minimum of two hours a day, attend weekly PE (Political Education) classes, and own two weapons with 10,000 rounds of ammunition."

Then he talked about how FBI Director J. Edgar Hoover and other authorities were on a mission to stop us.

"They're coming after you," Chairman Bobby said.

We were about to learn the foundations and principles of revolution from revolutionary leaders across the globe and throughout history. The Panther bible was the *Little Red Book* by Mao Tse-tung. It was full of revolutionary theories and principles vital to learning the ways of a revolutionary.

"Who's going to lead this chapter of the Black Panther Party for Self Defense?" Chairman Bobby asked.

As everyone looked around the room, all fingers pointed to Aaron.

"You'll be the Deputy Minister of Defense," Chairman Bobby said, later changing Aaron's title to Defense Captain. Our brother-in-law, Curtis Harris, became Co-Captain.

I was appointed Deputy Field Marshal, later changed to Field Lieutenant, in charge of security and the military. I had two bodyguards, as did anyone in a leadership position. With no official headquarters, we met in a building on the corner of Empire Way South and Madison.

Meanwhile, Chairman Bobby went east, setting up chapters in almost every state, including Illinois, where Fred Hampton joined in Chicago. He worked in cities like Kansas City and New York, and all points in between, growing the Party into a national organization. The Free Huey Movement became a battle cry as Comrades joined chapters in large numbers. The Party eventually expanded with chapters in London, New Zealand, Australia, and support groups in Japan, Denmark, Sweden, France, Germany, and in Algeria where Eldridge Cleaver went into exile and opened the International Section of the BPP.

During the summer of 1968, Chairman Bobby often called us down to Central Headquarters for opportunities to see the Party in action and learn how to organize within our own community.

On one such occasion, I had been talking to Chairman Bobby when someone called into the office and said, "The Richmond chapter is on the phone and the pigs are surrounding the office."

I followed Bobby out to a Ham radio transmitter and he got on a channel, talking directly to the Comrades inside the office.

"Where are the pigs?" he asked the Comrades on the other end of the radio. "Have they surrounded the office? What's the situation on the ground?"

I listened intently as he spoke to them for about an hour. After a couple of hours, the pigs withdrew from the office, never physically attacked, and the confrontation was settled without shots fired. This event and others were valuable lessons as we were learning the ways of the Party.

OUR MISSION: OVERTHROW THE U.S. GOVERNMENT

As we began to figure out how to grow and sustain our chapter, we were clear on our mission: to organize the people into a revolutionary force, to challenge the racist, brutal system of oppression, and if need be, to overthrow the U.S. government.

We were organizing on a grassroots level, and one popular slogan of the Black Power Movement was, "The revolution will not be televised." Meaning, our preparations for the revolution would remain under the radar until we were ready for all-out war. This slogan later inspired the poet Gil Scott-Heron to compose a popular song of the same title in 1970.

As I embarked on my leadership role in the Party, I was still in high school, focused on graduating and enrolling at the University of Washington. I didn't know how my plans of becoming a doctor would evolve, yet I needed to continue with my education. Poppy and Mommy would not have allowed me to just drop school altogether; I still lived under their roof.

At the same time, America felt like a tinderbox.

In early June, presidential candidate Bobby Kennedy was assassinated. Earlier that year, on March 26th, when he came to Seattle on a campaign swing, the Garfield High marching band was asked to play for his campaign stop at Seattle University. I was 10 feet away from him, awed by his presence—having no idea that I would soon be a revolutionary committed to overthrowing a corrupt and racist system.

A little more than a week after that, Dr. King was assassinated on April 4th, followed by the murder of Bobby Hutton on April 6th. Ironically, Kennedy died two months later.

Still, graduation was a big deal. It felt like freedom, a release from 12 years of primary and secondary school. College meant that I was an adult, at least in my eyes.

Plus, I had just turned 18 and had to register for the draft. If I were old enough to fight and die in an undeclared war, then I should have the rights of adulthood. At the induction center, I had one thing in mind: to make my intentions clear; if drafted into the military, I would not serve a racist government at the expense of my own life. I had spoken out against the war on several occasions and my attitude wasn't about to change now.

"When will I get my weapon?" I asked the sergeant in charge who was taking my induction form, which was required by law because of the draft. "How soon can I have a gun in my hands? Because I'm ready to do some damage right now, right here, without being shipped out."

I didn't directly threaten him or any superior officers, but he looked at me like I was crazy. I soon learned that I had been classified "4-F"— unfit for military service. I was elated, because I was about to become fit and qualified to do a different military service as a member of a different military—a revolutionary political army, the Black Panther Party.

Our training began at Central Headquarters in Oakland. Being around the Comrades and learning from Chairman Bobby, or the "Chairman" as we called him, was critical to our development. The first thing he taught us was the 10-10-10 Program, a method employed by Chairman Mao Tse-tung during the Chinese Revolution to organize the vast number of people in China. We would use that same strategy to organize our community, block by block, neighborhood by neighborhood.

The idea was to first divide the community into 10 large sections with a leader in charge of each. These section leaders would eventually organize Block Captains to serve as the eyes in the community and assist in organizing. Block Captains were community members who would participate in police lookouts and organize activities in their neighborhoods.

Organizing the young brothers and sisters who were coming to join the ranks of the Black Panther Party required a lot of work. They were coming from all walks of life: brothers and sisters who were working, raising families, and going to school. And of course, we welcomed the many brothers and sisters off the block—or as we used to call them, the lumpenproletariat, a term used by Chairman Mao to describe the people of the revolution—who were the downtrodden, disregarded, disenfranchised, and forgotten. Also joining our ranks were those who were unemployed or held menial jobs that contributed to the fabric of society.

The real challenge was getting them to understand the importance of discipline, study, and an organized, structural revolution. They came by the dozens, and while we had a system set up to register and qualify them for service within the Party, there were no such things as computers, background checks, or even references. We would interview every sister and brother to identify what their intentions were and why they wanted to serve the community. This proved challenging, because we wanted to trust that brothers and sisters were serious about the revolution, serving the community and people, body and soul.

At the time, we didn't even understand what that entailed. We learned as we went forward. Those of us who began the Party had seen the bloodshed. We had seen Little Bobby Hutton lying in his coffin. We were there to the death, but didn't know if the Comrades that we welcomed into the Party shared this commitment. We needed to believe that these brothers and sisters were also motivated to stand and fight after seeing the atrocities that had gripped Black communities across the country and throughout our history. But it would be a difficult learning curve. We would soon learn that the biggest challenge was these new Comrades having trust and belief in the Party's structure and leadership.

It was an election year, and the Central Committee of the Black Panther Party was challenging the political process by running members of the Party for political offices. Eldridge Cleaver was running for President of the United States under the banner of the Peace and Freedom Party, a new alliance formed with progressive whites and several prominent members of the Central Committee who were running for national offices.

In Seattle, we, too, were running members of the Seattle BPP for elected office. E.J. Brisker was running for a state legislative position. Curtis Harris was running for a Senate seat, as well as a number of other positions we had nominated at our own local convention.

The convention at the Sorrento Hotel, a popular historic hotel frequented by well-to-do white folks, drew hundreds of people, including a large contingent of Panthers dressed in leather jackets and berets. We looked like a formidable force to reckon with, even though we had no trust or belief in the political process. It was an exercise to expose the true nature of the decadent politics that ran this country, and an opportunity to put our platform and program out front, which was based on the Ten-Point Program of the Black Panther Party. We saw this as part of the organizing process and education of the Black community that we were engaged in.

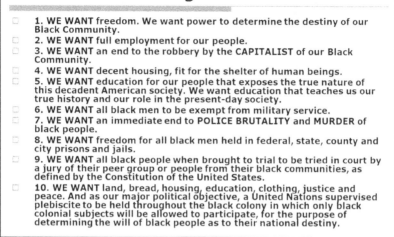

The 10 Point Program of the BPP

- **1. WE WANT** freedom. We want power to determine the destiny of our Black Community.
- **2. WE WANT** full employment for our people.
- **3. WE WANT** an end to the robbery by the **CAPITALIST** of our Black Community.
- **4. WE WANT** decent housing, fit for the shelter of human beings.
- **5. WE WANT** education for our people that exposes the true nature of this decadent American society. We want education that teaches us our true history and our role in the present-day society.
- **6. WE WANT** all black men to be exempt from military service.
- **7. WE WANT** an immediate end to **POLICE BRUTALITY** and **MURDER** of black people.
- **8. WE WANT** freedom for all black men held in federal, state, county and city prisons and jails.
- **9. WE WANT** all black people when brought to trial to be tried in court by a jury of their peer group or people from their black communities, as defined by the Constitution of the United States.
- **10. WE WANT** land, bread, housing, education, clothing, justice and peace. And as our major political objective, a United Nations supervised plebiscite to be held throughout the black colony in which only black colonial subjects will be allowed to participate, for the purpose of determining the will of black people as to their national destiny.

Chairman Bobby told us we needed to have a storefront office where we would be visible to the community and where people could come for information or support. Our first official office was located on 34th Street, just off Union Street and around the corner from our parents' home. It was befitting to launch our base of operation in the neighborhood where we had grown up. The community knew us, and many Comrades who joined came from that neighborhood. We had also attracted many Comrades from the South End, including students from Franklin High School.

Within a month, our ranks had swollen to more than 300 Panthers. This would require more of my time, and I still had to deal with getting into school. I was also in my first real relationship; Sherry Redmond was the sister of Joyce Redmond, who would play a significant role in the Party.

As part of my application to the University of Washington, I had to work a job for part of the summer. I was assigned to work with AT&T, or as we called it back then, Ma Bell. I started pretty early in the morning and was usually done by three o'clock, which meant that I could get out of my work clothes and into my uniform, get to the Party office, and start organizing in the community.

Of course, most of the development of the troops happened on the weekends, when the Comrades who were working on weekdays could attend and be a part of our drilling process. Many of our new Comrades had served in Vietnam. One was Mike Tagawa, who got all the rads lined up in military formation and drilled them as part of the process of developing discipline among the ranks. Mike was Japanese American, and one of a small number of Panthers who wasn't Black. But since we had all grown up in the same community, they were a natural part of the whole.

Our drilling process was a sight to behold. We were organizing these brothers and sisters into a fighting army.

Our formations of brothers and sisters—10 deep, 30 across—marching in precise formation sent a message that we were organized and ready for battle. Drilling also helped instill discipline and cohesion amongst our ranks.

"Attention!" Lieutenant Tagawa shouted. "Right face!"

The entire formation turned right.

"Left face!"

They turned left.

"March!" And they did.

We drilled long and hard on the weekends, often in a big field in the University of Washington Arboretum. We looked like a Black army, aiming to strike fear in the hearts of the police, who were filming us from a hill.

During these drills led by Lieutenant Tagawa, I was watching the troops on the sidelines, using a walkie-talkie to communicate with our leaders. We were proud and strong, ready for revolution.

CAPTAIN OF THE SISTERS

Since the sisters drilled separately from the men, we needed a woman to serve as the Captain in charge of drilling them, and the choice came down to Maude Allen, a sister from the East Coast, and Joyce, who was from the local Black community.

Maude was a short, stout sister with a fierce persona. She didn't take any shit. She had earned respect and a reputation for being tough-minded. She was articulate when it came to revolutionary philosophy, which gave her an edge over Joyce. On the other hand, Joyce came from one of the most notorious Black families in Seattle. Like Maude, she was a light-skinned, high-yellow sister with reddish-brown hair. All seven of her brothers and sisters (with the exception of her oldest and second to youngest sisters, Roberta and Edie) were light-skinned.

They had built a reputation for being tough and not to be messed with that stemmed from the complexion of their skin. Black kids would often make the mistake of thinking that light-skinned Blacks couldn't possibly be tough because they must be half white, as if their Blackness were somehow watered down. This was another example of the widespread colorism affecting Black communities, which was part of the dehumanization process to control Black people by racist whites. Huey often had to fight his way out of attacks and attempted beatings because of his light skin; he earned the same reputation. This reputation followed Joyce and her siblings, garnering immediate respect among the rank-and-file.

This was a dilemma: two tough sisters and only one position. We decided to split it down the middle and made them Co-Captains. This would prove challenging and volatile, but we were determined to make it work. We had to show the rank-and-file that we were organized in order to get their respect and inspire them to adhere to party discipline.

OUR MARCHING ORDERS

The Chairman explained that Huey had emphasized the need for the Party to capture the hearts and minds of the people in order to organize the masses into a revolutionary force, and that they needed to survive the conditions in the ghetto "pending revolution."

The first survival program was the police alert patrols. The patrols were a direct result of point number seven of the BPP Ten-Point Program, calling for an immediate end to the murder of Black people, an epidemic in Black communities across the country. One factor launching the patrols was the death of Denzil Dowell at the hands of North Richmond cops. Our response was for Panthers to arm ourselves with law books and guns to defend the community against the killing of unarmed and defenseless Black people.

During these early days, it was challenging to get the brothers and sisters to operate in an organized manner and not want to deliberately intimidate or bait the pigs into a gunfight. One of the brothers who was very active and committed was Buddy Yates, a native of Las Vegas who had a mixture of gangster mentality and machismo, a dangerous combination.

Once, we were out on police alert patrol, six deep in the car, when we pulled up to an intersection where a cop car was sitting at the light. Buddy pulled up alongside the cop car and started to rev his engine with six of us Panthers armed to the teeth.

Don't do it, Buddy, don't do it! I thought, as he sped through the intersection immediately before the light changed. The cops went in another direction.

Buddy was his own person and was hard to control. These kinds of interactions were happening in different parts of the country as well, and it wasn't too long before an order came from Central Headquarters to cease the police alert patrols because of their volatility.

That didn't stop us from monitoring the police. I was sitting in the Panther office one afternoon when the phone rang. The Officer on Duty, known as the OD, answered the phone. A woman was on the line, screaming:

"These pigs have got these young boys on the ground and are ransacking their car!"

I grabbed a couple of the brothers and jumped in the car. We sped to the intersection where this was going down. One of the young men on the ground later told me that he and his cousin had been cruising through the neighborhood around Empire Way, a major throughway in the CD. He was 13 years old, and his cousin was 16 and had a driver's license.

He said the cops had stopped them and told them they were robbery suspects because they fit a general description. They were hauled out of the car and thrown onto the ground face down, as the cops began ransacking their car, ripping out the seats, and tearing up the trunk. At this point, a woman came out of her house and, from her porch, yelled at the cops.

"Leave those young Black boys alone or I'll call the Panthers!" she threatened. Then she ran into the house, and within minutes, I and two of my Lieutenants came screeching around the corner.

We jumped out of the car.

We approached the cops.

"Why are you harassing these young brothers?" I demanded of the cops.

They responded that the brothers were robbery suspects.

"What proof do you have that they're robbery suspects?" I demanded.

The cops quickly backtracked and admitted that these young men did not fit the description and that they were just checking to make sure that they weren't up to any mischief.

"Uncuff them!" I ordered. "Get them up off the ground, put the car seat back in, and let them go!"

I followed our protocol by saying, "We're within our legal rights to observe you carrying out your duties and ensure you're not brutalizing innocent people."

A large group of people from the community were watching

along with us as the cops let the young brothers go before things got out of hand.

This exemplified the 10-10-10 Program in operation. I didn't know whether or not the sister was a Block Captain, but she knew the protocol was to call the Panther office if you saw someone being harassed or brutalized by the police. This was how control of police played out with action. It was one of many such instances where we were called on by the community and responded.

One summer afternoon, I had gotten off work and arrived at the Panther office where the street was full, from end to end, with cop cars. It appeared that they had just raided our office. As I stepped inside, the pigs were getting in their cars, driving away.

Aaron and Curtis had been arrested for theft of a typewriter. The word spread quickly throughout the community that the Black Panther Party Captain had been arrested. I jumped in the car with several Panthers and headed toward the police station, worried that they might try to harm him.

"Call the Panther lawyers!" I told the OD. "Tell them to meet us at the jail!"

When I arrived, Aaron was being processed and no bail had been set. Our lawyers, who included a young Black attorney Gary Gayton, and Michael Rosen, head of the local American Civil Liberties Union (ACLU), I told them to let me go with them to make sure he had not been harmed.

"I'm fine," Aaron told me. "Get the word out into the community not to riot, to stay cool. Tell the Comrades not to overreact."

That evening, we rallied at the Garfield Park swimming pool, a rallying place for many activities that we held in the Black community. We gathered Comrades at the office, and about 200 to 300 of us got in military formation— 10 abreast, 30 deep— and marched 15 blocks to Garfield Park. We were psyched to march through the Black community, straight down Cherry Street, in full uniform and in precise formation.

Years later, I met a man who had been an eight-year-old boy on that day, watching us through the window in amazement.

"Come to the window!" he called to his mother. She did, to watch us march in unity, shoulder to shoulder. His recollection of that day was that we were legendary heroes in our community.

We were on a mission when we arrived at the park, where hundreds of people from the Black community crowded the street. They were outraged over the arrest of Black Panther Party Defense Captain Aaron Dixon and Co-Captain Curtis Harris.

Kathleen Halley, whose African name was Nafasi, spoke first. She was an eloquent speaker and knew the fundamentals of the Party. Then she introduced me.

I spoke to the crowd about the principles of revolution.

"We don't advocate for spontaneous riot," I said. "I saw my brother. He's okay. He asked me to tell all of you to stay cool. Don't riot."

But the crowd wasn't hearing it. They were angry over the treatment of Blacks and the conditions within the Black community. They knew we were fighting for their freedom, and they were not going to let one of their leaders be harmed by the pigs.

They started throwing rocks at any passing car with white people inside. Across the street at the Bulldog Restaurant, a couple white cats were there, including a reporter and our attorney, Mike Rosen. I quickly dispatched a small cadre of Panthers to surround them and protect them from the crowd that was growing unruly.

By this time, the crowd was moving down the street toward Union, still throwing rocks at cars, breaking windows. Tear gas was in the air, helicopters were flying about, and Seattle's first full-scale riot was on.

CHAPTER 14

1968 – The Whole World is Watching

After the crowd dispersed and began moving up the street, trashing cars and anything in their path, the police quickly moved in with tear gas and riot gear. I gathered our remaining Comrades into the park.

"Watch out for spontaneous acts of resistance or confrontations with the pigs!" I warned. "If you engage in any acts of rebellion, travel in twos and threes, not in large groups." They knew that "twos and threes" was Panther code for launching strikes against the pigs without saying so.

"Aaron said stay calm," I reminded them. "Make sure the community doesn't get attacked." In essence, we were acting as a shield for the people who were upset because Aaron and Curtis were jailed on a stupid typewriter charge.

"Never turn your back on the pigs," I told our Comrades, repeating what Huey had told Aaron when he visited Huey in jail during a trip to Central, while getting schooled in the ways of the Panther.

At the time, Huey was in jail awaiting trial for the murder of one cop and the attempted murder of another. The two cops had confronted Huey on the streets of Oakland when he was alone without security; we believed the cops were trying to murder him. Huey defended himself and was now facing the death penalty. Aaron visited him in jail, and only able to see him through a small window, Huey had shared this advice that I now relayed to our Comrades.

"Stay alert," I said. "The revolution won't happen through spontaneous and unorganized attacks."

The summer of '68 would prove to be one of the most critical turning points in the short history of the Black Panther Party. The year before had been a critical year in that Huey was arrested and awaiting trial for murder. This led directly to the creation of the Free Huey movement and played a role in the death of the first member of the Black Panther Party, Lil' Bobby.

It was also the year that FBI Director J. Edgar Hoover declared the Black Panther Party the number one threat to the internal security of the United States, focusing his counterintelligence program, better known as COINTELPRO, on the Party. In an infamous memo, he directed his field offices around the country to "expose, disrupt, misdirect, discredit, or otherwise neutralize" Black leaders and Black hate groups to "prevent the rise of a Black Messiah who could unify, and electrify the militant black nationalist movement." This was particularly aimed at the Black Panther Party.

This was also the summer of the 1968 Democratic Convention in Chicago, which spawned, at the time, the largest anti-war demonstration against the Vietnam War that the country had ever seen. A series of rebellions had erupted by young white students protesting the war and the Chicago police responded with the veracity and violence that previously had only been used in Black ghettos across America. The fierce beatings and tear gas explosions were captured on camera. Unlike the "riots" of Detroit and Watts, these were the kids of White America, and the chant erupted among the students during the battle:

"*The whole world is watching! The whole world is watching!*"

This was an infamous moment in the struggle for human rights in the United States. These events would ultimately lead to the arrest and trial of Chairman Bobby.

Sadly, that summer proved the deadliest time for our chapter. We lost two Comrades, and later in the fall, a third. The first was Henry Boyer, who was from the South End group of Panthers known as "F Troop"—a large, tight-knit group nicknamed "F Troop" because they had attended Franklin High School. "F Troop" had been the title of a popular sitcom.

Henry had attended Franklin High School, along with the Noble Brothers, George and Richard, and two of the key members, Trolis Flavors and Charles Toliver, who had traveled to San Francisco when we met with Chairman Bobby to start the Seattle Chapter.

Some of those Comrades were still in high school in their senior year. George was the youngest of the two Noble brothers and he, along with Henry and several other Comrades, kept track of incidents and activities occurring at the high school. I first met the Noble Brothers when our band, The Regents, was competing against them in a battle of the bands at the YMCA in the C.D. They were called the Noblemen. As we were going back and forth with our music and talking trash to one another, the mood in the dance turned so hostile that the dance let out early. A large crowd had gathered, and people were expecting a fight, until Aaron stepped in.

"We need to be fighting the pigs," he told the crowd, "not fighting each other!"

This was before we had started the Party, but Aaron was always the one who had the cooler head and the ability to put things in context. We left shaking hands and acknowledging each other as brothers, rather than fighting in the streets for nothing more than trash talk.

Later, after they were in the Party, Richard would prove to be a die-hard Panther. He became a lieutenant and ran F Troop with a strong hand. During that summer, when the Comrades were restless, they kept approaching Aaron about taking some sort of military action. Aaron gave permission for the troops to go out and do individual acts of defiance and rebellion in twos and threes, or in medium-sized groups.

Once, I was out with a small crew and we were looking at potential targets when the sky in the South End glowed red. I thought, *That must be F Troop.* The next morning, I found out that they had set fire to a large lumberyard, striking fear into a long-established business. We often referred to these business owners as "the avaricious businessman who robbed our community and never gave back."

The other Comrade we lost that summer was Butch Armstead, who died at the hands of the pigs, and later Sidney Miller, shot by a West Seattle store owner.

Meanwhile, Richard was in charge of F Troop and reported directly to me. I had two other lieutenants, Steve Phillips and Wayne Jenkins, who were part of the squad keeping track of errant Panthers, or those we referred to as "rally Panthers," who had only joined the Party for fame and glory in order to catch girls. They would show up at rallies and wear the uniform without doing the work required of being a member of the Party.

That was enough to trigger disciplinary action, but worse was when they would use their power of being a member of the Black Panther Party to abuse women. We would not stand for that. I had been directed by Aaron to organize a special unit known as the "Goon Squad" to administer discipline to rogue Comrades. I would often dispatch the squad to straighten the brothers out. That usually meant that someone was going to get their ass kicked, or expelled from the Party, or both.

Two brothers from Louisiana had joined the Party. One was my high school classmate, Aaron Pierre, who had grown up just outside of the French Quarter. The Ninth Ward was a tough neighborhood and he knew the streets well. He had been a constant companion following the trip to Oakland that led to the formation of our chapter. On graduation night from high school, he was there driving my car, acting as chauffeur and bodyguard, as I was indulging in a bottle of Cutty Sark Scotch that he had bought me as a graduation gift.

Aaron had lent me one of his nice suits, as I didn't own one, and that Cutty Sark mistreated me, something terrible. I threw up all over Aaron's suit. I would have hell to pay if he found out, so I hid it from him until I could get it to the cleaners.

The other brother was Bo Lang. He, too, knew the streets well growing up in New Orleans and was a dedicated Panther. One evening, following a day of drilling and organizing in the community, one of the Panthers from a well-respected Black family, the Chapmans, was upset about my role as head of security and my role with the Goon Squad; he challenged me in front of the troops. He was so visibly upset and heated, some of the brothers took him outside.

I followed, and he lunged at me.

"I'm gonna kill you!" he screamed. "I'll get you after hours!"

Several Comrades knocked him to the ground. I let him cool down, and he was suspended for attempting to attack an officer in the Party.

After this, Aaron Pierre said, "I demand to be on your security detail. I'm not going to let this dude get near you."

So, I allowed him to be on my security detail that evening, throughout meetings, and other off-duty activities. When the evening was done and I headed home, he said, "I'm going to stay out in front of your parents' house."

"That's not necessary," I said. "You're off-duty and can go home."

However, the next morning when I walked outside, he was still in front of the house, sitting with his rifle across his lap with a keen eye, daring anyone to approach. That's when I realized the depth of his commitment and dedication to the Party.

"Thank you, brotha'," I said. "All power to the people! Let's go take care of some business."

Then away we went for the activities of the day. He realized that being a Panther was not a nine-to-five, but rather a twenty-four-seven commitment, something we all would soon learn.

This was why the Black Panther Party became recognized as the vanguard of the revolution. We weren't "Jive Time" nor "Armchair Revolutionaries" reading books of revolution only to spend hours and days espousing the rhetoric and never taking any action. It was our responsibility to show the way, to lead, to not back down, to not compromise our principles in the face of any opposition. This was the creed of the Panther: dare to struggle, dare to win, with no fear of death.

Meanwhile, our Comrades' deaths were grim reminders of our dangerous mission.

Henry's death was especially hard because he was well-liked and a good brother. He died trying to defend his mother from her boyfriend, who had been abusing her, and was shot in the process. We organized what would be the largest funeral in Washington state history at the time. This would cause many more young brothers and sisters to come out of the community and join the Party as our ranks continued to swell.

We had been drilling in Madrona Park across the street from our parents' house and around the corner from the Panther office. We also drilled in the large park at the University of Washington Arboretum. It was much larger and could accommodate the growing numbers of people now in the Party. This was an opportunity for the FBI and the Seattle pigs to observe us from the upper area surrounding the park. They were obviously photographing members of our chapter, but the real challenge was not knowing who the infiltrators were among our ranks.

On the day of Henry's funeral at the Angelus Funeral Parlor, which was owned and operated by a Black dude, uniformed Panthers lined up and down 12th Avenue. Each of them—with their Black leather jackets gleaming in the sun and berets cocked to the side—stood at attention, honoring their fallen Comrade.

Some of the sisters, including Kathleen "Nafasi" Halley, wore special powder blue dresses they had specifically made for the service. The Panther uniform showcased the colors of the Black Panther Party with our black jackets, pants or skirts, and powder blue shirts or blouses. This showed pride in our community and strength among our Comrades.

During the services, our lieutenants were on the street in front of the funeral home working to keep the Comrades in the "at ease" position—they stood silently with their heads and eyes turned to the captain. This was a show of discipline to the community. We came to observe the service and address the large crowd on the need for revolution. When the caravan formed for the long journey to the cemetery, it was ironically escorted by the Seattle Police Department; this was necessary because the funeral procession was the largest in Washington state history. The long line of cars behind us as we led the procession made us realize what a powerful impact we were having on the Black community.

This scene would be tragically repeated with the deaths of Welton "Butch" Armstead and Sidney Miller. After Butch's death, we held a rally at Garfield Park and renamed it Armstead Park in his honor. We didn't ask the Seattle Parks Department for permission, nor did we need their authority; we simply made it known that it was now called Armstead Park.

Services for many of our murdered Comrades were held at the Black-owned funeral parlor.

GUNS, BODIES, AND BOOZE

Late one night, the eccentric old brother who owned Angelus Funeral Parlor called Aaron and me.

"I have some weapons for you to fight the revolution," he said. "I only want to show them to yawl."

Under cover of night, Aaron and I visited the funeral parlor. We were very particular about our weapons and we only accepted them from outside sources whom we trusted. So, we met this dude in the embalming room, where he drank whiskey from a weird vessel that God only knew what it had been used for. Then he opened some coffins to show us the weapons.

"These are from the Brazilian military," he said.

They were an older model. Aaron and I were not familiar with them, but we accepted them. Everyone in the Party was responsible for getting their own weapons. So, this bounteous gift enabled us to provide weapons for large numbers of Party members who had no guns.

How did we pay for them? Well, Aaron and I had enrolled in the University of Washington, and we received federal student aid checks. So, we used our student loan money to fund our weapons and ammunition.

We purchased legal weapons, and back then, no gun registrations were required by the government. So, we bought significant and powerful weapons such as .44-magnum rifles with armor-piercing bullets. Thanks to my teenaged gun training with David's father, who made his own bullets, we obtained a loading machine to load shotgun shells and make our own, we didn't have to buy bullets.

My two shoulder holsters held a .45 under one arm and a .357 magnum under the other. I often carried multiple weapons so I could get to them quickly. Target practice helped me master how to fire each weapon, and how to unjam it if it jammed up. Anything could happen if you were in a fire fight, and if it jammed, you were in trouble. So, we did drills to take the gun apart and reassemble it. Likewise, we routinely cleaned our weapons, which we stored on gun racks up above, so—after we fortified the office with sandbags—the sand couldn't get in them. Mike Tagawa taught target practice, and I mastered my shot with pistols, long rifles, and long-range weapons, including an M1 carbine.

We were always ready so we would not be caught off guard. This was a matter of life and death.

We were also very aware of how the feds might try to incriminate us. The ATF—Department of Alcohol, Tobacco, and Firearms—justified attacks on Panther officers by accusing our Comrades of altering our guns to become automatic weapons, which was illegal. What's the difference? Normally, if you fire a gun that has a clip containing bullets, you are only able to fire one after another, making it a semi-automatic, which was legal. An automatic is a machine gun; it fires continuously as you simply hold the trigger down. You could make a semi-automatic into an automatic by filing down the mechanism. We never messed with that; it was too dangerous and made the weapons illegal.

MY FIRST REAL GIRLFRIEND

My relationship with Sherry became more serious. She had been working at Dag's, the burger joint across from Franklin High School, and the site of the riots where I was arrested for the first time.

I was attracted to her because she had a certain spice and fire to her, and was clearly someone that you didn't mess with. Eventually, I got up the nerve to talk to her and ask her out. She was my first real girlfriend, and we became tight, especially given the fact that her sister, Joyce, was in the Party.

By the end of the summer, Sherry and I got an apartment together on Capitol Hill off Broadway. This was my first time both living away from home and staying with a woman. On top of that, I became a sort of surrogate dad for her young son, André.

We had not yet advanced to organizing Panther barracks for the Comrades, as we were still in the organizing stages and needed only to have the storefront office in the heart of the Black community.

I loved having a woman. An important part of life. We enjoyed doing things as a couple, including seeing the Motown Revue in Seattle; the concert featured the Four Tops, Stevie Wonder, the Temptations, and Marvin Gaye and Tammi Terrell. I most wanted to see Marvin and Tammi, but to my disappointment, Tammi Terrell was replaced with Brenda Holloway. I later learned that Tammi was battling cancer and was too ill to make the trip. However, the show was still fantastic.

Growing up and living during the birth and development of Motown and R&B music was unlike any other era of music. Our parents grew up listening to the vocals of Billie Holiday, Sarah Vaughan, and others, but the birth of R&B and the rise of Motown was something totally different and new. This was the era of my generation. While others defined the era with "drugs, sex, and rock and roll," we declared, "drugs, sex, and Motown." I wasn't much into drugs, and sex was a new thing, but I loved my music, and I loved Motown and R&B.

TAKING THE HEAT

One evening I was out on patrol with my crew, and I made the mistake of not checking all of the car functions before we left on patrol. This was our protocol to avoid getting stopped for minor traffic issues.

We hadn't gone 10 blocks from the office when out of nowhere, a cop car swung in behind us, put on his lights, and pulled us over. The cop came up to the window.

"What did we get stopped for?" I demanded.

"You have a taillight out," he said.

"Fine, give us a ticket and I'll get it taken care of later," I said.

"You can't move the car and you're not allowed to drive it with a taillight out," he said.

I knew this was petty harassment, so I told my Comrades, "Get out of the car and stand at ease along the sidewalk." They lined up with their law books and weapons and observed while the pig gave me a ticket. We had no way of contacting other Panthers who were out on patrol, so I went to the phone booth and called the only person I could reach at the time: Poppy.

Within minutes, Poppy drove up and gave us all a ride back up to the headquarters. I later joked with my Comrades, "My dad was on police alert patrol."

Later that week, Nafasi came into the office and told me that she had been contacted by a Black cop who had something important to tell us. Of course, we were leery of any cop, whether Black or white. I grabbed a couple of Comrades and headed to the address that we were given. He welcomed us into his home.

"You're being targeted," he told us. "Whenever a Panther is pulled over and the cop reports it over his radio, one of your license plates or driver's licenses are called in, and we're to consider the occupants armed and extremely dangerous."

I thought, *That's motherfucking right! If you pull us over, we are armed, and we are extremely dangerous.*

As we were walking from his house, a pig car was driving by with four deep in the car, and one of the pigs pointed his hand out the window mimicking a gun, pretending to fire a round at us. We gave them the finger and said, "Anytime, mothafuckas!"

This back and forth between the pigs and Panthers continued wherever we went. One afternoon I was up on University Avenue—"the Ave" as we called it— looking for some new shoes or just hanging out. The Ave was like being in San Francisco on

Haight-Ashbury. Hippies were selling drugs every 15 feet in this free-spirited environment, with "flower power" and the whole thing.

As we came out of a popular haberdashery called Bluebeard's, two cops were coming up the street. One was as big as a bull and his sidekick was a little, skinny dude. The big cop reminded me of an oversized officer, Krupke, the cop in *West Side Story* who had a racist streak.

I was with Steve and Wayne. We often hung out in groups of twos or threes, just as we preached to the Comrades for security purposes. Steve was a tall and lean, handsome brother, with eagle eyes and a fierce persona. A dedicated soldier, he was not one to take shit from anyone. Wayne was short and strong-looking with no shortage of moxie. They were two of my most important lieutenants. These were dudes I would go to war with and die for.

As the two cops approached, they were blocking the sidewalk and weren't moving so we could get by. In a few steps, we were face-to-face with no place to go, left or right. It was like a showdown to see who was going to move to the side first and we knew we weren't moving.

Steve said defiantly, "Why don't you pigs get out the way and let us by."

Before you knew it, we were tussling with Officer Krupke and his little sidekick. We started to get the best of them. The sidekick called backup. When their reinforcements arrived, they overwhelmed us and got us pinned on the back of the cop car—eventually handcuffed.

They put the three of us together in the backseat of one car, but in their haste and excitement they forgot to thoroughly search us. We didn't always carry guns, but we always had some kind of weapon. Steve had a stiletto knife stuck down in the small of his back. He was able to get it out and slide it down in between the seats and the pigs never found it.

We were arrested for some bullshit charge and would later defeat the case in court. This was a constant off-and-on occurrence, and I was probably arrested 13 times that summer alone, never getting convicted.

This was the life of a Panther—being constantly vigilant, aware of one's surroundings, and never turning your back on a pig. We began holding target practice classes every weekend across Lake Washington in the woods near Issaquah, a small, rural, bedroom community of Seattle.

Many of our Comrades were Vietnam vets and we used their expertise to help train the troops. I led many of the target practice classes, as I had become quite proficient with weapons. Now as a Panther, I owned and carried multiple weapons at different times, sometimes a .45 with a snub nose .38, other times a .357 Magnum along with a .9-millimeter. I didn't want to be caught in the street with the pigs trying to kill me and not being able to defend myself.

I was determined to die standing and go down fighting. Most days when I went to classes at the UW, in my briefcase along with my psychology book, I packed a .357 Magnum. There were many racist right-wing students on campus, and I couldn't take a bodyguard with me to classes, so I made sure that I was armed. I wonder now what the professor would have thought if he had found out when I opened my briefcase and pushed over the .357 Magnum so I could get my psychology book.

The campus was roiling with angry students and protests. Several of us Comrades participated in the takeover of the president of the university's office, Dr. Charles Odegaard, as we were demanding the establishment of a Black Studies program.

Many of us were enrolled in Dr. Ed Jones' class, a Black professor who was teaching African and Black history. He was a renegade to many of his fellow colleagues, both Black and white, because he dared to tell true stories of Black and

African history. He was often ostracized. But to us, he was a hero because he told it like it was.

It was from him that I learned about the first Black Queen of England, Queen Charlotte, who was from the De Sousa family out of Portugal and had married Charles the Third. They had 15 children and a granddaughter, who at the time was the longest-sitting monarch on the throne, Queen Victoria. He told us when he had traveled to the Abbey in London to find her photo that it was not on the walls with the other monarchs; it was in the basement, he was told, because of a lack of space, when actually, they were hiding the fact that a Black woman was the queen of England. He eventually found and photographed it, then put it in his book.

Many of his colleagues ridiculed him and said it was a creation of his, but it turned out to be true. Several sites were named for her, including the Queen Charlotte Islands off of Vancouver, Canada and Charlottesville, South Carolina. I'm sure those racist Southerners never knew that the city was named after a Black Queen of England.

AARON TIES THE KNOT

Early that fall, Aaron's girlfriend, Donnie, got pregnant.

"You have to marry her," Pops told Aaron.

A shotgun wedding was planned, but Aaron was not sure he wanted to take that step.

"Swing by the house right when the ceremony is supposed to start," he told me. "Make up some story about a shootout, and scurry me off before the wedding can happen."

He was counting on me! I was ready to pick him up, but on the way back from the university, the wheels on my car caught fire. The ball bearings had worn out and the car had been on too many patrols and was sidelined.

I tried to get the tire changed and did my best to get to the house, but by the time I got there, it was too late. The deed had already been done. All I could do was sit on the stairs and observe, smiling while laughing to myself: *Boy, are you in for it now!*

PREPARING FOR THE REVOLUTION

We continued the process of building and organizing the chapter. Meetings of the central staff were held in the basement of the Madrona Presbyterian Church, just down the block from Madrona Park where we held weekend drilling exercises with the troops. There, we would discuss operations and tactics for organizing in the community. We discussed the 10-10-10 Program and other strategies.

Unfortunately, we felt a growing tension among the ranks, which was being played out across the country. Some Comrades were frustrated with all of the community organizing. They wanted to take direct military action.

The Mandate from Central was to organize among the masses. We understood that we needed to stimulate revolution in the community in order to build a revolutionary movement, to create a foundation for the overthrow of the corrupt U.S. Government. This was the premise of our revolutionary philosophy, based in the Declaration of Independence:

"*That whenever any Form of Government becomes destructive of these ends, it is the Right of the People to alter or to abolish it, and to institute new Government, laying its foundation on such principles and organizing its powers in such form, as to them shall seem most likely to effect their Safety and Happiness.*"

This meant doing the day-to-day work in the community of educating the people, but some Comrades wanted "revolution in our lifetime," and they wanted it now. As we continued to organize, it became apparent that two philosophies were competing to develop our launch for the revolution.

"Start organizing the community survival programs pending revolution," Central Headquarters instructed. The community survival programs were intended to stimulate revolution while providing programs for the community to exist and survive.

But many of our Comrades believed that the route to revolution was by taking direct action against the pig power structure. This paramilitary style of thinking—across the country in every chapter—would lead to some level of dysfunction within the ranks, and would open the door wider for the infiltration by agent provocateurs attempting to set up and frame members of the Black Panther Party.

We had identified most of the die-hard, to-the-death Panthers, including: Chester Northington, Billie Jackson, Louis "LouJack" Jackson, Bobby White, Bobby Harding, and Willie Brazier. Many others included my lieutenants: Warren Jenkins, Steve Phillips, Mike Murray, and Jake Fiddler.

With other Comrades, who seemed shady, we couldn't quite put a finger on who they were. We hadn't thought this through at the time because we were busy trying to organize the foundation of the chapter and keep the Comrades motivated and in the field.

I was receiving more reports of brothers running roughshod and needed to follow up with the squad. One thing that should have been a giveaway was the repeated demands by some Comrades to take direct military action because some of their actions were reckless. Some Comrades would go out and take it upon themselves to rob a store or beat someone in public, only giving the Party a bad name, while others took more serious action. I had heard that a group of Panthers in San Francisco had robbed a bank in broad daylight and engaged in a roving gun battle with the pigs as they were trying to escape.

This, of course, made headlines in the San Francisco newspapers: Black Panthers Rob Bank.

We were the only ones who knew that these were unauthorized raids. Those renegade Comrades were eventually expelled from the Party and labeled Jackanapes. But this was damaging our reputation and it needed to stop.

In a book *The Glass House Tapes*[2]—later written by a former agent for the California Conspiracy Section known as the CCS, which was created by the LAPD as a secret force to destroy the Party—Louis Tackwood stated that the role of an agent provocateur was to create the idea of a conspiracy by suggesting to members of an organization, like the Black Panther Party, during routine meetings, they should engage in bombing, sniping, attacking police, robbing banks, or other activities in order to create chaos and frame its members.

Aaron and I had grown increasingly suspicious of Panthers who were suggesting this kind of direct action, even though at the time we had not heard anything about Louis Tackwood. But we had been warned about being aware of potential agents infiltrating the Party and trying to create counter-revolutionary actions, which would result in both the defamation of the Party, as well as set people up for cases.

So, we had to be very vigilant, and one of our leaders was on the suspect list. We had heard stories about Panthers allegedly involved in brazen daylight hold-ups of grocery stores and banks in California and other parts of the country. So, when we got wind of a potential bank robbery in Seattle involving members of the Party, we brought the leader in question into a meeting and challenged him openly.

"Revolutionaries have to take direct revolutionary action," he told us defiantly during one of many confrontations that would ensue, causing a rift in the leadership that would only grow worse.

CHAPTER 15

The Purge

By January of 1969, things were getting intense, not only between the military-leaning faction and the community-based organizing efforts, but also with the growing threat of agent provocateurs and the ever-present FBI.

J. Edgar Hoover launched his COINTELPRO operation in full scale, and the first casualties were the leaders of the Southern California chapter of the Black Panther Party in Los Angeles.

L.A. was a key organizing point for the Party and was one of the three cities that J. Edgar Hoover had targeted for elimination. The other two cities, unbeknownst to us, were Seattle and Chicago. Central Headquarters had been under attack since the beginning and these three cities had now become the focal point.

Huey was facing the death penalty in Oakland, and Eldridge Cleaver was already in exile in Algeria with his wife, Kathleen Cleaver, the communication secretary of the Black Panther Party. As such, much of the Central Committee had been disrupted, so Hoover turned his attention on these three cities.

While attending a meeting on the campus of UCLA, the head of the Southern California chapter, Alprentice "Bunchy"

Carter and another leader, John Huggins, were gunned down by agent provocateurs. These agents were members of an organization led by Ron Karenga. They were known as "US," which we nicknamed "United Slaves." They were cultural nationalists imploring a philosophy of Black nationalism. They wore all black or African dashikis with shaved-bald heads and proclaimed themselves as the leaders of the Black Power Movement.

Ron Karenga was a CCS agent and was being used by them and the FBI to create a divide in the Black community and the Black Power Movement. It's the oldest tactic in the book; divide-and-conquer, create the illusion of a war among factions, and allow them to kill each other off. So, Karenga had instructed two of his agents, the Steiner brothers, to look for an opportunity to engage in a shootout with Black Panther Party members, specifically Bunchy and John, for the purpose of removing Bunchy Carter from the California scene.

Bunchy had previously been the head of one of the largest gangs in Southern California, the Slausons, a 5,000-strong gang organization that the FBI feared of being organized into revolutionaries. Bunchy had to be eliminated, and along with John Huggins, who had strong organizing capabilities, the two were targeted for assassination.

When we got the call that Bunchy and John had been murdered, it was devastating. We were pissed! It was bad enough that we were being targeted by cops, but to have two of our members murdered by a Black organization just made it that much more real as to how deep of a war we were in with a power structure that would go to any lengths to murder us.

We loaded up two to three carloads of Panthers from Seattle and traveled to Los Angeles for their funeral. On the way down, Aaron was driving the lead car and I was following behind in a vehicle with four Comrades: one was my bodyguard, two of my lieutenants, and the third was Joyce Redmond. As we got close to L.A., we were about to drive through the most treacherous stretch of the California highway, known as the Grapevine. We had been warned about this stretch of highway, and to be alert. It was my first time driving in that part of Southern California, so I was on point.

We lost track of Aaron's car and later found out that his car had gone over the side of the road. It was on its way to crash down the canyon when the back wheels of the car caught on the guard rail and held it from crashing over into the ravine. It was a miracle that they weren't all killed.

Just outside of L.A., prior to the funeral, we got a chance to see the Comrades at the L.A. chapter offices on Central Avenue, where Party members had built a fortress to stave off attacks from the notorious Los Angeles Police Department. Later that afternoon at the funeral, Panthers had come from all over California and other parts of the country to pay respect to Bunchy and John. It was a stark reminder of the dark days that lie ahead, and the need for us to be vigilant at all times.

Following the funeral, we met with Chairman Bobby to get any orders before we returned to Seattle.

"We want retribution!" we said. "We want to get some get-back!"

"That's what the pigs want," Chairman Bobby said, "to spark a bloody feud between the two organizations. You have to keep organizing in the community to build a foundation to launch a broad-based movement."

He also made it clear that the Central Committee had said there would be no retaliation against the Karangutang slaves, yet many among our ranks were ready to take direct action.

Still, we followed orders and knew a time would come for payback. During the long drive home, we reflected on the struggles ahead. Our emotions were high and everyone was on edge. We stopped briefly at Central Headquarters in Oakland as we came through the Bay Area, but Aaron had instructed us to get to Seattle, so we didn't spend much time there.

When we left Central, it was close to 3 a.m. and we were trying to get to a point up the freeway where we could stop and rest. As we were approaching the Bay Bridge, my bodyguard, Cornell, was fussing with Joyce, who was driving.

Cornell was a brother that was always agitating and talking jive. That was okay for most of us because we could deal with his jive, but when he was talking that way to Joyce, he had no idea who he was messing with, and he made the mistake of calling her a bitch. Joyce screeched on the brakes in the middle of the Bay Bridge, got out of the car, went around to the trunk, opened it, pulled out a tire iron, and came around to his side of the car, trying to yank him out and beat his ass to death.

I intervened and stopped her from killing the brother.

"Never, ever call this woman a bitch!" I told him. "And, quite frankly, you shouldn't be calling any sister a bitch!"

We got Joyce calmed down and back in the car, and away we went, up the freeway. By the time we got up to Grant's Pass in Oregon, we had been driving 10 hours since leaving L.A. The snow had started to fall and was getting deeper and deeper. We pulled off at a gas station to fuel up. Back on the highway, we came to a checkpoint where the highway patrol was holding up traffic.

"Everybody stay cool," I said, quickly looking around. We were carrying hot credit cards that we were given in L.A. by Aaron, so we would have enough gas to return to Seattle.

"The freeway is closed to any cars that don't have tire chains," the state police told us at the checkpoint. "You have to turn around."

We returned to the gas station 20 or 30 miles back, to see if we could get some chains. Using those credit cards, we got chains and snow tires for extra insurance to get through the roadblock. After putting on the chains, which really were too small for the snow tires, we drove up to the checkpoint. The trooper checked out the tires and the chains and waved us through.

As we got up the road about a mile or so, the chains were starting to pop off and hit the underside of the car, so we pulled off at a rest stop to pull them off. The snow was so deep, we could roll down the window, reach out, and pick up a snowball. But it didn't matter because the snow tires were so thick, they were like tractor tires, and we had good traction, even without the chains.

The drive was so slow, we stopped in a hotel for a night, using the credit card to get one room for five Panthers: four brothers and a sister.

"Stay away from Joyce!" I warned Cornell. "Don't say anything to her!"

We got through that night without incident and continued up the freeway. We later learned that the snowfall was a record snowfall in the Oregon mountains, all the way up through Washington State, and all the way into Seattle. When we got to Olympia, Washington, the state capital, we decided to check into the Motor Inn just outside of town.

As it turned out, the Motor Inn was full of state legislators who were laid over because of the snowfall. We showered and got cleaned up and went down to the gathering area where there were dozens of the legislators. We decided to walk into their gathering as if we belonged there, which is what we would normally do, anyway. We wanted to check these cats out and see what they were talking about.

Across the room was Dave Sprague, my childhood best friend's father! He had been a state legislator ever since I knew Mark and had been serving for quite some time. He recognized me.

"Come over to my table," he said. We chatted with him and he introduced us to some of his colleagues as members of the Seattle Black Panther Party.

"Are you really from Seattle?" one man asked me quietly. "You're too sophisticated for me to believe that. You must be California Panthers."

"All Panthers are organized and sophisticated in the art of revolution," I told him. "You'll be hearing more from us soon."

Back in Seattle, we were at a critical turning point in our young history. The FBI was not only escalating their assaults on members of the Party, but were also infiltrating the Party with an influx of unsuspected agent provocateurs. An agent provocateur cooked up a crime to entrap members of the Party to get long prison sentences.

"Let's plan a bank robbery," the agent provocateur might say, or, "Let's go plan a hit on some pigs tonight."

If he could get our Comrades talking about it, and record them on tape using a wire, then many Panthers were entrapped into getting arrested and busted. That was how Tupac Shakur's mother, Black Panther Party member Afeni Shakur Davis, was arrested as part of the original New York 21, who were charged with several counts of conspiracy to bomb police stations and other public places. She spent two years in jail before being acquitted.[3]

Prosecutors couldn't tie her into the room when the agent provocateur was planning to bomb the Bronx Botanical Gardens. We knew better than to talk about blowing up stuff. They also used a wiretap; we knew not to talk about that shit over the phone. We also knew that in any group larger than eight, someone was bound to be an agent.

We were wary of the enemies within our troops. But we remained committed to the tenants of Huey Newton's book, *Revolutionary Suicide: The Way of Liberation*.[4]

The goal of the 10-10-10 Program was to organize the revolution by capturing the hearts and minds of the people, block by block, section by section. But it was always thwarted by rally

Panthers who didn't want to do that work. Some only wanted to march in our military drills because it was cool and it looked good. Then they'd use it to go out and catch women by saying, "Yeah, I'm a Panther, baby, come on with me."

And others took the idea of our military organization literally, by announcing, "We're a Black army. We go out and attack motherfuckers!"

"No!" I argued. "You can't just go out and shoot at pigs. We're going to be organized. The pigs are the aggressors. We defend the community."

The lack of discipline among the ranks was aided by the ongoing internal debate about taking direct action against the industrial-military complex of the United States through a variety of actions.

We were continuing to build a foundation through the community survival programs in order to stimulate revolution among the masses. While other movements had targeted the proletariat or the working class in organizing their struggles, we learned through our studies that it was the lumpenproletariat, the bottom of the heap, the disenfranchised, the forgotten, the hustlers, pimps, prostitutes, and the jobless, who were most in need of a revolution and desperate for survival.

Many of these lumpen had come into the Party and had, throughout their lives, borne the brunt of racism, segregation, and oppression. They were ready to fight back. But many of them conducted acts of spontaneous revolution in full Panther uniform without any orders. Eventually, a directive came from Central Headquarters ordering members of the Party to come out of uniform and to not wear the leather jacket and beret casually every day, but only at sanctioned special events, such as large community giveaways or Panther funerals.

"We need to dress more like the people to make it easier for them to relate to us," Huey said.

The ideological differences were growing in our chapter. Some of the brothers were taking actions into their own hands and not following the organizing strategy of the 10-10-10 program. This was about to come to a head as the co-captain of the chapter, Curtis Harris, our brother-in-law, stood with the brothers who wanted to take more direct action. It became increasingly difficult to discern or identify whether someone was part of the more military-focused apparatus, operating to stimulate revolution, or whether they were agent provocateurs. It was an uneasy time.

As this was unfolding, we received a request from Eugene, Oregon, from some brothers who wanted to start a Black Panther Party chapter. We had already assisted some brothers and sisters in Portland, Oregon, in starting their chapter under the direction of Kent and Sandra Ford. So, Aaron instructed me to travel to Eugene to speak on the campus of the University of Oregon, and to work with the brothers there to start their chapter. It was a rough time for me, as I had broken up with Sherry a few months earlier. She later revealed some information, and I received news about our relationship that was upsetting to me. This left me depressed.

I wanted to travel with two of my trusted bodyguards, Steve and Wayne, but Wayne could not come, and a young Panther by the name of Cornell, whom I had already been grooming, stepped up and volunteered for the duty. Cornell was ambitious; he was always asking us, "When can I be a lieutenant?" and my lieutenants always said, "Naw, you ain't ready."

We rode the Greyhound bus to Eugene, a place that I had never visited, and were met by a few brothers and sisters who were organizing the chapter, one of whom was Bill Green. We spent the day talking about the chapter requirements to join the Party.

"You have to read two hours a day in PE, that's political education classes," I told them, "as well as being armed and proficient in weapons use and having thousands of rounds of ammunition."

The next day I was scheduled to speak on campus at the University of Oregon. After my speech, as I exited the auditorium, a student was approaching me.

"We should take that white motherfucker's leather jacket," Cornell said.

"C'mon," I said. "What are you talkin' about?"

"Oh, we ought to take this motherfucker's jacket!" Cornell insisted. "Look, he's on this university campus, all high and mighty."

"Fuck it, leave me alone," I said. "I'm getting ready to leave."

"Naw, man, we need to take this jacket. C'mon! Here, you get it. You take it!"

I didn't turn around and say, *Why don't you take it?*

"Man, we need to get this dude!" Cornell persisted. "He's one of them. We can teach him a lesson."

Without thinking about the consequences, and perhaps due to the fact that I was still depressed and being egged on by Cornell—who had a gun—I told the guy, "Hey, motherfucker, give me the coat!"

Before I knew it, we ended up with the guy's coat. Later that afternoon, we boarded the bus to Seattle. During the long journey home, I felt uneasy about having acquired this leather jacket. But Cornell was still laughing and joking: "Oh, yeah, he had no business coming up to you that way!"

I didn't think much of it. As we pulled into Seattle's Greyhound bus station, I immediately spotted dozens of police at the Greyhound station and I knew that they were coming for us.

"Give me your weapon," I told the young bodyguard. I hid it in the small of my back as we got off the bus. The cops were standing there and said, "We've got him. We've got Elmer Dixon."

They were so elated that they were arresting me for

something, they didn't search me. They just handcuffed me, stuck me in the back of the car, and drove me to the police station where they put me in a holding cell.

"You're under arrest for armed robbery," they said, as they read me my Miranda rights. They walked away gleefully because they had achieved what they wanted to do, but they didn't know that I still had a gun tucked in the small of my back.

Now, uncuffed, I could get the gun out of my back. As I watched them laughing and joking with each other, I wiped off all the fingerprints and stuck it in the corner of the holding cell, out of sight. When the pigs came to get me from the cell and take me to the jail block, as I was walking away, I heard a loud commotion.

The sergeant was cussing out several of the police officers because they had found the gun and he was pissed off that they had allowed me to bring a weapon unchecked into the police department. It was a point of contention that I would later use at my trial, stating that I never had a weapon because they never saw it on me. I would not be charged in Seattle because the alleged crime of armed robbery had taken place in Eugene, Oregon, so I was held without bail, waiting to be extradited back to Oregon.

Within a couple of days, there was an extradition hearing and the judge granted the state of Oregon the authority to transport me back to Eugene. When the two detectives arrived, they handcuffed me, put leg irons on and ran the chain around my waist, and up around my neck area. I was basically shackled from head to toe.

They put me in the backseat of a car for the six-hour drive to Eugene. A couple of days later, I made bail and was out on the street before members of the Eugene chapter picked me up.

When I got back to Seattle, I tried to explain to Aaron what had happened, but it was still a blur. It wasn't until 40 years later that we discovered that Cornell was an agent provocateur and had planned to look for the opportunity to get me involved in some sort of criminal activity so that I would be arrested. I discovered that he was an agent provocateur when I saw Cornell's name on a list of informants in Aaron's FBI file, which he had obtained while writing his book. But at the time, I didn't give it a second thought. I trusted him to protect my life as my bodyguard. Instead, he was trying to destroy me.

COMMUNITY SURVIVAL PROGRAMS CONTINUE

As things continued to intensify between the two different ideological perspectives, we moved forward with plans to develop our survival programs. The second survival program that we started was the Children's Free Breakfast Program. We had been told by Central Headquarters that we needed to step up our organizing, as Panthers were being arrested across the country for a variety of both petty crimes and larger crimes, including hold-ups and bank robberies.

The first breakfast program was organized in the Madrona Presbyterian Church, where we held our Central staff meetings. The pastor had always been a strong supporter and gave us access to the kitchen and fellowship hall to offer breakfast to school children.

This was viewed by the military-leaning Panthers as a soft touch and not part of revolutionary practice. But if they had studied in the PE classes as they were supposed to, they would have read about how Mao Tse-tung, in the Chinese Revolution, had organized the lumpenproletariat by helping them to survive. The people needed a way to survive oppression at the hands of greedy businessmen driven by the need to occupy our community. The Ten-Point Program spoke to our desire to control the institutions within the Black community and to put Black people in a position to take care of our own needs.

The Children's Free Breakfast Program was a manifestation of us taking back control of our community. We demanded that the avaricious businessmen, who had been taking resources out of the community without putting anything back, contribute food and other necessities, so that we could run the breakfast program. This, in fact, was the most revolutionary of acts, and with help, would lay the foundation for rebuilding a revolutionary movement.

TAKING A STANCE AT THE STATE CAPITOL

It was during this time that we had gotten wind of a bill that the state legislature was attempting to pass into law, which said it was illegal to carry a loaded weapon in public. We planned to spontaneously go to Olympia and disrupt their hearings, but on the morning that we were to travel to the capitol, my younger brother, Michael, who was a legislative page in Olympia, called us.

"The National Guard was called out," he said. "There are soldiers and police everywhere, including a .50-caliber machine gun mounted up near the Dome of the state capitol."

"Turn around!" Aaron ordered. "Don't go! We'll find another way to show our opposition to the bill."

In Olympia that afternoon, the state police and National Guard were bewildered because they had prepared to confront us, and perhaps wipe us out, but we were a no-show. The next morning, we gathered several of our key Panthers, including several of my lieutenants—Steve Phillips, Warren Jenkins, and Larry Tesino—along with other Panthers, including Warren Meyers and Anthony Ware, who is now Frank Muhammad. and we headed to Olympia.

When we arrived, the state police were caught completely off guard because the National Guard was not there. We marched right up to the capitol and positioned ourselves on the capitol stairs while Aaron was escorted inside to address the legislature. Once he got inside the door of the assembly, we blocked the door so that no one could get out, in order to give him the opportunity to speak, while myself and the other Comrades took up position on the capitol stairs.

As we were about to position ourselves, a state trooper approached.

"It's illegal to have loaded weapons on the capitol grounds," he said.

I knew the other brothers' weapons were loaded, so I took my weapon over to him, opened the chamber, pulled out a round, and said, "See, not loaded."

He was okay with that and we took up position; he never checked the other weapons. We had caught them totally off-guard. After Aaron finished his speech, we drove back to Seattle with our loaded weapons in the trunk. We headed over to The Checkmate, one of several places designated as Panther hang-outs. Black people gathered in this popular nightclub where they were comfortable with Panthers sitting in the booths, as we had a personal relationship with the owner, Sonny Booker.

That night, there was no parking on the street, but the gas station across from the club had empty spaces. It was always closed at that hour, so we pulled into the parking lot as we would on any other night. A brother still inside the station was apparently closing.

"You can't park there!" he said.

"Why not?" I asked. "You're closed, we always park here."

He went back into the gas station office, came out with a gun in his hand, and said, "I told you, you can't park here, you crazy nigger!"

As we drove off his lot, somebody said, "Why the fuck did he want to say that and pull a gun on us?"

So, when we parked, we went to the trunk, we pulled out all the weapons that we had, and looked at the brother at the gas station. He ran and ducked and hid in the gas station. We didn't make any moves towards him but let him know by our actions that we were more than capable of defending ourselves if he wanted a shoot-out.

We walked across the street with our weapons and went in The Checkmate. The music stopped. Everybody froze. We walked to the bar where Sonny was waiting.

"Hey, Sonny," I said, "we need to check our weapons in."

"No problem," he said.

We checked our weapons in. The music played. People danced again. We sat down and ordered our regular drink—a Loganberry flip—and started getting into the groove.

Minutes later, there was a lot of commotion outside. Sirens were going off and lights were flashing. About 10 police cars were outside. Again, the music stopped. The police captain came to the front of the club. Sonny met him at the door.

"Sonny," the cop asked, "is everything alright?"

"The Panthers checked their guns in at the bar and everything is fine," Sonny said.

All the cop cars loaded up and drove away, and the party commenced. Again, it was just another typical night as a member of the Black Panther Party.

STREET JUSTICE FOR MY SISTER

Yet the turmoil that surrounded us was in full swing. A few months earlier, as tensions began to grow between Aaron, myself, and Curtis, I had gotten information that he had assaulted my sister and had been abusing her.

When I went to talk to her, the bruises on her face let me know it was time to make a statement.

Later that afternoon, with my security guard, Cornell, I went up to their house and knocked on the door. When Curtis answered, I remembered what I had always been taught growing up: to land the first punch.

I was already infuriated that he had been beating on my sister, so I knocked him clear across the room into his couch, onto the floor, smashing the lamp. My sister came out screaming, "What's going on?"

Standing over Curtis, I warned, "Don't you ever touch my sister again or I'll kill you!"

I turned and headed out the door.

"Where's my gun?" Curtis screamed. "Where's my gun?"

Cornell and I dashed to the car. As we got in, Curtis fired his weapon into the air. I gave my .357 to Cornell.

"Don't fire at Curtis, or the house, because my sister is up there," I said. "Just fire a shot into the air."

This would set off another series of events. Curtis was questioning Aaron's leadership. Before long, Aaron wanted to confront Curtis and the other members who were aligned with the philosophy of direct action.

"The efforts you're planning are counter-revolutionary to the efforts of the Party," Aaron told Curtis and others during a tense meeting. I was there to back Aaron up in case things got heated.

"You're acting like fake Panthers," Curtis accused, referring to the capitol steps drama. "You didn't have loaded weapons and had allowed a pig to check your weapon without confronting him."

"You stupid motherfucker," I said. "You can't have a round in the chamber anyway. The weapons were loaded."

Curtis countered: "We ain't stupid, motherfucker."

I got in his face. "You motherfuckers are trying to get us all killed! You go out here robbing banks and holding up stores. That's not revolutionary. That's counter-revolutionary."

Aaron reminded Curtis, "We weren't there for a gunfight. The day before, when the state troopers were waiting for us, they had an armed encampment that could have easily wiped all of us out, which is what they wanted. Our purpose was to challenge the legality of passing a law that would prohibit people from carrying guns in public, knowing that the law was targeted specifically towards the Black Panther Party."

While Aaron was the voice of reason, I didn't feel it was necessary to respond to Curtis's claims because I knew that I allowed my weapon to be checked so the other Panthers' weapons would not be, as their weapons were, in fact, loaded. But the die was cast.

All this occurred while we were taking the fire from Eldridge Cleavage's reputation as "murder mouth"—always talking about whom he was going to kill. Plus, we had just returned from the funeral for Bunchy Carter and John Huggins. And Huey had ordered a nationwide purge of counter-revolutionary Panthers. Curtis was one of them, and his renegade behavior made us suspect he was an agent provocateur.

One fall afternoon, we heard a radio report that a bank robbery had gone down in broad daylight on the South End near Franklin High School, with suspected members of the Party involved. The robbery went awry and several key members of our organization were arrested, facing federal charges.

Of the four Comrades involved in the robbery, the only ones to get caught were Willie, LouJack, and John. Curtis was never identified. This further convinced Aaron and me that Curtis was the informant.

Willie B., LouJack, and another brother, John, were some of our most trusted and important leaders, and to see them get caught up in this concocted scheme that we believed was set in motion by an agent provocateur, was very disheartening.

Those three ended up getting prison terms. Willie B. was sentenced to 25 years at McNeil Island Federal Penitentiary, John was sentenced to 20 years in a federal prison, and LouJack got the same sentence. LouJack would be transferred to Lompoc, another federal penitentiary outside of the state of Washington, where he would be attacked and stabbed to death. When he left the courtroom after sentencing, it would be the last time we saw him alive. We later found out that John had turned Capital Witness and made some sort of plea deal, fearing the long prison sentence.

Yet even with this deal, Curtis was somehow still unnamed. Further feeding our suspicions was when another Comrade, Mike Murray, told us of several questionable situations involving Curtis.

"Come into the office," Curtis had called to a group of young Comrades, which included Mike.

"Here," Curtis said, handing them pistols. "Go around the corner to ambush the fire station on the corner of 33rd and Union." The station was a frequent target of random attacks because it was a staging area for the pigs when they wanted to vamp on our office. Mike said he and the brothers left the office to go do the deed, but decided that it did not make sense, and returned to the office. Curtis checked their guns and told him that his and the other Comrades' weapons had not been fired.

"I always suspected him of being an agent provocateur," Mike told me, "for ordering senseless attacks that could result in him getting shot or put in jail for a senseless, random act of violence."

This ultimately led to Aaron expelling Curtis from the Party.

THE PURGE

As tensions within the Party grew around the country, it was clear that many of the Comrades who had joined in a rush—including several hundred in Seattle, and thousands nationwide—were not used to the discipline and regimentation of the Party. They were routinely either breaking the rules of the Party, or confronting the police openly with renegade actions.

As a result, Central Headquarters issued two orders. One

was that we were to immediately come out of uniform and no longer wear the leather jacket and beret in public, with the exception of previously sanctioned events, and the second was a purge of our ranks aimed at rally Panthers and renegades.

This became known as "The Purge," an effort to rid the ranks of counter-revolutionary opportunists and agent provocateurs. This would result in a sort of fine-tuning of our ranks and whittle us down to a dedicated core of Panthers we could count on, and who were well disciplined.

For the Seattle chapter, this meant a reorganization of sorts, so Aaron called for a weekend retreat where several remaining key leaders traveled to a remote mountain cabin, lent to us by one of our white liberal supporters. Though we were far away in the snow-covered North Cascades, we brought weapons to clean, do target practice, and keep us secure.

During our meetings, we first laid down our understanding of the principles and foundations of the Black Panther Party. This was critical as one of the most important factors of being a revolutionary in a Vanguard Party was being principled. That meant no compromise on any of our ideals or other things that we stood for, which was serving the people and building a revolutionary movement.

We fueled our fire for a strategic revolution by reading *The Little Red Book*, also known as *Quotations from Chairman Mao Tse-tung*, the former Chairman of the Chinese Communist Party. We stood outside the cabin in the snow, reading this book and quoting our favorite one-liners, such as:

"Dare to struggle and dare to win!" and

"Beware of paper tigers."

I loved that one, referencing people who pretended to be tough, but weren't like the pigs.

The retreat—which included deep talks around the fireplace each night—provided some of the most productive PE classes and discussions that we had ever had since we formed the chapter. It provided us with the impetus for moving forward in an organized and disciplined fashion. The attacks that were being launched against the Party were coming in waves and we needed to be prepared and disciplined to survive.

MUSIC AND MAYHEM

I had moved out of my parents' house for the second time and hoped it would be the last time. I took an apartment up on Capitol Hill and shared it with Michael Dean, a Comrade and brother who had been a high school classmate. Dean, as we called him, was a tall, lanky, gangling young man who had joined the Party after Aaron and me and others started the organization.

He often would accompany me when I played in the band, as I was still a member of the group known as the Regents. On one occasion, we were playing at Club Ebony, a popular dance venue on Capitol Hill. Hundreds of young people packed this large venue that evening, so my lieutenants were there, just in case things got out of hand.

Sure enough, a fight broke out in the auditorium. A few brothers quelled the disturbance and settled people down. The fight re-started with multiple people, raising the possibility of a riot.

"Go get your weapons," I told my Comrades, "and line up on the stage."

My band members were in shock when my armed Comrades positioned themselves on the stage.

"The dance is over," I announced over the microphone. "Get outside and leave before the pigs come and vamp on everyone. You know the pigs are looking for any opportunity to come in with billy clubs and tear gas and create a riot scene."

People quietly gathered their things and left in an orderly fashion. There was no incident with the police. It soon became clear that my band members were uneasy with me needing a security team to travel with me, so I soon parted ways with the band. The revolution was becoming more serious, and it was time for me to put down my adolescent activities and fully commit as a revolutionary. Despite that, I still longed for the days of playing with my bandmates.

That spring, James Brown was coming to town for another concert. Aaron and I had met Mr. Brown during the summer of 1968, after approaching his manager after a concert.

"We're seeking a donation for our Children's Free Breakfast program," we told the manager.

"Mr. Brown will see you at his hotel at the airport Hilton," the manager said.

When we arrived at the hotel, we were escorted to Mr. Brown's large, one-bedroom suite. In fact, it may have been the presidential suite. His manager told us:

"Mr. Brown is eating breakfast and will be with you after he finishes."

Aaron and I sat there in our leather jackets and berets wondering what it would be like to meet James Brown.

"Never address him as James," his manager said. "Only address him as Mr. Brown. Mr. Brown was raised in the South, and having formal etiquette, it shows a sign of respect to call someone mister."

When Mr. Brown came out to us, we introduced ourselves and told him about the Black Panther Party's Children's Free Breakfast program.

"I want to give you a donation," Mr. Brown said, but before he got to writing a check, he wanted to give us some advice.

"If you ever want to get anywhere with your revolution," he said, "you need to take off your leather jackets and berets, and put on a suit."

Aaron and I tried desperately not to roll our eyes and to maintain respect, so we just nodded without saying much. Once

Mr. Brown wrote the check, we thanked him.

"We respect you and your music," we told him. "You're a legend in the Black community! We wish you farewell and good luck in your engagement."

The next time we met with Mr. Brown at the concert venue, his manager recognized us right away.

"Wait here," he said. "Mr. Brown will be out."

What was ironic was that we were no longer in Panther uniform. We were trying to dress more like ordinary people in the Black community. But because we were also in a more heightened sense of security, we often wore battle fatigues, which was also common among Black activists.

So, there we were, standing in green fatigues when we met Mr. Brown for the second time. He took one look at us and chuckled.

"Well," he said, "at least you're out of the leather jackets and berets. But you need to put on a suit."

He gave us a check for $5,000, which was 10 times more than the $500 he had given us the year before.

CHAPTER 16

Body and Soul

Following the retreat, we honed in on studying the *Red Book* and learning to put revolutionary theory into practice. We also studied one of my favorite books, *Wretched of the Earth* by Frantz Fanon. He explored dialectical materialism and the fact that everything within the universe was in a constant state of flux.

"Man, this is confusing," brothers and sisters complained.

"Wait, let me break it down," I said during meetings. "Fanon is just saying that we have to understand that change is possible and the conditions that we live under will inevitably change."

This elicited glimmers of understanding in their eyes.

"We have to be the catalyst for that change," I said. "Huey taught us that power is the ability to define phenomena and make it act in a desired manner. This is the difference between revolutionaries who practice the art of revolution, and those who only talk about it. Those jokers are armchair revolutionaries. But we are the real revolutionaries!"

Thankfully, our Comrades became excited about how to apply this philosophy to our work in the streets.

We also knew that defining phenomena meant that we had to do an analysis of the conditions within our community. This analysis inspired our free breakfast program. Feeding hungry kids was a deliberate response to the conditions that poor Black, brown, white, and Asian youth faced every morning when going to school and struggling to learn on empty stomachs.

This analysis also led to the creation of the original survival program: the police alert patrols, the community control of police initiative, and eventually, our free medical clinic.

These endeavors contradicted the philosophy espoused by the military-minded members of the BPP. They believed that direct action against the establishment would ignite revolution, failing to see that such insurrections in the past only tended to isolate the group further from the community, and made it possible for their eventual extermination.

This was the path that J. Edgar Hoover wanted the Black Panther Party to take so that he could set us up for extermination and annihilation. But the Central Committee was hip to his game and knew that this would only lead to further attacks on our offices.

So, we had to engage in building a strong revolutionary philosophy that would allow us to build a protracted struggle, one that would organize the lumpenproletariat, and eventually lead to a showdown with our oppressors. This was how our Revolution was to be built.

We continued to have our regular meetings with Chairman Bobby in Oakland, and I looked forward to those trips because they gave me the opportunity to hang out with the Comrades at Central Headquarters, who I knew were down for revolution.

Aaron was spending a lot of time at Central learning about the Party, which was important to gain the knowledge and understanding of Party operations. The small cadre that we still had intact stayed behind to initiate other programs.

"Organize the Summer Liberation School while I'm in Oakland," Aaron instructed. This would be the first of many for the Seattle chapter. I got together with Jake and Anthony, an old friend from the Madrona neighborhood and now a trusted Comrade, to organize the school.

"Educate to Liberate" became our motto, inspired by Chairman Bobby's instructions to make educating our youth a top priority. We drew inspiration from Central, which had organized the first Liberation School. This put point number five in our Ten-Point Program into action.

I was happy to work with Anthony, whose awakening happened alongside mine after we heard Stokely Carmichael speak at our high school. I'd known this soft-spoken brother since we attended Madrona Elementary. He lived a few blocks from us, but we didn't hang out much because he was quiet and unassuming. But in high school, we started talking about what was going down in the community. We'd joined SNCC at the same time and he was among our trusted Comrades who helped me form the Black Student Union at Garfield High.

Now, our first task in organizing the Summer Liberation School was to find a location. Thankfully, Anthony's progressive-minded parents, John and Jerry, were staunch supporters of the Party and very supportive of their son. They were well connected in the Black community and had access to several properties, including a large house on the corner of 32nd and Union in Panther territory.

Anthony and I organized a small cadre of teachers, and in that large house, we began to teach Black history classes, math courses, reading, writing, and the basics of a good education. The Panthers' school was all about giving the youth a hand up so they would have a chance of surviving the schoolyear with a leg up on their basic skills. We also instilled some foundational learning about who they were as African kings and queens, so they could develop a high level of self-esteem—a proven launching pad for kids to achieve high levels in school.

We also provided free lunch and breakfast to the kids. This became a real-life lesson on how to execute the Panthers' Ten-Point Program, so the boys and girls would understand what the Black Panther Party stood for, and why it was important to have a purpose and be organized.

We demonstrated this by creating a lesson around our meal program and point number three, which stated that we wanted an end to the robbery of the Black community by capitalist businessmen. This referred to store owners and other businesses that exploited the Black community for profit, but gave nothing back to the people. So, we took the kids to two of the largest grocery stores that occupied the Black community. Both were Safeway; one was on the corner of 23rd and Union, and the other was at the intersection of 23rd and Jackson, like bookends occupying our community.

"Can we have a contribution for the breakfast program and the lunch program for the school?" we asked the store managers.

Both stores responded the same: "We don't give donations directly from the store. That's handled by headquarters."

"Headquarters are in Bellevue," I countered to both store managers. "We don't care about what they give to Bellevue, because they don't need it, anyway. We care about the fact that your store is in the Black community right here, and you should give back to the community that keeps you in business."

Again, they refused.

So, I asked the kids, "What strategy should we use to convince these stores to help us?"

"Boycott the grocery stores!" the kids said.

Back at school, the kids made signs and crafted a strategy. That afternoon, we went to boycott the two big stores that would not give food to the free food program.

As we stood in front of the store with our signs, some of the 11- and 12-year-old kids were talking to adults who were entering the store. They later revealed the boycott strategy that they conceived by applying the teachings of the Liberation School. They told me:

"We asked the shoppers to fill up their grocery carts with bags of groceries, mostly perishable and frozen foods, and when they got to the checkout counter after all of the groceries were checked through, to say that they changed their minds and they didn't want the food."

I was awed as these young people explained: "So then the people who work in the store have to put all of the groceries back on the shelves, over and over, every time somebody abandons a basket full of groceries at the check-out. This will jam up the check-out and all people who are waiting in line will be so mad, they'll leave!"

Their brilliant boycott strategy worked magic.

Two weeks later, the giant food chain closed both stores! They eventually went out of business. This was a brilliant strategy by 11- and 12-year-old kids who were putting what they learned in the Liberation School into practice.

Meanwhile, all the shoppers went around the corner to a small grocery store run by a Jewish gentleman, Jack Richland. He had been in that neighborhood for many years, as the Central District was once a Jewish community. When many of the Jews fled to the suburbs, Jack remained, because he had built relationships with many of the Black people who had moved into the neighborhood.

"Jack," I asked, during a store visit. "Can you please donate food to the breakfast program?"

"How much do you need?" he asked.

"Jack, whatever you can give us. We understand you're a small business and any help that you give will be greatly appreciated by the community."

At the time, Jack's store was called Jack's Mini Mart. After the big Safeway had closed, Jack's business skyrocketed, and he eventually bought the grocery store and gas station on the corner of 23rd and Union; his establishment then became Jack's Super Mart. That resulted from his commitment and service to the community.

A NEW TYPE OF BUSINESS MEETING

After the long, hot summer of 1968, the anti-poverty programs established by President "LBJ" Lyndon Johnson were in full swing, but the funds weren't making it to the Black community.

Specifically, the Model Cities program was seen by many as a way to appease Black people and keep the natives from getting restless.

Aaron and I wanted answers. So, armed with shotguns, we and several Panthers marched into the office Seattle's Model Cities Director, Walt Huntley.

"These funds are not being used to benefit the community!" we told him. "They only serve to create an upper class by feeding the deep pockets of those like you who are benefitting from high-level positions."

We viewed him as an "establishment Negro" who cow-towed to the institutionally racist power structure that kept Black and brown people in poverty and struggle.

Mr. Huntley wasn't happy about our meeting method, or the fact that we were telling him how to run his program in a way that would help the people who needed it most.

The irony of this was that my father was now working at Model Cities because Boeing had laid off many workers, and he had taken a job as an artistic marketing person of some sort. But our beef was not with the employees; we knew that they needed jobs. We just didn't want the head of the organization establishing programs that would not benefit the community to the fullest.

We were a group to be reckoned with. One of the most important aspects of being a Panther was standing on principle, so we didn't accept or apply for any government funding whatsoever, because Panthers couldn't be bought off.

We confronted this at every turn and we didn't stop there, even taking issue with Black churches that were exploiting Black people for their own profit. This would rub the establishment Blacks the wrong way, but we were standing on principle, and we told it like it was and like we saw it. This caused many standoffs with some who thought they could challenge us, but we would not be compromised and often found ourselves having to face down would-be challengers.

ON PATROL FOR ROCK 'N' ROLL

When Aaron finally returned from one of his long trips to Oakland late in the summer, he informed us that he had arranged for us to provide security at a rock concert. It was highly unusual for members of the Black Panther Party to take on this kind of assignment, but it was a promise he had made to a friend of our sister, Joanne.

One of her childhood friends was Thane Hellmuth, a slightly built young white girl from a well-to-do family across the red line in Denny-Blaine. Thane was artistic, intense, and very loyal to Joanne. She had a younger sister who was mentally disabled, and an older sister who had married a local promoter who was bringing together bands from around the country to create the Northwest version of Woodstock.

He didn't want law enforcement officers to be security at his event. He didn't trust them and had seen disasters with uniformed police officers at these big hippie fests. This would be a big one, so he had asked Aaron if members of the Party would provide the security for this event.

Because we knew him and he was Thane's brother-in-law, Aaron agreed to take a small core of Panthers who were not officially on Party business and provide security for this event. My cousin, Mark, from Chicago was visiting along with one of his best friends, Ron, so we brought along Ron and Mark, and a couple of other brothers, to provide security for an event that had 40,000 people attending.

The headline groups were Jefferson Airplane, Santana, Ike and Tina Turner, Chicago, Led Zeppelin, Jimi Hendrix, The Doors and The Grateful Dead. This three-day event was located in Woodinville, Washington, a farm area located about 15 minutes from Seattle. When we arrived, our main objective was to make sure that everyone was orderly and that no one was trying to rip off the event.

I tucked my .357 tucked underneath my shirt for backup, but for the most part, things went pretty smoothly. We dispersed the Comrades around the ticket booths and the entrance ways into the area, while Aaron, Michael Dean, and I went over to Tent City to see what was shaking over there. Tent City was an area that had probably more than 1,000 tents, where some of the hippies would be staying over the three nights. When we first came into the area, we entered the first tent.

"Security!" we announced. "We're here for tent inspection."

Weed started flying, and pills were being thrown out the door.

"Hold it everybody!" I shouted, "Stop!"

I reached over and grabbed the joint from one of the hippies and took a puff off of it.

The hippies watched in shock.

"Okay, this is good shit!" I announced coolly. "You pass inspection."

Then we were on to the next tent, where I conducted more joint-testing. After I smoked just enough not to be too high, I went to inspect the entrance area.

My cousin Mark was up a trail talking to Ron, who had hippies lined up longer than the queue at the ticket booth. I hurried over to discover that Ron was reselling tickets that he had taken at the entrance from people going into the event. He hadn't torn them in half and had started his own ticket line up in the woods.

Wads of money were hanging out of his pocket, thanks to his ghetto entrepreneurial spirit from Chicago.

"Everybody!" I announced. "Go back to the gate."

Meanwhile, during the long, laid-back afternoons in the hot sun, the music was some of the best we had heard.

Then, what a sight to behold: Aaron, having just smoked a fresh joint, riding a big white horse through thousands of hippies as they listened to the rockfest, making sure they were cool and relaxed.

On Saturday evening, the crowd was especially large and boisterous because The Doors were about to come on stage. Their lead singer, Jim Morrison, was known to incite crowds with his spontaneous words and music.

I positioned myself to watch the crowd from a chair in front of the stage, separated from the crowd by a large fence. I positioned myself to expose my .357, in case the crowd had any ideas of getting unruly. There were thousands of people, and if they started to push forward, I wasn't about to be crushed. All I had to do, I thought, was lift my shirt, wave my finger back and forth, and say, "Nope," so the crowd would back off.

Fortunately, the crowd grooved into the night with Jim Morrison's music, including "Light My Fire." It was one hell of a scene.

CHAPTER 17

The New Headquarters

Aaron continued his frequent trips to Central Headquarters working with leadership there to understand ongoing strategies for the next several months.

The FBI had begun to step up their activities around the country attacking various offices using Alcohol, Tobacco, Firearms and Explosives (ATF) Agents to raid our offices. We were not yet in a secure living situation that summer, and I was living on Capitol Hill with one of my Comrades, Michael Dean. We watched each other's backs while we were working in the Panther office and out in the street.

I had purchased an M1 carbine with a banana clip and wire stock that made it look like an assault rifle. I kept it in my apartment for self-defense as we had moved on from having bodyguards or security and needed to stay vigilant and ready to defend ourselves at all times. This particular apartment on Capitol Hill was facing the street and had long windows that reached from the floor to a high vaulted ceiling. There was a loft bedroom up above the living room, and I would hang my carbine upside down on the wall as if it were a wall ornament, hanging over the living room below.

One afternoon after Michael and I had been out selling Panther papers and organizing in the community, I came back to my apartment and it was full of FBI agents. They had ransacked the apartment and had my weapon in their possession. When I came in, I asked them: "Show me the warrant for why you're here," I ordered.

They produced a warrant.

"We're investigating a report that you have an automatic weapon," they said.

"That's ridiculous!" I said.

"The weapon that you're holding is my personal property," I said, "and you have no right to take it. Plus, you have no proof that it could be an automatic weapon."

I glared at them. "You don't know what the fuck you're talking about. Unhand my weapon!"

One of the agents who looked like a rookie opened the chamber of the weapon and said to the lieutenant, "See, sir? It looks like it's been filed down. I'm almost certain it's been made into an automatic weapon."

"Listen, rookie pig, who must have escaped from the academy before graduation," I said. "You don't know shit. The M1 carbine was a semi-automatic weapon, which meant that it would rapid-fire every time you squeeze the trigger, but in order for it to become fully automatic, someone would have had to file down a portion of the trigger mechanism, so that when you held down the trigger, it would fire like a machine gun." I knew I had not done this and it was very unlikely that someone would have tampered with it unless it had been those agents who were in my apartment.

"Go ahead and test it," I told them. "But I want my attorney present when it's being tested. And I want it to be filed with a file number so it can't be tampered with while it's in your possession."

Michael Dean was with me in the apartment and we both agreed to examine the weapon and make sure that it was in the same condition in which we left it. We then could inform our attorney, John Caughlan, that there were no markings on the weapon when it left our apartment. That way, he could inspect the weapon before they tested it, and observe the test that was being carried out. The rookie officer looked like a kid in a candy store, like he had captured something significant and was all excited about the fact that they had gotten ahold of my weapon. They thought they were going to go and prove that I had an automatic weapon so they could arrest me and lock me away, but we knew that that was not going to happen.

Some weeks later, I got a call from the FBI saying that I could come downtown and pick up my weapon. So, Michael Dean and I went by the apartment and got a banana clip, then went down to the FBI offices in downtown Seattle. When I walked into the FBI office, that lieutenant was there, along with his sidekick.

"See?" I told them. "That little dude didn't know what he was talking about. Give me my weapon."

They handed the weapon over the counter. As I walked out, I had the banana clip in my back pocket so they would know that once I got outside, I would be putting my banana clip in my weapon. They watched as I left the building, and when I got outside, I inserted the banana clip, we got into our car, and drove off.

That kind of tit-for-tat was going on that year, as if the ATF was looking for a reason to attack our office or to confront us. As a result, we were on alert most of the time while out doing our work, and other duties, throughout the community. The atmosphere was shifting in the community, as we had become a smaller, more compact group of revolutionaries. It came time to move into a more secure site.

We found a location on 20th and Spruce streets, which became our barracks and our central office—one of the most notorious Panther offices in the country. There we would prepare to make our final stand if necessary.

First, we began fortifying the location. The building was a duplex with two entrances at the front; one door led into the lower apartment (which would become our offices, and later, the site of our first free medical clinic). The door to the right led upstairs, which would become the Panther barracks.

I worked with members who were former Green Berets in 'Nam, including James Redmond and his brother Randolph. Randolph had been pronounced dead four times on the operating table before he was brought back to life, surviving a machine gun strafing across his midsection. He and James were from the notorious Redmond family. His sister, Joyce, had been one of the original members of the Seattle chapter, and one of the first women to join. She was in the car with me when we drove down to Bunchy's and John's funeral, so they, as a family, didn't take no mess. Their backgrounds provided insight into how to best fortify the office, starting with sandbags.

We went to the Fisher Flower Company and purchased several hundred empty flower bags. Late at night, we went to Alki Beach with a shovel and a truck, then filled sandbags. In our office, we lined the downstairs and upstairs walls with sandbags.

To fortify the windows with something that would deflect bullets from a police attack, we got large sheets of plywood and found corrugated steel wherever we could get some. We used manhole covers, appropriated from wherever we could find it, and sandwiched that between two sheets of plywood. This created steel and plywood barriers on all the windows upstairs and downstairs.

The window barriers had "gun flaps." They were about six inches wide and we could flip them up, secure them with a hook, and have gun slots all the way across the bottom of the window, which came up to the top of the sandbags. This would give us protection in the event of an attack and allow us to fire back and defend the office.

We then built barriers for each of the two doors in the front and the rear of the downstairs apartment. The barriers that we constructed were about eight inches thick and made the doors very heavy. We fortified the door hinges to support the weight of the door. We bolted two-by-fours into the floor, and built a doorstop that would fall into place, locking the door. It was just bolted against each of the fortified doors in case the doors were being hammered from the outside.

Inside the downstairs door, we placed a desk, so when anyone entered, the Officer of the Day greeted them. Every Panther office had an Officer of the Day who protected the front of the building during the normal working hours. In the drawer of the desk was a .357 or .45, and under the desk was a sawed-off shotgun, so the Officer of the Day had ample weapons to prevent any immediate attack.

The office doors usually stayed open during the day, so community members could freely enter and ask about programs or inquire about the activities of the Party.

Upstairs, we had arranged the rooms into sleeping quarters. The kitchen in the back was a central location to meet, have meals, and do community study or our political education classes. It quickly began to feel like a Panther home and would remain that way for the next several years.

In the fall of '69, Leon Valentine Hobbes joined our group. He was a very important addition to our team, largely because he was fearless, took no shit from anyone, and became a die-hard Panther. He was from New York City and had a very brash way about him.

"Don't fuck with James," I warned. Valentine was a bad dude, but he didn't want to cross James. But when James came to the office and met Valentine for the first time, Valentine immediately got in James' face and said, "I heard you think you're a bad mothafucka."

Oh shit. I told him not to do that, I thought.

Before I could blink, James threw a right punch, knocking Valentine out cold. He dropped like a sack of potatoes. When he regained consciousness he asked, "What happened?"

"You met James and I told you not to fuck with him," I said, "so get over it 'cause we got work to do."

We welcomed him to our ranks. Aaron recognized his background in medical care made him perfect for helping us start our free medical clinic in the fall of 1969. We had heard of a doctor, Dr. John Green, who had worked with Students for a Democratic Society (SDS) at the University of Washington.

During huge anti-war demonstrations, when 40,000 students would march and block the freeway, Dr. Green and his medical students followed behind. If anyone were struck by a billy club or a tear gas canister, Dr. Green and his students administered first aid. He was legendary after gaining some notoriety for his work and his commitment to the struggle.

So, one afternoon we met with him to talk about how to set up and staff a clinic. He invited Valentine and me to his home in an affluent neighborhood.

"Come on into the living room," he said. "Let's get our head right." We followed him into the living room, where he pulled out a hash pipe to share.

Then we rapped to him, explaining our mission. Valentine shared what he had learned after being assigned to start the clinic. We had done our analysis of the problem and found that the C.D. in Seattle had the second highest infant mortality rate in the whole state, and we had to do something about it.

"We have to address this," we told him. "The rate of sickle cell anemia is increasing, and nobody is doing anything about it. We want a clinic to focus on sickle cell anemia and we want a well-baby clinic."

Dr. Green agreed. "You need a well-baby clinic to get young, expectant mothers the prenatal care they need, so we can arrest this epidemic in the Black community. They don't have any place to go for healthcare, and they don't have any support."

Back then, teen pregnancy was taboo. Teenagers wouldn't tell their parents that they were pregnant. While white families put their pregnant daughters in private schools where they received good prenatal care and delivered healthy babies, Black girls were sent to alternative schools that lacked prenatal care, resulting in the state's second highest infant mortality rate.

This conversation occurred as we smoked on the bowl of hash that he provided. (I didn't think anything of it at the time because I thought, if a neurosurgeon can do it, so can I!) We had long discussions over that hash pipe about the importance of free medical care. And he agreed to help us.

"The first thing we need is some equipment," Dr. Green said. "Rent a big truck. Next Wednesday at three o'clock, come back to the university with a truck. When you pull up to the loading dock, ring the bell to get the door rolled up. Just tell them you're there for Dr. Green."

Valentine and I did just that. Up came the door, and there was Dr. Green, standing with all the medical equipment, including exam tables, that we needed.

"Damn, John, where'd you get all this shit?" I asked.

"I appropriated it from the hospital," he said. "They weren't using this stuff, anyway. You can put it to good use."

Along with exam room tables, medical cabinets, and medical equipment, Dr. Green also staffed the clinic with third- and fourth-year medical students whom he had assigned to us from the school. They brought whatever medicines they thought they would need in the clinic. All were supervised by Dr. Green.

These doctors, including Meredith Mathews, MD, made it possible for us to provide free medical care to the community. Our first program was a well-baby clinic, so women who were pregnant or thinking about becoming pregnant could learn about nutrition and the proper healthcare required to deliver healthy babies. This enabled us to address the infant mortality rate in the Black community.

The Sidney Miller Free Medical Clinic was named after one of the first Seattle chapter members who was murdered. Shot by a grocery store owner in West Seattle who claimed that he thought Sidney was going to rob the store, the murder appeared to be a set-up, because Sidney was shot in the back. Sidney had been a rank-and-file member of the Black Panther Party, dedicated to selling papers, working in our community-based programs, and politically educating the community. He also worked on the police alert patrols. It was a heavy blow when Sidney was shot.

The clinic proved successful, as many young Black women began seeking medical services.

"Walking by the Officer of the Day," one woman said, "and being escorted back to the clinic, and past the sandbags, I feel totally safe."

We had achieved one part of our goal—a safe environment for women to receive healthcare.

CHAPTER 18

Prevent the Rise of a Black Messiah

It had been several months since my arrest in Eugene, Oregon. The chapter there had been running for a while, and it was time for me to return to Eugene for trial.

My attorney had developed a strategy to try to draw attention away from me as the suspect, without shifting blame or causing my bodyguards to become suspects. What we were not aware of at the time—and didn't find out until 40 years later—was that my bodyguard, Cornell, was actually a police informant and had orchestrated the whole situation. Without knowing that, we had no idea of an effective way to mount a defense other than mistaken identity.

When I arrived in Eugene, the Comrades had already set up a Panther house and were doing the daily activities of a small chapter, which included selling papers, running the breakfast program, doing political education, and trying to educate the population on the finer points of capitalism, oppression, and the need to organize and build revolution.

Two members of that chapter, Bill Green and his wife, Alice, were responsible for organizing most of the chapter's efforts, along with another brother named Lee, who had helped them organize arms training in the back hills of Eugene.

Eugene was a small college town with a major university, the University of Oregon. Its population was mostly students who attended the school, the faculty, administration, and of course, the small townspeople. It was in a rural part of Oregon, which provided the perfect opportunity for an outdoorsman to actually enjoy the outdoors and do some hunting and fishing, while also doing political and arms training out in the field.

"I'll participate in the daily activities," I told them when I arrived, "as I would in any chapter. I'll travel to the extent that I can, since I'm here for a trial."

The next morning, while I was sleeping in the barracks, I was awakened to the blaring music of Santana's song, "You Got to Change Your Evil Ways." When my eyes popped open, there was Bill Green dancing through the living room, singing, "You got to change your evil ways! Wake up, Comrades, it's time to go to the breakfast program!" Everybody swung into action as if I were in Seattle. We rose at 6 a.m. and went to the breakfast program to feed the kids.

Then, for me, I had to get ready for trial. Downtown, the courthouse resembled something out of the Perry Mason TV show, as did the courtroom. We did jury selection and took our chances on an all-white jury, hoping that we could convince one of them that I wasn't the perpetrator. The judge looked like any other old white dude presiding over a Black man's life and freedom, but I had confidence in my attorneys and wasn't afraid of the outcome.

The trial lasted a few weeks and the jury deliberations lasted several hours. When the verdict came out, I was pronounced guilty and sentenced to six years in prison for stealing a leather jacket. I thought it was a harsh sentence, but they said, being that a weapon was involved, they were able to give me six years. My lawyers and I immediately appealed, and I was let out on an appeal bond. After spending some time with my Comrades in

Oregon, I returned to Seattle later that fall.

The Eugene chapter soon closed. Bill and Alice came to Seattle, lived in the Panther barracks, and helped operate the office. Lee was left in charge of a small troop in Eugene. Because he was in a strategic location, he was not transferred out.

That same year, we organized a chapter in Tacoma, Washington, and we designated a brother out of Philadelphia named Tyrone Byrdsong (we called him T) as the leader. T was an important and inspirational figure to lead that small cadre. He was released from the United States Army in Tacoma, where he resided when he joined the Seattle chapter of the Black Panther Party in 1969. He then proposed there be a chapter in Tacoma that functioned like the Seattle headquarters. There in Tacoma, they organized in the same way as all the chapters did, with the running of breakfast programs, selling papers, and providing tests for sickle cell. Running that chapter proved challenging as T was the only one responsible for keeping the Comrades motivated and in line. He was the primary leader and often lacked the back-up he needed, as we were focused on Seattle's operation. He called Aaron and gave him the low down.

"Take Jake and Valentine to go straighten them out," Aaron told me.

With Valentine always ready to kick some ass and Jake providing the necessary back up, I delivered Aaron's message: "Straighten up or get the fuck out."

The chapter ended shortly after that. T went to Oakland to work out of Central Headquarters, as the Comrades there were under constant attack by the FBI and many members were being arrested.

Chairman Bobby had given us responsibility for either organizing or working with the chapters in Tacoma, Portland, Eugene, and other parts of Washington. This designated us as the Washington state chapter and the smaller affiliates were designated as branches of the BPP. In Eastern Washington, a cadre of Panthers were headed by the Bell Brothers, James and Larry, who were attending Eastern Washington University. They had grown up in the C.D., running the Chain Gang, and were one of the more notorious Black families that came out of the Central District. Plus, they were staunch revolutionaries who understood the Marxist-Leninist philosophy of Mao Tse-tung, the theories of Frantz Fanon, and other revolutionaries.

The Bell Brothers had us speak on campus, which was surrounded by a very right-wing, white, working-class community. On one such occasion, I flew to Eastern Washington as a featured speaker on the Black Panther Party. James and his older brother had organized this event, and when I spoke, it was like speaking to a sea of white folks because there weren't many Black people on campus, nor many who lived in the small college town of Cheney, Washington.

I was railing on the FBI and J. Edgar Hoover, when a woman in the audience said, "My husband is an FBI agent and he's a good man!"

"I have no doubt that he's a good man," I responded, "but he's working for a very evil man, J. Edgar Hoover, and the actions they're directing towards the Black Panther Party through the COINTELPRO program are unconstitutional and illegal."

Aaron was sending me to speak at these universities more and more, and each time, I gained confidence in my ability to articulate the philosophy of the Party, the sins committed against Black and oppressed people, and the illegitimacy of the Nixon regime.

"Our struggle is not against a single FBI agent nor all white people," I told the woman, "but against a corrupt government that has no understanding of the common man or woman's struggle to exist."

THE CASE AGAINST CHAIRMAN BOBBY

One day that fall, Chairman Bobby disappeared from his home in Oakland. We later learned he had been kidnapped for charges that arose from the riots that occurred at the Democratic National Convention in 1968. He was charged along with seven other radicals, including Abby Hoffman, with the conspiracy of inciting riots at the convention; they became known as the Chicago Eight.

At the start of the trial, as the attorneys for each of the eight defendants would be introduced, Bobby Seale stood.

"I will not be represented by any of the attorneys at the table," he announced, though accompanied by counsel who included William Kunstler and others. "I'm going to represent myself based on my constitutional right to defend myself."

"I refuse to allow you to represent yourself," said the acting judge, Julius J. Hoffman. "You need a lawyer, and if you don't want one of the lawyers at the trial table, then one will be appointed to you."

Bobby refused and said that it was his legal right to act as his own attorney, and that he intended to do so. The judge told him that he would not be allowed to defend himself, that he was not to disrupt the court proceedings, and it was his choice if he did not want to have an attorney represent him. However, Bobby would not relent.

The chairman was very well-versed in the law and legal representation. He knew his right to act as his own attorney. When the prosecution began to call witnesses, Bobby would stand up and attempt to cross-examine the witness, and Judge Hoffman became very upset, ordering Bobby to take a seat and be quiet.

"I'm not going to be quiet," Bobby said. "I'm defending myself and I have a right to do so."

"If you don't be quiet, I'm going to order you to be chained and gagged!" Judge Hoffman said.

Bobby continued to defend himself, so Judge Hoffman ordered sheriff's deputies to remove Bobby from the courtroom. When they brought him back in, he was chained and bound to a chair with a gag across his mouth.

But that didn't stop the chairman. When another witness was called, Bobby would yell from underneath his gag, trying to question and cross-examine the witnesses, screaming that he was being treated like an animal in a United States courtroom, and that he was being chained and bound just for trying to carry out his right to defend himself. Every time a defendant or a prosecution witness took the stand, he would yell through his gag to try to question the witness. It was a mockery of justice in the United States court system and the whole world could see it.

Judge Julius Hoffman declared Bobby's trial a mistrial and ordered him removed from the rest of the defendants. The Chicago Eight became the Chicago Seven. Bobby would be tried separately. This of course angered Panthers across the country. In Seattle, we were very upset at how our chairman was being treated and wanted to travel to Chicago to exact some revenge.

But of course, orders from Central Headquarters were to the contrary. We were told not to attempt to take out any acts of vengeance in support of Chairman Bobby. We had no other option but to allow the court system to work its course, knowing that Judge Hoffman and the Illinois court system were an embarrassment to the judicial system and the United States. In the end, we were confident we would be proven right and that they would look like fools.

So instead, we protested from 2,000 miles away, and did not attempt to drive to Chicago. But the news only got worse. We later learned that Bobby had been kidnapped the second time from that Chicago courtroom, charged with conspiracy to commit murder, and transferred to New Haven, Connecticut to stand trial and face the death penalty.

He had been framed along with Ericka Huggins, wife of slain Panther Comrade Jonathan Huggins, for allegedly orchestrating the death of a New Haven Panther, Alex Rackley. Rackley had been identified as an informant and shot to death. It would later be revealed that the person who shot Rackley and made the accusation against Bobby and Ericka was, in fact, an informant himself—George Sams, a ruthless provocateur, who orchestrated the conspiracy charges. Ericka gave birth while incarcerated, shackled to a prison bed, as she was pregnant when arrested. The plot to eliminate the Party leadership was in full operation. Now, the two BPP founders were facing a possible death sentence at the same time, Huey in Oakland and Bobby in New Haven.

On the morning of December 4th, 1969, we got a phone call from Central Headquarters telling us that Comrades Fred Hampton and Mark Clark had been assassinated by the Chicago Police Department. It was a very sobering moment as we heard the detailed reports in the early hours of the morning.

ATF Agents and members of the Cook County District Attorney's Office, under the direction of Ed Hanrahan, known as the Red Squad, had gone to Fred Hampton's apartment, knocked on the door pretending to be a telephone repairman, and began firing through the walls.

It was reminiscent of the attacks that the likes of General George Custer led when they were raiding Indian villages, murdering innocent women, children, and men.

We later learned that the setup had begun long before, with the infiltration of an agent into the Chicago chapter; this particular agent had become very trusted in the Illinois state chapter. He was not only Fred Hampton's bodyguard, but was also head of security for the Illinois state chapter. He had drawn a diagram of Fred Hampton's apartment, with details of where the bedroom was, where his bed sat, and on which side of the bed he slept with his girlfriend and soon-to-be wife, Deborah Hampton. The night before the raid, he had drugged Fred, and some of the Panthers who were in Fred's apartment, with a sedative, Seconal—or what we called Red Devils—so when the raid came, they would be unable to defend themselves. This was an act of premeditated murder.

In Hoover's memo, where he said to prevent the rise of a Black Messiah, we knew that this was directly aimed at leaders like Fred Hampton. We also didn't know at the time that three cities were targeted for specific elimination: L.A., where Bunchy and John were murdered; Chicago, where Deputy Chairman Fred was murdered; and Seattle. We didn't know it at the time, but we were next on the Hit List.

The morning of the raid, as the ATF agents and Red Squad of the Cook County District Attorney's office surrounded the Panther office, Fred Hampton and the other Panthers lay motionless in the apartment, unable to respond because the agent had drugged them.

When the shooting began, several Panthers tried to respond. Mark Clark, who was the head of the Peoria chapter, was killed instantly as he slept on the couch. Several other Panthers were wounded. The shooting raged for 45 minutes to an hour. When it ended, the agents entered the apartment. As they approached Fred Hampton's bedroom, they found him bloodied and unconscious in the bed.

His fiancée, Deborah, was awake and alive. She had not taken the Seconal because she was pregnant. She later testified in court that the bed was shaking so violently from the bullets hitting it that it felt like an earthquake. The agents had known where Fred's bed was and which side he slept on, so they were targeting their bullets through the walls to strike him. Deborah had been hit several times in the legs, but not the torso. They told her to walk to the other room. She said she couldn't walk. As they dragged her out of the bedroom, she heard an officer say, "He's still alive," referring to Fred. Then she heard more gunfire as one of the pigs shot Fred point blank in the head. She heard the pigs say jubilantly, "He's good and dead now." This was all part of J. Edgar Hoover's initiative to destroy the Black Panther Party by any means necessary.

The following morning, the cowards led by district attorney Ed Hanrahan held a press conference where they stated that there had been a shootout at the Black Panther headquarters, the apartment of Fred Hampton, and that two Panthers had died. He claimed that the officers were there to serve a warrant, were fired upon, and that the agents returned the fire.

Unbeknownst to him at the time, a group of white liberal attorneys had gone to the site of the shooting to hold a press conference of their own and were conducting a straw test. A straw test is where you take pieces of straw and stick them into the bullet holes to determine the trajectory of the bullet, and of the 300 or more bullet holes they found in the apartment, all of them, with the exception of one, were going into the apartment, which meant that not only were the pigs and the agents the aggressors, but they were, in fact, the only ones firing. The one bullet was an exit bullet that came from the trajectory of one of the other bullets entering the apartment from the other side. They stated in their press conference that there was no shootout, that, more accurately, it was a shoot in and that it was premeditated murder.

Years later, after several trials, no police officers or agents were ever charged with Fred's or Mark's murders, but in a civil suit, they were ordered to pay the family in excess of two million dollars for the wrongful deaths of Fred Hampton and Mark Clark. Justice to this day still has not been served, but this is nothing new. The lynchings, the church bombings, the countless innocent civil rights workers, Black men and women, brown men and women, shot in the street by police, have gone unaccounted for. No one has been held accountable. It is the same story over and over and over again.

In our Seattle headquarters, we were devastated by the loss of Chairman Fred. We were angered by the outright, blatant murder and wanted to take action, but we knew that we were targets and had to be vigilant. They were looking for any reason to attack us. We couldn't seek retribution for the murder of one of our Comrades; we had to maintain our dignity, our cool, and our resilience. So, we hunkered down.

Four days later, the L.A. Police Department, along with the ATF agents, launched a four-hour attack against the L.A. chapter office. This was the first time that the pigs had deployed their new weapon, the SWAT team. It had been specifically designed to attack Panther offices and annihilate our members inside. But the L.A. office, like ours in Seattle and other offices around the country, had learned from previous attacks and were prepared. Their office was well-fortified and had been designed with the help of Vietnam vets who understood tactics of at-war invasion.

Coming into the L.A. office, they had dug a deep trench, which would cause unaware invaders to collapse and fall on their faces. The trench was dug straight back and had a sharp turn right, then a sharp turn left, and after about 10 feet at the end of that stretch was a large desk where the Officer of the Day sat. This was a heavily fortified and well-armed battle station which would allow the Comrades to defend the office entrance.

When the SWAT team was finally able to battle-ram the door open, they all fell on their faces into the trench. As they got up and proceeded forward, first to the left and then to the right, they were met with a barrage of gunfire when the Comrades defending the office, blew them back out of the office, causing them to retreat.

The pigs then brought in a tank and helicopters, fired from above the office, as this battle raged for four hours. But the Comrades were never breached. After sustaining some wounds, the Comrades put out the white flag and surrendered. They were all paraded in front of the press as if the pigs had won and conquered the Panther office. But in reality, the community that was watching knew that this band of revolutionaries had defended themselves and had held off an army of 400.

Later, when the Panthers were brought to trial, they were charged with assaulting the police at their preliminary hearing. The judge overseeing the case made an astonishing announcement. He said that from his assessment of the events, the police were in fact the aggressors, and that all the Panthers would be acquitted of any charges, and their cases were thrown out.

Days later, we were next on the list. While we didn't know it at the time, we were prepared for the eventual attack that we knew would come. This did not stop anything—not our resolve, our activity, the Children's Free Breakfast program, the free medical clinic, or our political organizing in the community. This only strengthened our resolve. We began to store more weapons and ammunition and prepare for the eventual attack.

CHAPTER 19

Preparing for War

During that fall, we had added several key Comrades to our ranks. In addition to Valentine, they included Melvin and Asali Dickson, a couple who had moved from the East Coast. They were a key component in expanding our community organizing and outreach efforts, and working on various other projects.

Melvin's laid-back style enabled him to easily relate to people. Asali was the opposite; she was vibrant, lively, and outgoing, with a magnetic personality. This combination made them excellent community organizers. When they met with Ike Ikeda at the Atlantic Street Center, he was immediately impressed with them, and they worked together to develop the foundations of a new program, working with people involved in the prison system.

One evening, Jake and I headed up to Seattle University to go check out a function that the BSU was holding. I spotted this fine sister wearing an African dress with a zebra print and a headscarf. She looked regal and revolutionary, so I decided to check her out. Vanetta Molson would later become a trusted member of the cadre.

The Party had strict rules concerning relationships outside of the cadre. Starting a relationship with someone outside the Party was frowned upon, unless they had been vetted to alleviate security concerns. We couldn't just have a relationship with someone, then bring them into the fold without knowing whether they were a potential security risk.

This was especially true for the sisters in the Party, which was upsetting to some women because it reeked of chauvinism. The feeling was that if a sister met a brother, somehow, she was more likely to be taken advantage of, and if he were a security risk, it might be missed. This, in my view, was flawed thinking because a brother could be taken advantage of just as easily as any woman, if not more so. Still, the restrictions were not as heavily enforced with the brothers as they were the sisters. The bottom line was, I needed to make an effort to get to know a sister, to see whether she could possibly become a Panther.

Vanetta had already been very active in the community through the BSU and other endeavors. A dedicated activist, she soon became a dedicated revolutionary. Our personal involvement was brief, but it lasted long enough to see that she was committed to the struggle and wanted to give her life to the people and join the Party.

She later entered into a relationship with Valentine, which was good for him because he needed a calming factor in his life. Vanetta was very kind-hearted and caring. The basic foundation for being a Panther was that you served the people out of love, rather than hate. We called it "an undying love for the people," and it was evident early on that Vanetta had a very deep love for her community. She came from a stable family with a strong father and mother, and she had two younger sisters.

Adding her to the ranks was a good move for our chapter. It was also beneficial for me, because Aaron had me holding down multiple duties, including the role of breakfast program coordinator. He shifted that responsibility to Vanetta.

By this time, Bill and Alice Green had moved up to the Seattle office and lived in the cadre house after the Eugene chapter closed. A feisty couple originally from L.A., they were hardcore, dedicated revolutionaries. No one wanted to mess with Alice. Bill was a big, kind-hearted, teddy bear of a man who espoused a lot of revolutionary theory and worked hard to serve the community.

Unfortunately, their relationship was sometimes rocky, and it was hard to get between them when they got started. Bill was somewhat of an alcoholic. His favorite drink was Mogen David 20/20, one of the fortified wines that the alcohol industry flooded into Black and low-income communities for people who couldn't afford to buy a fifth of whiskey; they could buy this cheap wine and get the same high, or a worse one. We called it "Mad Dog" for its propensity to make people angry and mad as hell.

We had also developed a relationship with Malcolm Williams, an ex-football player who had played with the Dallas Cowboys. A mountain of a man, his nickname was Big Malcolm. His wife, Jerry, was Native American, from the Alaskan Aleut tribe. She was beautiful, with movie star features, and they had three kids. Starla was the oldest, Shamsudheen was about two years old, and Ali was the baby.

Along with those Comrades, and others who were already part of the chapter, we had strong coalitions in the community, some of whom acted as a quasi-backup security force. One of those individuals was Milton Norwood, head of Seattle's Black contractors. He had organized a group of hard-nosed Black construction workers who were part of a larger group, and they all packed weapons. But Milton was the toughest of them all—a committed, die-hard revolutionary. While the group didn't serve directly in the Party, they were a force we could count on if we were under attack, because they would take care of our flank.

When we had community meetings where we were confronting issues like the misuse of public funds that were allocated to the Black community, or challenging the construction of a bridge that would divide and separate the Black community, they were always there, very vocal, challenging the status quo and ready to back us up during a confrontation.

On one occasion, local developers had devised a plan to build the Thompson Expressway project to essentially seal off the C.D. The Black community was furious about this highly contentious plan, and the Black contractors expressed their opposition to dividing our neighborhood.

The freeway plan reminded some people of how the Jews were cordoned off in many European communities during the rise of the Third Reich and Adolf Hitler. Our community launched the Freeway Revolt with Party spokesperson Kathy Halley, speaking on behalf of the Panthers at city council hearings. Our uproar was so loud, the Thompson Expressway project was struck down in a vote before the council. A victory for the people!

Meanwhile, a lot of characters came around stressing their support and wanting to join the revolution, but we had to be cautious about agent provocateurs among us. One of these dudes was the Bishop—an old pimp, probably in his sixties or seventies. He still had a couple of young girls as prostitutes that he called his wives, so we didn't intervene. He had kids with them and they seemed happy.

His main thing was hanging around the office, talking to Aaron and me, and trying to impart what he called his "wisdom." He was a player from way back and had mastered "the paper game." He would find ways to get authorized checks, forge you an identity, and cash them. He kept his game alive through schemes like this. However, we weren't into that kind of action and suspected he might be a low-level police informant.

But he never came at us with any provocateur shit, and often gave us inside tips as if he were a double agent. We never gave him any pertinent information anyway, or engaged in any of his schemes. He just kind of hung around.

Another interesting character was Jack, a Cuban who claimed to have fought with Fidel Castro. He wore a red beret and a leather jacket, and seemed pretty legit. He never seemed to be prying about information or trying to suggest any crazy shit, so we were usually happy to have him around because he would come to rallies and offer support or back up if we needed it. There was always someone who showed up wanting to be a part of things, and we had to be extremely cautious.

Because we were the Washington state chapter and responsible for building chapters and branches in the region, we helped Kent Ford and his wife, Sandra, establish and organize a chapter in Portland. They operated like all Panther offices around the country, with a breakfast program and other services for the community. They also had a free dental clinic, which was unique to their chapter.

In early January 1970, following the recent attacks on the Chicago office where Fred Hampton was murdered, and with the L.A. police attempting to finish the job that they had started when they murdered Bunchy and John, we were on constant alert. One ordinary day of working in the field, we returned to the office and got a call from a local reporter, Don McGaffin. A popular newscaster for KOMO News, Don was feisty, progressive, and always looking for a storyline to expose the truth.

"What's up, Don?" I asked.

"I'm in the police station downtown," he said in a hushed tone on the phone. "I saw the cops standing around, stacking their ammo, getting their weapons together, pulling out their gear, including armor. It looked like they were preparing for something big, so I asked them, 'What are you guys getting ready for?' and a couple of the cops responded, 'We're going to go get those Dixon Brothers tonight.'"

"We're on it," I said. "Thanks for the call."

I turned and informed my 10 Comrades who were in the office: "Tonight's our night. They're coming to get us." The excitement was electrifying. We wanted revenge for Fred Hampton's murder, and this felt like the big payback.

"We gon' get them suckas tonight," I said.

We went on "red alert"—a heightened level of security where everyone on hand was to prepare for combat. We already had 24-hour guard duty in the office but no one was going to sleep that night. The red alert meant that everyone would be awake, with gear on, stationed at strategic positions, and combat-ready. Ready for war.

We also alerted our outside forces that an attack was imminent and that they should be prepared for counter activity behind the police lines once they were set up. Since our phones were tapped, we had messengers go out to inform an array of revolutionary activists who were prepared to help defend our office. All heavily armed, they included: "Big Malcolm," the Black contractors, and Milton Norwood and his crew.

"Keep an eye out," we told them. "Be outside the perimeter, so when things go down, and the pigs are attacking us from the front, you can strike from the rear. We need your fire power later if this goes down."

As the night wore on, a couple of Comrades had disappeared. One was Michael Dean, who had been a running buddy, quasi-bodyguard, and Panther operative. We didn't suspect that he was an agent, but we did believe that he had just lost his nerve.

As dawn arrived, no one showed. We had been up all night, but we did not let down our guard because they could come at any moment. As it got time for the breakfast program, we decided which Comrades needed to be at a particular breakfast program site. Because many of those breakfast programs were staffed by community members, we were still able to keep a combat squad ready at the office.

Still, nothing happened. We were ready for an attack that never came.

Later that morning, we heard a news broadcast that the mayor had refused to give the ATF agents permission to get back-up from the police department. We later learned that when the ATF had approached the mayor for tactical support from the Seattle pigs, he asked them why they wanted to attack our office and they replied that we had illegal weapons. The mayor, after retorting that his informants had told him that our weapons were legal, declared:

"There will be no bloodbath in our city."

The ATF left town with their tails between their legs like the cowards they were and never got permission to attack the office using Seattle police.

We were sure that a lot of pigs were discouraged and disappointed that they wouldn't be able to attack our offices with large armaments, or with the ATF on their side. We were confident that if there was a bloodbath, it wouldn't only be our blood that would be spilled.

No, fresh in our minds and hearts was the murder of Comrades Fred Hampton and Mark Clark, just a month earlier, caught off guard by a pre-dawn raid by the pigs in Chicago; that, along with the attack on the L.A. office, made us more than ready for payback. We did not let our guard down. Attacks on Panther offices were intensifying across the country, so we continued to organize around our survival programs and remained ready for an inevitable attack.

We had no fear in our hearts, or doubt in our minds. We were ready to defend ourselves, the community, and stand on our principles and our right to revolution.

CHAPTER 20

The Protracted War – Organizing the Community for Revolution

Vanetta had been designated as the breakfast program coordinator, relieving me of those duties. Aaron decided that I would be the distribution manager, so he put me in charge of ordering our weekly lot of the Black Panther newspapers, and determining the number of papers that we could sell each week.

Setting this sales goal was important. We had to be as accurate as possible, because for every paper that we ordered, we had to pay a percentage of each copy's cost of 25 cents. Extra papers that did not sell were our responsibility.

Our strong cadre could sell a lot of papers, so we always focused on upping our distribution with a goal of being amongst the chapters that sold the most papers. This was not a competition or a quest for superiority; it was always based on wanting to educate the community.

"Educate to liberate," declared Sam Napier, the national distribution manager for the Black Panther newspaper, who had a very colorful and outgoing personality and was based at Central Headquarters.

Whenever I met with Sam, we discussed ways to increase circulation, such as identifying businesses throughout the Black community that would carry the Panther newspaper. Every week, we went down to those areas. One was a strip of businesses, clubs, bars, and hole-in-the-wall joints down on Yesler Avenue, between 12th and 14th streets. It was known as the Hoestro, for the prostitutes who roamed the street to sell their business. It was a very lively part of the neighborhood. The city had placed pink bulbs in the streetlights, which is how it became known as the Red Light District.

In this same six block radius was one of the early hubs of jazz music in Seattle. One nearby building was Washington Hall, which had seen the likes of Billie Holiday, Duke Ellington, and Marcus Garvey. In the other direction was an organization of Black men who had their own club called the Esquire Club, where they put on cabarets for the community on Friday or Saturday nights.

This was a natural place for us to organize because it was where the lumpenproletariat would hang out. These were the lost souls of our community. Brothers and sisters who couldn't find jobs, or didn't have jobs for one reason or another, and needed a hand up from someone to stand up for them and show them the way. So, it was easy for us to relate to them as we organized among them and the people.

Often, after breakfast program duties, which started at 6 a.m. and finished around 9 a.m. and after the kids had gone to school, some Comrades would go down to the Hoestro, to the local joints, to eat breakfast and relax. Then they embarked on a typical day of organizing and selling papers, which often began downtown on 3rd and Pike, which was probably one of the most popular places to find a Black Panther newspaper because we were always there.

We were also constantly present in the University District

up on the Ave. The Ave was full of hippies, yippies, and would-be revolutionaries, many of whom were supporters of the Party. Standing among the anti-war demonstrators, the peace lovers, Hare Krishnas, and the flower power children, the Black Panthers were selling the Panther paper. I often hung out there with a few of my Comrades. We frequented Bluebeard's, buying some men's clothing, but more often walking out with pants or shirts that we didn't pay for. For that, the owner, a tall, redheaded woman, didn't like to see us coming.

Bluebeard's, like many other businesses, were a symbol of capitalism, and since we were against capitalist exploitation and the robbery of communities, we justified our actions as a way to ensure that businesses gave something back, whether they wanted to or not.

Meanwhile, we continued to challenge the anti-poverty programs and their leaders who were absconding with money intended to solve poverty rather than making sure the funds got back to the community where it belonged. It was important for us to stand up for people who had no voice, and demand that the funds get to the people who needed them. Some of these CEOs and program directors did not necessarily approve of our tactics, which were to go in and tell it like we saw it, but that was the Panther's nature. And it was the nature of the vanguard to serve the people and make sure that the community was not being abused.

The people in the community knew that we couldn't be bought off, and they knew that we weren't part of the upper crust of the Black community. Instead, we were for them, for the people. As such, we got to know all the people who lived around us and they became part of an extended family.

One family that lived near our office had eight or nine kids. Their mother was Shirley and her mother, who was the kids' grandmother, was called Moon Pie, perhaps because she was a large Black woman with a large face shaped like a pie and she always had a smile. Twelve-year-old Andre and his younger siblings became Panther prodigies of sorts. They hung out at the office and we provided them with PE—political education—as they were learning about living in a Black community in America. We built a bond with them and established trust with their parents, as we did with many people within the community.

We also formed allies with folks like Big Malcolm, and Kiev Bray, who had a newspaper, *Northwest African American Journal*, with Cliff Hooper, a dedicated Black journalist who covered the tough stories. We formed a camaraderie as they reported on Panther programs, as well as community meetings, about the city's anti-poverty programs to challenge the status quo and ensure that funds weren't being misused or misrepresented.

Kiev's buddy was a big, tall, muscle-bound, bald-headed Black dude known as Bone Crusher. I never knew his real name, but he looked like a Bone Crusher, and everybody called him that. Once, when he challenged Valentine over some bullshit, Valentine knocked him to the ground, proving that Bone Crusher wasn't as tough as he looked.

Meanwhile, a business group called Black Front, organized a couple of Black grocery stores in the Central District to replace the Safeway supermarkets that we had run out of the neighborhood. One was not far from the Panther office on 20th and Yesler, while the other was on Empire Way, at the site of an old grocery store that we frequented as kids. One of the main people in that business was Dean Falls, a good friend of Milton.

We supported the stores as much as possible, until one of the business owners ran off with a bunch of the profits, and the stores were forced to close. This scene was happening across the country in many Black neighborhoods where funds would come into the community to build it up, but because either opportunists had taken advantage of the Black community, or banks that supported these businesses would pull their funds, the businesses would fail. Sometimes a brother who was not prepared to commit to the community would end up leaving those businesses in a hole.

The soundtrack to this era was Marvin Gaye's most critical album, *What's Going On,* recorded in 1970. It includes iconic songs like "What's Going On" and "What's Happening Brother," which were relevant to our struggles. Other songs like "Save the Babies," and the ecology song, "Mercy, Mercy Me," provided a profound analysis of the ills of society that would affect generations to come. It was in this backdrop that every day we would go out into the streets and organize among the masses, reminding us that we were fighting for better days, even as we realized that dark days lay ahead.

This included the absence of Chairman Bobby at Central Headquarters. I took many trips down to Oakland, often after Bobby would call us in the middle of the night or day, and say, "Get down here in the morning, or right away."

Without question, Aaron and I and a few Comrades would load up in the car, take a couple of black beauties, and drive straight to Central Headquarters without stopping. Once there, we would go out back and talk about the shit that was going on and how we needed to organize.

Bobby would often reach into his back pocket, or inside his coat jacket, pull out a pint of whiskey, and pass it around as we were talking. Those seemed like good old days now, even though they were just a year or so earlier. Now our chairman was in prison, facing the death penalty, but we knew the deal; the Revolution would be like this, and we were confident that we would get him free.

Central Headquarters had moved from Shattuck Avenue in Berkeley, over to Peralta Street in Oakland. So, on one visit, I headed over to meet with the chief of staff, David Hilliard, to talk about some of the work that we were doing, and to get direction on some of the things that we were planning.

When I walked into the office, this fine sister was sitting at the piano playing some tunes; I had never seen a piano in Central Headquarters, and I had never met this woman before.

"What's your name?" I asked.

"Elaine Brown."

Little did I know that she would ultimately become the leader of the Black Panther Party. She was a kind, warm, and loving—yet fiery—revolutionary. As I sat waiting for my meeting, she was playing some of the music from her soon-to-be-released album, which included a song that she wrote that would become the Black Panther Party's national anthem.

Later that day, all the Comrades met at one of the many cadre houses for a backyard barbecue. A group of Panthers had formed a musical group called The Lumpen. The group included Clark (Santa Rita) Bailey, Michael Torrance, Bill Calhoun, and James Mott. There was a platform set up in the yard and I was about to hear them for the first time. They were the official musical group of the Black Panther Party, and they wrote and sang revolutionary songs. Now, they performed one of those songs, entitled, "Bobby Must Be Set Free."

This was a time when Comrades could forget about the troubles of the day, pop open a cold beer, chat with Comrades they hadn't seen for a long time, and listen to The Lumpen, who would also be singing soul favorites by The Miracles, The Temptations, and other popular tunes of the day. These times took our minds off what was happening around us, such as the murders of Party members, informants, the Karengatangs (Karenga's group), and raids on our offices. Still, everybody had a strong, revolutionary spirit, and these times would only strengthen our resolve. They also deepened the strong connection between all of us, enabling us to focus on what it would be like when the revolution was won.

CHAPTER 21

HUAC, Pigs, and Counter Revolutionaries

Hoover was intensifying his attacks on the Party, but rather than break our revolutionary spirit, it only made us stronger. They were trying to come up with new strategies and ways to divide-and-conquer us.

We were contacted by a Senate investigator who wanted to interview us about the work of the Black Panther Party in Seattle.

"You'll talk to him," Aaron told me.

When the interviewer came, I sat down with him, and ran down the survival programs.

"Why do you feed kids breakfast?" he asked.

I told him, "It's simple, dude. When kids don't have enough food to eat, and when their parents can't afford to put a hot breakfast on their table in the morning, kids go to school hungry and on empty stomachs. When a kid can't concentrate on their studies because their stomach is growling or hurting, their school scores are going to suffer. It's common sense. 'We serve the people.'"

A few weeks later, during the Spring of 1970, I was subpoenaed to testify before the House Un-American Activities

Committee (HUAC) in Washington, D.C. I contacted John Caughlan, our attorney, and he connected me with one of his colleagues in D.C. who would represent me as I went before the Congressional Committee.

I flew to D.C. and checked in with our Panther office there. My Comrades welcomed me as if I were a long, lost brother. I had never met any of them before, but that didn't matter. I was a member of the Party. Central Headquarters had alerted them that I was coming. However, I did not arrive as if I were someone special. In the spirit of our revolutionary communalism, I was just another Comrade carrying out his duties, and that was the natural atmosphere I experienced in other chapters.

That night, I pulled a three-hour guard duty shift. As I sat in the back of the Panther house from midnight until 3 a.m., guarding the rear of the office, I had a shotgun, watching for any movement or suspicious activity. I had pulled guard duty hundreds of times in Seattle, so this was routine.

A long fence ran down along the backyard, and as I sat there staring out into the cold chill of the night, a huge rat came up out of a garbage can, scurrying down the fence toward me. *Should I blow it away?* Firing my weapon would cause all kinds of hell to break loose, so I just hoped and prayed that he wouldn't come too close. I figured if he did, I would simply knock him off the fence with the shotgun, but he stopped and turned around.

I continued to look off into the night and keep a close eye. When my shift was up, I joined some Comrades in another part of the house, just as a sister was getting off guard duty from another section of the office. Her name was Ukali. She was from the D.C. area and had joined the Party, like most of us, because she was deeply committed to fighting oppression. She was proficient in weapons and could defend herself. In a few brief moments, we discovered a mutual affection for one another. Perhaps we related to the fact that we were at war and knew how rare these moments were, not knowing if death was around the corner or what else lay ahead.

This was living in the moment, capturing precious seconds for some measure of peace. The Party rule was that two Comrades could "relate" to one another, which was code for having a sexual relationship, as long as it was mutual. But as we talked, she told me that she was pregnant. She wasn't showing, and I wouldn't have known otherwise, but I looked into her eyes and said, "Well, let's just lie down and get some rest." So, we lied down, side-by-side, hands on our weapons, and fell asleep. It just wouldn't be right to have a sexual relationship with her while she was with child, and I was content to just lying down, closing my eyes to rest, and getting up the next morning to head to the Congressional offices.

"I'm not going to be testifying in front of no pig senators," I told my lawyer when I arrived in the chamber of the Congressional offices, where the HUAC was meeting.

"You have to say your name and address," he said, "then you can take the Fifth Amendment."

"Cool, let's do it," I said.

I went into the offices and sat down in the chambers as the senators lined up to begin their questioning. One of the clerks asked, "Will you say your name and address for the record?"

I stated my name and address.

A senator asked, "Are you a member of the Black Panther Party?"

"I take the Fifth Amendment."

"Do you serve children free breakfast?" he asked.

"I take the Fifth Amendment."

Another senator named Strom Thurmond asked me, "Do you teach target practicing classes to members of the Black Panther Party?"

"I take the Fifth Amendment."

Agitated, Thurmond turned to someone on the panel and said, “I thought we had a cooperative witness.” Then, he turned back to me and asked, “Do you advocate for the overthrow of the United States government?”

“I take the Fifth Amendment,” I said, thinking, *This pig ain't going to get me to respond,* all the while knowing and wanting to say, *“Fuck yeah, all of you mothafuckas need to go.”*

He continued with questions like this, and each time I answered, “I take the Fifth Amendment.”

After I proclaimed my rights 17 times, he was pounding the table with his fist, screaming and yelling because I wasn't the cooperative witness that he and the others were expecting. The room was in chaos, yet my lawyer and I sat composed.

“Fifth Amendment!” I repeated. “Fifth Amendment. Fifth Amendment.”

It was a surreal scene. And once they figured out that I would not be answering any of their questions, the hearing was over. I was then excused from the chamber. In my leather jacket, with my big afro, I walked out feeling victorious—at least in some small measure—for standing up against a high-ranking senator and his cohorts on this fascist committee.

I wanted to tell them that: if it was Un-American to serve kids breakfast; if it was Un-American to provide free healthcare; and if it was Un-American to provide free food and clothing to the starving masses; then this America was not the America it pretended to be. But I knew to refrain from stating this because, if I had said anything beyond my name and address, I could have been held in contempt of court and imprisoned until I answered their questions.

Later that day, I returned to the Panther headquarters and shared my experiences with my Comrades, along with the visiting chapters from other parts of the country. Times like this always felt like coming home, because you were among people with genuine intentions. Without a doubt, these people would sacrifice and shed blood for the cause. I flew back home later that evening to join my Comrades in Seattle.

These efforts on the part of the pig power structure to annihilate and to set us up for long prison sentences were an ongoing reality that would consume many of our Comrades. We lived under constant threat of attack on our offices, or some random set-up or assault every time we stepped outside the office. But we did not live in fear. To the contrary, we were fearless, almost as if daring them to fuck with us.

Upon arriving back in Seattle, I learned that the pigs had shot a brother named Larry Ward in another instance of a police set-up. Larry was a decorated war veteran who had recently returned from 'Nam. As the story unfolded in the media, the press tried to paint him as a violent Black Panther caught by the police trying to blow up the Hardcastle real estate offices on 24th and Union, across from Liberty Bank, the first Black bank on the West Coast. He had apparently been caught placing a bomb device at the real estate offices' front door, and when called out by the pigs, was shot trying to escape.

Panther attorneys, including Lem Howell and John Caughlan, immediately launched their own investigation and represented the family in the inquest hearing into the death. The device or package that was found on the scene was apparently dynamite, but as it turned out, it had a dummy fuse. When he tried to ignite it, there was no spark.

An informant came forward and told us that the cops had approached some brothers in the jail to seduce them in finding a high-level member of the Party to blow something up. It was a classic agent provocateur move, complete with a concocted conspiracy. They would supply the dummy dynamite, which would be given to the unsuspecting Panther with instructions of where and when to launch the attack. The pigs were already staking out the scene, waiting for him in the bank parking lot across the street, ready for him to show up so they could catch him red-handed and gun him down. There was no plan for capture.

When he went to place the dynamite and tried to light it, he had no idea of the fate that awaited him. The pigs lay in wait like animals stalking their prey, knowing they would murder him. As he struck the match on the dummy fuse that wouldn't light, the pigs shot a spotlight on him.

Surprised and confused, he ran. They fired a shot. He turned and faced them with his hands in the air to surrender. Another shotgun blast rang out, mortally wounding him. He turned from the impact of the shotgun blast, and they fired again, hitting him in the back.

Larry Ward had been assassinated.

The pigs believed that a Panther leader was being targeted to be coerced into blowing up the real estate office. The word had gotten out in the hood that a police informant had been recruited while in jail and was working to set up a high-profile Panther for assassination. By this time, the pigs' mission was to take down one of our leaders. When the informant could not get a high-profile Panther to carry out this act to blow up the real estate office, he then turned to Larry Ward. It was believed that Larry had agreed to place the bomb to prove his loyalty to the movement.

The community was outraged that a Vietnam veteran, who had come back from fighting for his country without a blemish, came home to be murdered in the streets. When the pigs held their inquest looking into the shooting, the evidence—through rigorous cross-examination by the families' attorneys—exposed that bullet holes in Larry's armpits showed he was trying to surrender when he was gunned down and murdered. The evidence was so overwhelming that the inquest jury had ruled the shooting as death by criminal means.

The King County Prosecutor, Charles O' Carroll, however, refused to indict the pig, throwing out the verdict on a technicality. This was an all-too-common occurrence across the Black community. It was clear that we were at war, and that the pigs would stop at nothing to murder us in the street, then find ways to justify it through their corrupt criminal justice system. These incidents would continue as the pigs sought to carry out COINTELPRO. The pig who murdered him was John Hannah, who was never prosecuted and was later promoted to lieutenant.

One afternoon, I was sitting at the front desk as the Officer of the Day, keeping an eye out for any surprise attack, while also greeting members of the community who wanted information about our programs. In the desk drawer was a .357 Magnum, while a shotgun sat out of sight beside the desk.

"The pigs are after me!" a Comrade yelled. "The pigs are after me!"

I dashed to the porch. Valentine Hobbes was running up the street with the pigs in hot pursuit. Valentine jumped over the top of the wall and into the office, just as I slammed the door behind him and secured the bolt.

We immediately went into Attack Mode, going down our checklist in preparation for an assault. Ironically, DJ Robert L. Scott from the local Black radio station, KYAC, was in the office for a feature story. Robert L. was a 17-year-old, popular DJ in the Black community. We trusted him, and regardless, there was no time to put him out. We let him continue taping live on the radio station while we prepared for attack. We made sure he did not broadcast details about what was going on inside.

Above our heads, the trap door to upstairs opened, and weapons began being passed down to the offices below, along with rounds and rounds of ammunition, body armor, and gas masks. We had cut a hole in the floor from the barracks upstairs to the offices below because the only way to access the upper level was to go outside the duplex and enter through a separate door. In the event of an attack, we needed to get additional weapons and ammunition downstairs without going outside.

Now, one Comrade got on the phone to initiate the phone tree that we had set up for attack situations. We would call 10 people, who would then call 10 people, and so on, to alert them of the attack. One of the first people on that list was Gloria Martin. She and her Comrade, Clara Fraisier, had formed "Radical Women," a group of hard-nosed women fighting male dominance and oppression. Gloria Martin was a small, short, white woman with a fiery persona, as was Clara, an outspoken radical. They were staunch supporters of the Black Panther Party.

Within 20 minutes, dozens of people gathered in front, to stand between the pigs and the Panther office. Many of them came with their dogs: Doberman Pinschers, German Shepherds, and other large dogs. Plus, I always believed that Gloria had a pistol in her purse; she was that audacious.

Meanwhile, our backup team—whom we called "lowriders"—were taking up positions behind police lines. Inside the office, Robert L. broadcasted live—his eyes as big as saucers—as .44 Magnum rifles, M1 carbines, gas masks, and bulletproof vests came down through the trapdoor. We weren't going to let an assault take place without getting him out the door first, under a waving truce flag. But we wanted him to see what was going on inside the office.

At some point, the police captain outside sent a messenger to the office, requesting that we negotiate. Aaron designated me as the negotiator, along with Jake Fiddler, to watch my back. We stepped outside the office to talk to the police captain in the sunlight, among throngs of people. It must have been an incredible sight for community folks to see us in our battle fatigues and bulletproof vests, with gas masks dangling from our shoulders, as if we were in a scene from the TV series, *Combat.*

When I approached the captain, he said, "My officers say Valentine snatched a woman's purse. They were trying to arrest him."

"Panthers don't snatch purses," I said. "It's ridiculous to think Valentine would be involved in such a petty crime."

"I need Valentine to surrender," the captain said.

"Valentine isn't going anywhere," I retorted. "We're not going to give him up. Produce a witness." I knew he didn't have one, or that his officers had fabricated the whole thing. We went back and forth for a minute about the lack of a witness.

"Can you come to a lineup?" he asked.

We knew that Valentine wasn't going to be picked out of the lineup because he hadn't done anything. So, we agreed to go to the lineup that evening with our attorney.

"We'll be coming in force," we said.

That ended the standoff, and the pigs left. Later that night, a group of us, about 40-strong—which included our back-up team, the Black contractors—went downtown to the police station. Armed to the teeth, we were suspicious to enter the silent police lobby, where there wasn't a person in sight. This was highly unusual to allow Panthers to walk unchecked into the police station, let alone a group of 40, but we were able to just walk right in. We went into the lineup room, as planned, and sat waiting for 30 minutes for them to appear.

"This is a bunch of bullshit," I said. "They never had a witness in the first place." So, we left, and never heard about that case again. It was another episode where we challenged the pigs and won.

This was just another day in the life of a Panther. We always traveled in twos and threes, as we had been instructed early on by Central Headquarters. Only rarely did we get caught without backup, which was how Valentine got caught that particular afternoon. We always sold papers in a group, which discouraged the pigs or anyone else from messing with us.

Attempts on our lives continued, as did the pigs' efforts to set us up. Aaron had told me about an attempted set-up early on by a cat named Davis, who had tried to get him to buy dynamite late one night before we got our fortified headquarters, but he had sniffed it out.

Then, one evening while we were in the office, a dude rode up on a big Harley Davidson and said he needed to talk to us outside. We thought this was a good idea to talk outside because we weren't going to let a white dude, that we had never seen before, riding a motorcycle, into the office. Besides, we were constantly under surveillance and wiretapping. So, we found a spot on the side of the office in the dark shadows to talk to this cat. My .357 was inside my jacket in case something went down.

"I just came from a rock concert in Southern Washington," he said, "and some FBI agents had approached me to hatch a plot to lure you Panthers into the woods outside of Seattle to buy machine guns. They told me to tell you that I had advanced weapons that were fully automatic that you could purchase, and all we'd have to do was go out into some wooded area to make the transfer."

He topped off the story by warning that the feds wanted to ambush and assassinate us while purchasing illegal weapons.

"I told the feds no," he said, "but they were still trying to get me and some other dudes to carry out this plot. So, I'm here to tip you off instead."

With the feds getting more brazen, our visits to the shooting range remained a top priority. I usually went to keep my skills sharp and educate our Comrades about weapons.

"The shotgun," I said, "should not be used like a rifle firing from the shoulder, unless you're hunting quail or duck. But it's more useful in close-range combat and should be fired from the hip, especially if the barrel has been sawed-off."

One particular afternoon, Aaron would be firing a shotgun, among other weapons. He had put it up on his shoulder to fire, and at the last minute, he remembered to fire it from his hip. When he squeezed the trigger, the gun exploded, ripping his arm to shreds. Had he fired from the shoulder, he would have likely been killed.

Someone had doctored his shotgun shells. This was a clear attempt on his life. Aaron was rushed to Harborview Medical Center and immediately sent to surgery to save his arm.

When I found out, I met the family and Comrades at the hospital. I was pissed off! But I was glad that my brother was alive, and made sure that guards were present during his hospital stay.

I wanted to know who had access to the shells. Eventually, we realized it was impossible to know who had tampered with the shells. Our solution was to get a shell reloader that enabled us to load our own shells, thus limiting the possibility of sabotage.

We had always known that death was a certainty, but we weren't going to go down like that. We would rather die fighting and seeing the enemy clear in front of us, than being sabotaged. So, we intensified our security.

Our presence in the community was having an impact. People knew that we would not stand for anyone being ripped off, abused, or misused.

This came with being the Vanguard party. When Huey and Bobby initially founded the Party in 1966, they called it the Black Panther Party for Self-Defense. However, many community members interpreted that as the Party being its own private defense force. So, Huey and Bobby quickly dropped "Self-Defense." The Party's intent was to demonstrate the right to bear arms by openly carrying our weapons in defense of the community, and teach Black men and women to defend themselves against racist brutal attacks. They didn't want the Party to become known as a response team, but rather as the Vanguard Party, an organized political party representing the needs of the Black community. Though we were not a private defense force, that reputation continued to stick.

When someone called us for a problem, we had to do something. People called us about all sorts of problems, including abusive landlords. They would take apartment doors off their hinges, trying to intimidate people into moving out, or getting jacked up by the pigs for an obscure reason. So, we would go re-attach the door and help the wronged family get in touch with a tenants' rights group or get legal support.

If a woman feared an abusive spouse, we tried to intervene, or in extreme cases, go straighten out the spouse to make sure the sister wasn't brutalized again.

And then there were the prostitutes. Back on the Hoestro, prostitutes would sometimes come to us and ask, "How can I get off the streets?"

"All you have to do is say the word," we told them, "and we'll move you from the streets and get you back to your home, your parents, or whomever you were staying with before you got into this life. Tell your pimps that you're out of the game and you don't want to hoe for them anymore, and that if they don't leave you alone, you'll tell the Panthers."

The word got out on the street that the Panthers were protecting these prostitutes who wanted to get away, and by doing so, were breaking up the pimping game. We let it be known that we were not trying to interfere with their lifestyle or their business, but that if a woman was tired of being pimped and wanted to get away, then we would help her.

One evening, a carload full of pimps challenged us at our headquarters. We saw their long Cadillac coming down the street. As the pimps cruised in front of the Panther office, I stood in the doorway with the sawed-off shotgun, while upstairs, Jake and Valentine flipped up the gun flaps. The pimps just drove by. They clearly understood that they were messing with the wrong dudes and decided to go on about their business.

On several occasions, Aaron, Valentine, and I confronted pimps out on the street, and too many times, I had to put a gun to their head in case they were wanting to make a false move. But ultimately, no one challenged us.

"You can't respond to every complaint," Chairman Bobby had told us back in '68. "Be leery of being taken advantage of. But you can't just stand by. You have to do the work of the Party."

CHAPTER 22

A Change is Gonna Come

The cadre house on 19th above the office was starting to get crowded. Bill and Alice Green had moved in and were a part of the everyday operations. Aaron decided that we would establish another office and barracks on the other side of the C.D., on East Roy Street. In this location, the community didn't get much attention from our efforts and we thought it would be a good area to do outreach work.

While it felt like we were splitting up our ranks, it was a necessary strategy and would give us a presence in a strategic location in the C.D. We also knew the focal point of any attack would be targeted primarily at our headquarters on 20th, but we fortified the new cadre house, as well.

Anthony was put in charge of the location, and we moved several other Panthers into the house. They were to follow strict Panther rules and guidelines, which included keeping the house clean and orderly at all times and being mindful of their weapons. Having a satellite office on the northernmost tip of the C.D. didn't last long, and we eventually moved the Comrades back to our original headquarters.

In July, 1969, the Party had brought together nearly 5,000 activists from many organizations, including BSUs, the Communist Party, SDS, Third World Liberation Front, Young Lords, Young Patriots, and others, to organize a United Front Against Fascism.

Bobby knew this would help to further the Party's ability to organize the community around our platform in critical areas, such as our control of police programs. The goal was to use this new organization to guide radical whites and other groups to organize within their own communities to launch efforts to fight oppression.

Central Headquarters had ordered us to become a chapter of the National Committee to Combat Fascism (NCCF). Some misunderstood as Central Headquarters' intention for us to cease being a Black Panther Party chapter. The truth was that we were to remain intact while organizing an NCCF to enable white radicals and others to fight back in their own communities. We put National Committee to Combat Fascism on our sign in front of the office; in our minds, this simply meant that we were the initial NCCF site while maintaining operations as a chapter of the Black Panther Party. We would have to fight for this distinction because it was important for us to remain a BPP chapter.

THE SUMMER LIBERATION SCHOOL IS BORN

In the summer of '69, I joined our longtime Comrade Anthony Ware and a few other people to launch the first of several Summer Liberation Schools. Anthony's mother secured a house near the Panther office, and we created a simple structure that included classes for math, reading, and history lessons. We provided a free lunch and activities beyond the classroom to keep them engaged during the summer.

We posted flyers around the community, alerting parents that they could enroll their children in this program. And we encouraged mothers to attend our history lessons, as most of them had not learned the expansive history of Black people and the extraordinary accomplishments of African societies.

The next summer, in 1970, we expanded into the South End, where Anthony and I opened the Summer Liberation School in the Rainier Vista housing project. Here we were already operating one of our five breakfast programs.

One day, I was walking through the hall when a woman caught my eye. I was stunned by her raw beauty—no makeup, a big afro, and a sweet, innocent smile. Her name was Dee Dee, and she would come and observe us working with the kids and bring her small son to the reading classes.

She would later tell me that when she first saw me walking by, she felt frightened by an eerie sense of recognition; we had never met, but she felt that she had met me in another life. She went home and told her grandmother, a Black Cherokee who had "the juju," a term that originated in West Africa that describes having psychic ability.

"If it's meant to be, it will be," her grandmother said. "Just go with the flow. If you're connected through the universe as a soulmate, then it would be."

Later, while riding through the housing projects as my bodyguard and Comrade Jake drove, I spotted Dee Dee.

"She's cute," I told Jake. "Pull over."

"Hey," I called to her, "I noticed you in the Liberation School today. What brought you in?"

"I heard about the Black Panther Party when I was in Spokane," she said, "while attending classes at Eastern Washington University. After I moved to Seattle to live with my grandmother, I wanted to see what you're all about. It was very interesting."

I smiled. "If you want to learn about the Black Panther Party, you can come to the office and see the programs we offer."

Whenever I saw a sister who caught my eye, I wanted to inform her about the BPP and get her interested in the Party. We had a rule: no relationships outside the Party, for security reasons. So, any romantic prospects for male and female members had to join the Party. Women in the Party didn't like this rule, but we had to ensure security as our top priority.

"I'd love to tell you more about who we are," I told Dee Dee. "Give me your number and I'll invite you out."

Dee Dee vividly recalled our first outing.

"He came by my grandmother's house with his friend, Jake," she said during an interview for this book. "I was happy to see him. I decided to take a ride with him. When I got in his van, I was surprised because all the seats were gone in the back. So, I asked him, 'What happened to your van?' Elmer said, 'We took the seats out so we could carry stuff. Newspapers, groceries for the elders, and whatever else we need to carry.'"

As we rode around in the car, I told her about the Ten-Point Program, the struggle for liberation, and the life of a freedom fighter.

"Have you ever considered it?" I asked her.

Dee Dee recalled that, as we talked, she was smitten. "We talked and I got to know him on a personal level," she said. "I liked everything about him. After he took me home, I didn't see him anymore. I didn't hear from him; I thought, 'Well, he was nice.'"

My reality was that being a revolutionary didn't give me time to court or date someone. I had already testified before Congress, we knew the cops were hot on our tail, and every week something was going down.

So, I lost track of Dee Dee pretty quickly.

JIMI HENDRIX

Later that summer, Jimi Hendrix's manager approached us and said, "Jimi wants the Seattle BPP to be security for his next concert this summer at the Sick's Seattle Stadium."

We had done security for another event and decided that this would be a good opportunity to get to know Jimi and ask him for a contribution to the breakfast program and other programs, so we accepted.

On concert day, it rained as usual, but rain doesn't stop nothing in Seattle. As we covered the grounds and made sure that no one got unruly, it was apparent that Jimi did not want the pigs there because Jimi himself was a revolutionary.

I had heard him before in concert, but this was different. This cat was on stage playing the version of "The Star-Spangled Banner" that he had played at Woodstock, which was a uniquely twisted version of the national anthem to illustrate the contradictions in American society. Another one of his popular songs was "Machine Guns," a protest of the Vietnam War. As he stood under a tarp on the stage, he shouted to the crowd: "If you stand in the rain, I can stand in the rain!"

He stepped out from underneath the tarp with no concern over electric shock, and played with his guitar, aiming it like a machine gun into the audience, the twang from his guitar mimicking the sound of machine gunfire. It was the most revolutionary scene of defiance I'd ever seen at a concert, and the whole place was rockin' and rollin'.

That same year, we had seen groups like the Chicago Transit Authority, which changed its name to CTA, then Chicago, after a lawsuit filed by the Chicago Transit Authority. We also saw Santana and the Doors, but Jimi was special. He was like our own, homegrown revolutionary artist who was at the peak of his career and became the most critical and advanced guitar player of his generation.

After the show, I went backstage and sat with him in his dressing room.

"Jimi, we went to the same high school," I said.

His face lit up. "You cats are from Garfield? I didn't even know Seattle had a Black Panther Party."

We grinned, and he marveled at the thought of a Black Panther Party chapter in his hometown of Seattle, and that it was started by cats from the high school that he had attended several years earlier.

"Here, I got a doobie," I said, as he pulled out beer. The vibe was like two old friends who were excited to reunite and chat about the good old days and the revolution.

As our visit wavered between laughter and serious talk, I told him about our Children's Free Breakfast program and our free clinic.

"Jimi, we need money for the Children's Free Breakfast program, and our other programs," I said. "Would you consider making a contribution?"

He looked at me with a big smile and said, "Hell, I'll do one better than that. I'll do a whole benefit concert for the Party and the breakfast program right here when I get back from Europe."

I was thrilled! "Good luck on your tour. We'll be waiting for when you get back."

Several weeks later, news broke that, while in London, 27-year-old Jimi had choked to death on his vomit. We would never see him again, and—given the era of assassinations—were convinced that his death was not an accident. Nobody believed the story that Jimi was that stupid to vomit and choke in his girlfriend's flat. Reports said his girlfriend was with him, but if she were there, all she'd have to do was turn him over. Many suspected that she was in on it.

We believe Jimi Hendrix was assassinated, just as Bob Marley was, according to a CIA agent who gave a deathbed confession that he infected Bob Marley with cancer. While this theory has been disputed over the years, the story goes that the agent masqueraded as a reporter, gained Bob's trust, then gifted him with tennis shoes. In the heel was a small nail that had cancer genes or cells on it. Once you put your foot in the shoe, and the nail pierced the skin, cancer entered the body. Bob Marley died of skin cancer that started in his foot; he was only 36 years old.

His music, like that of Jimi Hendrix, was too inciteful and too revolutionary. And for that, I believe he was killed.

CHAPTER 23

Dark Clouds on the Horizon

Another profound artist of that era was Curtis Mayfield. The lead singer of Curtis Mayfield and the Impressions since the 1950s had more recently become a single recording artist, like many Black R&B artists of that time. He had always been a prolific writer, but more recently, his words were profoundly prophetic of the Black condition in America. In his song, "We the People Who Are Darker Than Blue," he became one of the first artists to vocalize the pride, racism, and oppression that Black people were enduring socially and politically.

This song was part of the soundtrack for Black America on August 5th, when the word came down from Central Headquarters that our leader and Minister of Defense, Huey P. Newton, had been released from Alameda County Jail.

This unexpected good news felt like things were finally turning in our favor. It was like a huge cloud had lifted from over the Black Panther Party.

"Huey is free!" Jake and I wrote in large black letters on a huge piece of plyboard. Then we borrowed a truck from a neighbor near the office and drove throughout the community, honking with the sign displayed in the back of the pickup truck.

"Our leader is free!" we shouted through the open windows. "The revolution is on!"

This euphoria was short-lived. Two days later, a shootout was unfolding in front of the Marin County Courthouse.[5]

The younger brother of George Jackson, Jonathan, had gone into the Marin County Courthouse to free three of his brothers, who were testifying in the trial of William McClain. For some reason, George did not make the trip from the prison, and only two Panthers, William Christmas and James McClain, were in the courtroom.

Jonathan had an M1 carbine assault rifle under his long jacket, along with a sawed-off shotgun and several other weapons in his belt. He was a tall, handsome, young revolutionary who was committed to the death, to right the wrongs committed against his people, and in particular, his brother and the other members from Soledad prison.

He burst into the courtroom, pulled out his weapons, and calmly said, "I'm taking over!"

He disarmed the sheriff's deputies while assuring any innocent bystanders that they would not be harmed. The plan was to have backup outside when they exited, so they could get away in the van that was awaiting.

They took several hostages, which included the prosecuting attorney and the judge. Jonathan had wired his sawed-off shotgun around the judge's neck, with the shotgun pointed directly at the judge's head, so that if police snipers were intending to shoot him, the judge would be killed instantly.

This was a daring move to secure the freedom of the Soledad brothers.

What Jonathan did not know was that a police informant named Louis Tackwood had been working with other undercover agents from the famed California Conspiracy Section (CCS) to put this whole process in motion. The CCS had orchestrated this in expectation that members of the Party would be at the scene and killed in the escape attempt to further discredit the Party. The CCS plot was to have a high-ranking Panther sanction the use of a backup team, but the informant was sniffed out and no backup team was sent.

Jonathan was convinced that he had an opportunity to free his brother and the other members of the Soledad crew and went along with the plan, but there was not enough time to get word to him to call off the escape. It was a set-up for murder from the very beginning.

As Jonathan and the others headed out of the courtroom and stepped out into the broad daylight, there was no back-up team. The world got one last glimpse of this true revolutionary.

As they made their way down to the van, surrounded by their hostages, they entered the back door. While the van began to take off, snipers opened fire, pummeling them with machine guns and rifle blasts from their positions without any concern over who would be killed inside.

Jonathan was killed instantly, as were the judge and his two Comrades.

As the sun set in Alameda, and the dust rose from the battle, the judge, William Christmas, James McClain, and Jonathan laid dead. It was a stark reminder that dark days were ahead in the revolution.

Huey had stepped from prison into a Party vastly different from the one that he had left when he went to jail in '67. At that time, the Party was a local organization in Oakland with just a handful of members. Now, the organization had chapters and branches across the country, in parts of Europe, and an international section in Algeria.

This was largely due to the work Chairman Bobby had done in the early days of the "Free Huey" movement, beginning with the Seattle chapter as the first one outside of the state of California, and moving across the country. And the revolution was in a heightened state of activity. The combination of a large multistate and global organization and two conflicting ideologies presented enormous challenges for our newly released leader.

The Central Committee was moving forward with plans to further ignite the revolution, and began making plans to hold a Revolutionary People's Constitutional Convention (RPCC) in Washington, D.C., later that fall. Meanwhile, raids were continuing on Panther offices around the country. In Philadelphia, the site of the RPCC's Plenary Session, Police Chief Francis Rizzo had organized a raid on the Panther offices. When his SWAT team descended upon the offices in a pre-dawn raid, they eventually broke through the Panther defenses and made all the Panthers stand naked while lined up on the street outside of the Panther Headquarters.

The brothers and sisters inside knew that when they surrendered, they needed to strip down so that the pigs couldn't claim they had a weapon, as was the case when Little Bobby was murdered in the streets in Oakland two years earlier. It was a lesson learned all too well. The attack was meant to disrupt the Central Committee's planning sessions for the RPCC.

Aaron was requested to attend that planning session as they made preparations for the fall event. It was during this time that factions began to grow inside the Party. Some members in San Francisco and New York had begun to defect and there were huge headlines in the Black Panther newspaper; "Enemies of the people," and the term "Jackanapes" became common references to those who defied the Central Committee, wanting open-armed struggle as opposed to organizing in the community. This was the beginning of the most troubled time of our existence and soon blood would be shed.

CHAPTER 24

The Revolutionary People's Constitutional Convention

The Party was under siege by police agents and the ATF, while local police departments continued to murder our Comrades across America. Earlier that summer, an attack on our Houston office killed one of our Comrades.

Meanwhile, internal strife continued, dividing the Party.

First, Party members who advocated open warfare only became more vocal. But the Central Committee insisted that we continue the task of winning the hearts and minds of the people, while taking care of their needs. So, in addition to our clinic, food banks, and the breakfast program, we had launched a free clothing and free shoe program in Seattle. And we were preparing to expand other programs into the community.

Additionally, some former Panthers were angered that Huey P. Newton was now being called "The Supreme Servant of the People," a title that the Central Committee bestowed upon him after his release from prison. Huey lobbied against being called "The Supreme Servant," because it set him too far apart from the Comrades. So, the Central Committee decided to simply call him "The Servant."

He had been ordered to live in a penthouse apartment overlooking Lake Merritt for his safety. Unfortunately, a page one news article in *The Oakland Herald* revealed that the Black Panther Party's Minister of Defense was living in a penthouse apartment. This was a major security breach, because our leader was under constant threat of assassination both from the pigs, as well as from defectors in the organization. Our mission was to protect our leader's life.

As fall approached, we began planning the Revolutionary People's Constitutional Convention, the RPCC. Chapters and branches organized across the country to mobilize thousands of people to attend this very important event in D.C. We assembled a large contingent of Panthers, community workers, and volunteers who would travel by van to attend.

Among this group were some remaining Panthers from the Tacoma office, including Tyrone Birdsong, known as T, and Valentine, who would be in charge of the cross-country caravan. Central Headquarters wanted me to fly ahead of our group to work with the local chapter and organize part of the security force. When I arrived in D.C., my East Coast Comrades greeted me with open arms, as they had months earlier when I had been subpoenaed to testify before HUAC.

While there, the Party's distribution manager, Sam Napier, met with other distribution managers from chapters across the country.

"Circulate to educate!" Sam urged, stressing the need for us to go deep into the community to get the paper, which he called "The Voice of the Vanguard," out to the people. Sam was a highly energetic, thoughtful, and caring revolutionary who had been responsible for pushing the circulation of the Black Panther newspaper to its highest levels across the country. He emphasized the necessity to teach the people the true nature of this decadent society and to make sure that they were informed about news nationwide involving the struggle, as well as on revolutionary movements across the globe.

I was assigned a group of Panthers who would be part of the security detail that I was leading, to protect The Servant on the night that he delivered his speech to the convention. The night before, a huge rally in Malcolm X Park drew thousands of people who had come from across the country to witness our historic Constitutional Convention, where the needs of the people would be addressed, not only of Black people, but for all oppressed people across the country.

On a huge stage for the speakers and entertainment, our revolutionary group, The Lumpen, performed "Bobby Must Be Set Free," the first single release of their upcoming album.

During these festivities, it was a sight to behold: security teams drilling and preparing for the convention the following day. In uniform, marching and drilling on the sidewalks surrounding the huge park that covered two or three city blocks, our Comrades let the authorities know not to fuck with Party members or the community of those who had gathered from across the country.

The next day, as we prepared for the conference and our security detail, June Hilliard gave orders that I would be positioned with my security team on the east side of the church where Huey would enter to deliver his speech. The 20 or 30 Comrades assigned to my detail were spread along the perimeter where Huey's transportation detail would arrive.

June issued his order to me: "Secure the area and let no one in who is unauthorized." That basically meant no one could enter but me.

While I waited for someone to let me know via my walkie-talkie when The Servant's detail would arrive, a man approached the checkpoint with a tall, slender, redheaded woman.

"This is Jane Fonda," he said. "She needs to get into the church."

My reply to him was, "I don't care who the hell she is. She's not coming in this area. This area is sealed off. She has to go somewhere else."

It didn't dawn on me that I had just turned away a renowned actress and supporter of the Black Panther Party, because it just didn't matter. I was in charge of that security detail, and no one was getting in through that side of the church. Soon after that, my walkie-talkie squawked:

"Heads up, The Servant will be arriving in minutes."

I put all the Comrades on alert to look up at the windows and rooftops to make sure there were no threats. Everyone was in position. As I turned around, three black cars sped up to the side of the church. The front car and the back car unloaded 12 to 15 Panthers. As they surrounded the middle car, the door opened and more bodyguards popped out, along with Huey.

This was my first-ever glimpse of The Servant. The group moved quickly into the church and he disappeared into the building. A sense of pride and honor rolled through me, knowing that the Servant had arrived and would deliver the speech after we had successfully protected that side of the church to ensure his safe entry.

The church was filled to capacity, and the overflow crowd of thousands was eagerly awaiting hearing his speech over an outdoor speaker system. Their anticipation was electrifying, because they were about to hear Huey deliver his speech to this important and critical Revolutionary Constitutional Convention. This moment seemed as if we were at the height of the struggle, and that the world was going to take notice.

The next day, I met with my Comrades to discuss their long journey back across the country.

"You have a long drive ahead of you," I said. "Keep a watchful eye and be safe. I'll see you back in Seattle."

When I returned to the headquarters in Seattle, our office felt like a ghost town, because so many of our Comrades were still driving back from D.C. A day or so later, we got a call that the vans had been held up in Oregon on the east side of the state, where all the Panthers and community workers had been detained in jail. Apparently, someone had tried to shoplift shotgun shells out of a gas station and the pigs had arrested everyone. Jake and I hopped in the car and drove 500 miles to rescue our Comrades. It was late November, and the freeway on the eastern side of the state was treacherous.

On the way down, our car slid off the road, into a ditch. Neither Jake nor I were injured, so Jake waited with the car while I hitchhiked into town to get a tow truck. The town was Vale, Oregon, a small community of about 1,400 people. The jail, the courthouse, and the police station were located in a small building near the center of town. I went to the jail and identified myself as the person responsible for the group that had been arrested.

"I'm here to either bail them out or come to some resolution to get them released," I told the jailer.

"The only way you can get anyone out of jail is to talk to the judge," the jailer said. "Since it's Sunday evening, the presiding judge is at home, relaxing. Go to his house."

When I arrived at the judge's house, he told me to come into his study, which served as an impromptu courtroom. The whole thing had a neighborly feel as the judge explained what the police report stated: that someone was caught shoplifting merchandise from the local gas station store.

"They had just returned from a convention in D.C.," I told the judge, without divulging details or that we were Black Panther Party members. "We'll pay whatever fine or retribution for the stolen property, and you'll never see us again."

The judge agreed, and the police officer took me down to the jail's holding cells where all my Comrades and other people from the community were jailed. They were glad and relieved to see me.

"We'll deal with whoever stole the shells later," I said. "For now, you're all getting out. The vans are outside. Stay out of trouble. And get on back to Seattle!"

This was a startling conclusion to the euphoria that we had felt just days earlier at the RPCC.

Back in Seattle, we investigated what happened: the perpetrators were a few Panthers from the now-closed Tacoma office. They were disciplined and expelled.

Meanwhile, the RPCC triggered a renewed direction for organizing in the community.

We expanded our efforts in areas where we had our breakfast programs. In Holly Park, High Point, Yesler Terrace, and Rainier Vista, we drove a truck through the neighborhood with a bullhorn and loudspeaker.

"The Revolution is here!" we announced. "Play your part. Join the Black Panther Party, and fight the powers for justice and equality for the Black community!"

This campaign drew people into our officers, where we worked daily to educate the masses and stimulate revolution. This inspired more people to come forth, wanting to fight back and address the conditions within their communities.

This also led to more young women stepping forward to escape from their pimps. One was an underaged girl named "T Baby." She had been in the state's juvenile detention system, then swooped up by a pimp. We allowed her to stay in our headquarters for a few days, but it was not safe for her to stay long, and it was against Panther rules.

"We want to help you," I told her, "but the only way you can get out of trouble is to go back to the youth center where you're supposed to be right now." She agreed to go finish her time at Fort Lawton in the northwest part of the state, then return to Seattle and contribute to our programs.

Lil' Bobby Hutton was the first Black Panther Party member killed by police during a shootout alongside Eldridge Cleaver in Oakland, California. It happened on April 6, 1968, two days after the assassination of Dr. Martin Luther King, Jr.

Photo Credit: Stanford University BPP Collection/ David Hilliard.

My brother, Aaron Dixon, in front of the Panther office and medical clinic in Seattle.

Photo Credit: Rick DuPree.

Movie star Marlon Brando attended and spoke following Lil' Bobby Hutton's funeral, which I attended in Oakland, California.

Photo Credit: Stanford University BPP Collection/David Hilliard.

Working the phone in the Seattle Panther office, which housed our free medical clinic, in front of a picture of BPP Co-Founder Huey P. Newton around 1970. Standing are Vanetta Molson and my brother Aaron Dixon, whose arm is in a sling, following an assassination attempt in which his shotgun blew up while he was training on the gun range.

Photo Credit: Stanford University BPP Collection/David Hilliard.

Our Information Secretary Kathy "Nafasi" Halley speaks at a Panther protest. To her far right is Guy Karose. We had strong support from the Asian community and the Karose family lived in our neighborhood, Madrona. That's me on the right. The young white woman in the center, Karen Bodemer, babysat for Panther children.

Photo Credit: Museum of History & Industry, Seattle (MOHAI)

Speaking at a Students for a Democratic Society support rally. From left: me, Aaron and Steve Phillips.

Photo Credit: Museum of History & Industry, Seattle (MOHAI)

A press conference in the Panther office. With me (from left) are Lewis "LouJack" Jackson, Willie Brazier and Curtis Harris.

Photo Credit: Museum of History & Industry, Seattle (MOHAI)

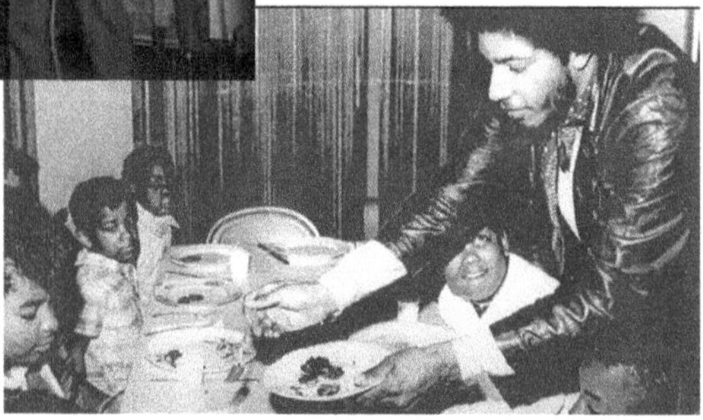

My brother Aaron Dixon serving a hot, nutritious meal in our Children's Free Breakfast Program.

Photo Credit: Museum of History & Industry, Seattle (MOHAI)

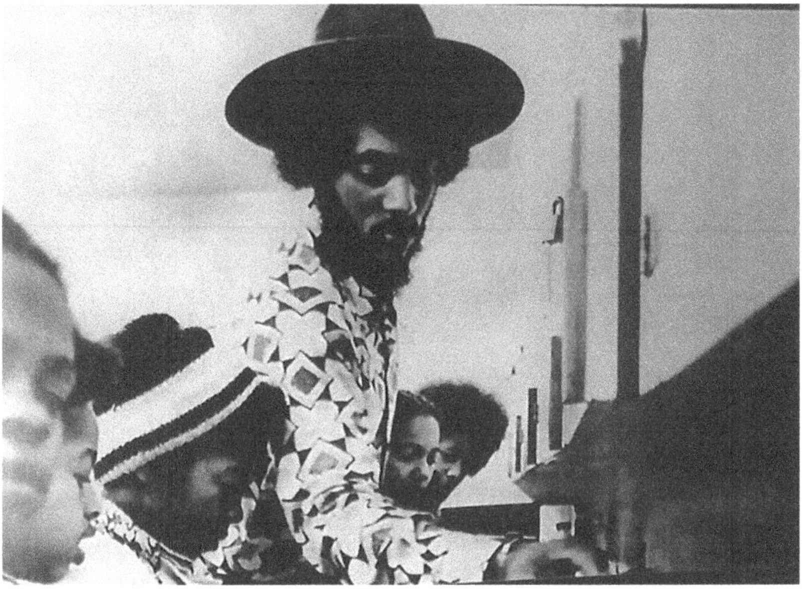

That's me providing kids with a hot meal before school in our Children's Free Breakfast Program in the Holly Park neighborhood.

Photo Credit: Museum of History & Industry, Seattle (MOHAI)

Me with one of my bodyguards, Tony, in the Black Panther Party barracks above our offices.

Black Panther Party Co-Founder Bobby Seale fills grocery bags with food as part of the Panther's free food give-away, during his campaign for mayor of Oakland, California.

Photo Credit: Stephen Shames

Our Panther house in Seattle was fortified with sandbags to protect us in case of attack.

Photo Credit: Museum of History & Industry, Seattle (MOHAI)

Information Secretary Kathy "Nafasi" Halley speaks at the Seattle City Council meeting during our "freeway revolt," protesting plans to build a freeway through the Black community. Beside her is my brother Aaron Dixon and between them is Comrade Garry Owens. I was there, but am not pictured. We succeeded in stopping the freeway construction.

Photo Credit: Dixon Family Collection.

My Comrades and I frequented The Checkmate, known as "The Panther Club." From left: Kathy "Nafasi" Halley, Mike Murray, Aaron Dixon, me, John Anderson and Willie Brazier.

Speaking at a rally at Garfield High School.

Photo Credit: Museum of History & Industry, Seattle (MOHAI)

Panther kids.

Photo Credit: Stanford University BPP Collection/David Hilliard.

My bodyguard, Jake Fiddler (left) with Kathy "Nafasi" Halley, marching to protest the FBI kidnapping of Chairman Bobby Seale.
Photo Credit: Seattle BPP Collection/Univ. of Washington Civil Rights Project.

My brother Aaron Dixon reading the Black Panther Party newspaper, which the Party published and all chapters distributed, with a cover story about Chairman Bobby Seale being kidnapped by the FBI.
Photo Credit: Rick DuPree.

This is the poster from the rock festival we were hired to provide security for in 1969.

That's me in the front with our Comrades on the state capitol steps in Olympia, Washington, in 1969. We were standing up for our right to bear arms.
Photo Credit: Stanford University BPP Collection/ David Hilliard

The eyes of a revolutionary.

Photo Credit: Museum of History & Industry, Seattle (MOHA

A police officer stares down two Panther Comrades during our protest at the state capitol in 1969.
Photo Credit: Museum of History & Industry, Seattle (MOHAI)

Panthers on the way to Rainier Beach High School to stop Black kids from getting beaten up. In front, left to right, are Bobby White, Curtis Harris, Chester Northington, Aaron Dixon and Lewis "LouJack" Jackson in the back wearing dark shades.
Photo Credit: Museum of History & Industry, Seattle (MOHAI)

Treating kids to a fun, informative experience at the Revolutionary Youth Festival in Bobby Hutton Park in Oakland in the spring of 1971.
Photo Credit: Stephen Shames.

Our Seattle BPP Chapter ran E.J. Brisker for the 37th District legislator, demonstrating our contempt for those in office who weren't properly representing the Black community.
Photo Credit: Museum of History & Industry, Seattle (MOHAI).

Comrade Ron Johnson, one of our top lieutenants (left), with our chief attorney John Coughlan, at our "Justice for Joe" rally before the trial of the police killing of Joe Hebert, a 22-year-old Black man. This was the first verdict of unjustified homicide from an inquest jury. The prosecuting attorney Charles O. Carroll, whom we viewed as racist, refused to bring charges.
Photo Credit: Museum of History & Industry, Seattle (MOHAI).

My sister Joanne Dixon in the courthouse lobby during Aaron's typewriter trial. To her right is Cathy Jones, one of the founding members of the Seattle Black Panther Party.
Photo Credit: Museum of History & Industry, Seattle (MOHAI).

Me in the courthouse during my brother Aaron Dixon's typewriter trial. The woman on the right is Joyce Redmond, Co-Captain of the Women in our BPP Chapter. Photo Credit: Museum of History & Industry, Seattle (MOHAI).

My mug shot after being arrested after my bodyguard set me up to steal a leather jacket in Eugene, Oregon. I was sentenced to six years and served 14 months in an Oregon state prison.

Lem Howell (left), a longtime champion of the people, activist and one of our attorneys, at Aaron's and Curtis Harris' infamous typewriter trial.
Photo Credit: Museum of History & Industry, Seattle (MOHAI).

Testifying before the House Un-American Activities Committee (HUAC) in the spring of 1970 in Washington, D.C. I took the Fifth Amendment 17 times.
Photo Credit: Museum of History & Industry, Seattle (MOHAI).

With the fireplace that I built in prison. The instructor in the bricklaying class told me, "Elmer, I don't know what you've got, but you ought to bottle it and sell it."

My beautiful wife and partner Dee Dee watched the Panther kids and earned the nickname, "Panther Mama."

My first picture after being released from prison in 1972 in my parents' home.

With Dee Dee shortly after we married in 1972.

Serving as a pallbearer (front left) in 1971 at the funeral of Sam Napier, the national circulation manager for the Black Panther Party newspaper.

Photo Credit: Stephen Shames.

BPP Chairman Bobby Seale and Black Power Movement leader Stokely Carmichael (left) lead a rally.

Photo Credit: Stanford University BPP Collection/ David Hilliard.

Original Panther Frank Anthony Ware with Asali Dickson, who joined the Party in Seattle with her husband, Melvin Dickson. Her art was often featured in the Panther newspaper.

Photo Credit: Stephen Shames.

Alprentice "Bunchy" Carter (left) headed the Southern California BPP Chapter, and John Huggins, husband of Ericka Huggins, was his Deputy. In 1969, Bunchy and John were murdered on the campus of UCLA by Ron Karenga's goons. Three men were convicted of second-degree murder and imprisoned.

Photo Credit: Stanford University BPP Collection/David Hilliard.

Comrade Garry Owens, a member of the Seattle Black Panther Party.

Photo Credit: Museum of History & Industry, Seattle (MOHAI).

Willie Brazier, Information Secretary for the Seattle Black Panther Party.
Photo Credit: Museum of History & Industry, Seattle (MOHAI).

Speaking as a teenaged leader in the Student Nonviolent Coordinating Committee (SNCC).
Photo Credit: Museum of History & Industry, Seattle (MOHAI).

A speech by Black Power Movement Leader Stokely Carmichael first awakened me to become a revolutionary after I heard him speak when I was in high school.
Photo Credit: Stanford University BPP Collection/David Hilliard.

Fred Hampton, deputy chairman of the Illinois Black Panther Party, was murdered by police at age 21. His life story was told in the 2021 film, Judas and the Black Messiah.
Copyright @ Alan Copeland

Photo Credit: Dixon Family Collection

The Regents, a band I played in during high school. From left: the saxophone player who formed the band, Gary Hammond; in the back, drummer Ralph Brooks; guitarist Biggie Lewis; in front on the bottom, manager Garvin Terry; Michael Dean with flute; organ player Dennis Blackmon; and me with my double-barreled Dizzy Gillespie trumpet. I played in a second band, The Majestics.

Our Black Panther Party singing group, The Lumpen, put out an album and a song called, "Bobby Must Be Set Free," after Chairman Bobby Seale was chained and gagged while awaiting trial in Connecticut, where authorities were trying to put him on death row. From left: Bill is sitting down, James Mott, Michael Torrance and Clark "Santaria" Bailey. I'm not in the photo. We wore Panther buttons and colors—powder blue with black.
Photo Credit: Stanford University BPP Collection/David Hilliard.

CHAPTER 25

Divided We Fall, United We Stand - The Resiliency of the Party

Later that fall, we got word that June Hilliard was coming to Seattle to do an inspection of our headquarters and our barracks. It was a routine practice for a Party leader to come and inspect the operations of each chapter.

We had been lobbying to make sure that our standing as a BPP chapter was intact, because we didn't want to be designated as just a chapter of the National Committee to Combat Fascism. We had worked too hard for that to happen.

The day before June arrived, we were busy making sure that everything was in order. We had added an extra cleaning detail to make sure that the cadre house was spotless, the weapons secured, and everything operational.

When June arrived, Comrades were doing their routine activities; I was on the staircase leading up to the barracks, mopping the steps. It was a typical day. We discussed our operations with June, the programs that we were running, and our outreach into the community. After reviewing our daily operations, we completed the day and were in the kitchen preparing for an evening meal.

Valentine pulled out a bag of brother rugy, the Party name for marijuana. We had just fired up a couple of joints when a loud thumping on the wall, with screaming and shouting, drew our attention to the back bedroom where Bill and Alice slept.

The door burst open. Alice and Bill were punching each other, screaming, yanking, scratching, and trying to gouge each other's eyes out. They battled right past us.

Startled, June looked up.

Aaron and I gawked, like, *What the fuck is going on?*

They fought down the hallway and stairs, onto the street and down the block, screaming into the night. It was surreal. We all just looked at each other and shook our heads. And while we acted like we were not shocked, we knew something had to be done.

"This is a normal occurrence," we told June. "Both of those Party members need to be expelled."

Soon, they were, and a steady stream of new brothers and sisters showed up to join our ranks. A brother from the Block, as we used to call it, came by one afternoon to commit to the Party.

Valentine introduced him to me. "This is Alfred Postell. He wants to be a Comrade. He wants to serve the people."

"Power to the people, brother. What's happening?" I asked.

Alfred explained how he'd had a rough life and had been battling drugs, and he seemed like he had no axe to grind, and was not likely an informant.

"You gotta attend PE classes," I told him. "We have a strict schedule. If you're willing to go through our strict schedule, we're glad to have you."

"Right on, I'm down," he said.

Alfred came around every day to sell papers and work the programs, so we welcomed him with open arms. Then we'd be in a PE class, and Valentine would share information that made it clear, Alfred was still battling a heroin addiction, like many sisters and brothers in Black communities across the country, the result of the man sledding drugs into our neighborhoods.

"We're going to help you through it," we told him.

"I got experience dealing with this from my days in New York," Valentine said, "working in a healthcare clinic, and being in the military. We need to help him quit cold turkey."

"How can we do that?" I asked.

"We're gonna take him to his apartment and lock the door, make sure we have food and ice, and make sure he's safe," Valentine said. "We won't let him out 'til he's done."

We went to the brotha's apartment. He was willing to go through the pain. Knowing it would be a struggle, he was ready to get off drugs.

We took 'round-the-clock shifts, with Comrades wrapping our arms around him, as he suffered shakes and chills.

"Let me out of here!" he shouted. "I can't take it! What the fuck yawl doin'?"

"We're here for you, Comrade," we assured him. "We're not gonna leave you."

Valentine took care of his medical needs and violent reactions as Alfred expelled this demon from his body.

Alfred got off drugs and became a strong, contributing member of the cadre—until his sudden death. We never knew the actual cause of death, but assumed his years of drug abuse contributed. He was a good Comrade. We hated losing him and were saddened to see him die after he had come so far.

Around that time, one of the sisters who had come to our office for information began to work closely with Valentine. Rosita Holland had a small son and was married to an abusive man. Eventually we would have to intervene as he continued to get violent with her. Jake and I found the dude near the Jack in the Box fast food restaurant on 23rd and Union.

I called the office and when Valentine got on the phone, I said, "We got him." Valentine met us at the location and we told him his options. "You keep your hands off Rosita, motherfucker," I told him. "Or you'll get your punishment from us. Your best move is to get out of town. Fast."

Soon thereafter, he did, and Rosita joined our ranks.

By December, Valentine and Rosita had made plans to move the clinic out of our headquarters and into a large house several blocks away, on 18th and Union. It was bigger and could accommodate more patients. And being in a separate building would make it secure and safe from police raids.

SPEARHEADING SICKLE CELL ANEMIA AWARENESS AND TESTING

At that same time, we announced that we were launching our sickle cell anemia effort. It became a national campaign to raise awareness around the deadly disease, which primarily affected Black people.

Many people had this painful disease, but did not know it, because back then, little was known about sickle cell anemia. No funding was allocated for research to find a cure.

So, our unprecedented campaign aimed to test as many people as possible to see if they either had the disease or carried the sickle cell trait. If they had this disease, there was no cure, but they would know to seek various treatments that were available to ease their pain and enable them to survive as long as possible. And if they carried the sickle cell trait, then they would know the likelihood of passing the trait or the disease to their children. Because of our efforts, the National Sickle Cell Disease Association of America was formed in 1971.

AVERTING A GUN BATTLE

Since things were so dangerous, we formed a tighter bond among the Comrades. Aaron, Valentine, Jake, Anthony, Vanetta, James Redmond, and several other comrades all traveled in packs, whether it was selling papers or going out to check out some entertainment.

One place we frequented was The Blue Post on 18th and Madison. This place was a little different from our earlier hang-out back in '68 and '69, The Checkmate. It was a different time and the crowd was younger and hipper. We could go up there and get our dance groove on. Our other favorite spot was the Eagles Ballroom in Downtown Seattle. We knew the promoter, so we could get in without paying. We saw groups like Chicago, Santana, Blood Sweat & Tears, and others.

Jake, whose full name was Jake Fiddler, Jr., had become my main running dog. He was from East Saint Louis, right outside Chicago. Since I was originally from Chicago's South Side, we had a lot in common, including the same taste in music. When we found time to chill in the barracks after hours, we listened to the Chi-lites: "Have You Seen Her" and "Write a Letter." Another favorite group was The Main Ingredient, whose album was *Tasteful Soul,* with songs that included "Spinning Around" and "I'm Better Off Without You." Their lead singer at the time was Don MacPherson, reputed to have the purest voice in the business. When he died suddenly of cancer in '71 and was replaced by Cuba Gooding, we mourned his death.

We also dug the Delfonics and The Stylistics, who were part of the new Philly Sound that originated with Thom Bell and Kenny Gamble, two dudes out of Philadelphia who popularized falsetto harmonizing with smooth love songs, like "Didn't I Blow Your Mind" and "Betcha By Golly, Wow." Our jazz favorites included Miles Davis' "Bitches Brew," John Coltraine's "My Favorite Things" and "Naima," tunes by Pharoah Sanders and Sun Ra, and Grant Green's hypnotic "Cease the Bombing" and "A Time to Remember." These love songs were like soothing tonic to revolutionaries who longed for love while accepting the likelihood of an early death at the hands of the pigs.

We would often end up doing errands together, partying, working, or just chilling. But we always tried to heed the rule—traveling in twos and threes. My license had been suspended several times due to minor infractions, so Aaron had put me on driving restrictions to prevent me from getting arrested. That meant I had to be with somebody else who could drive if I were going someplace; often it was either Jake or Valentine. Hippies were always donating vehicles, so we always had a Volkswagen van or a couple of VW Beetle Bugs as transportation to and from the breakfast programs and places where we sold papers. One of the Beetle Bugs had no seat on the passenger's side, so when we went for a run, Jake drove and I sat on the floor. What a sight to see, the two of us riding down the street with one up in the seat and someone sitting with only his head popping out of the window.

One evening, Malcolm came by the office with his family in his huge, green panel truck, whose large, domed backend made it look like an old bakery delivery vehicle. He had it decked out as a perfect hippie mobile: green exterior paint, while inside, it had a small sofa and a refrigerator for cold drinks.

On this night, he thought the pigs were following him, so he stopped by our headquarters to get them off his tail. He came in with Jerry, his wife, daughter, Starla, young son, Shamsudheen, and his new baby boy, Ali. After chilling out for a while and talking shop, Malcolm thought it would be okay for them to leave, so he could get the family home.

"Okay, bro," I said, walking them outside. "Peace. Be careful."

Soon after everyone was in the van, the pigs showed up. Their sirens blared as they approached Malcolm.

"We have a warrant and you're being placed under arrest," they said.

I quickly got his wife and kids out of the van and into the office, where they were safe behind our walls that were fortified with sandbags.

I dashed outside to help Malcolm. But he was wrestling with the cops as they struggled to put handcuffs on his big arms.

The tow truck driver was already there, trying to hook up the van to the tow truck. I jumped up on the tow truck, shoved the driver out of the way, and began to unhook the truck.

"What's in the van?" the cops demanded.

"I ain't done nothing wrong!" Malcolm protested.

The pigs were pounding on Malcolm, and the tow truck driver continued attaching his chains to the van.

I couldn't stop them, and we were outnumbered.

So, I ran into the office, grabbed the shotgun, and headed out the door.

The cops drew their weapons.

Aaron yanked me back inside.

"This ain't the time!" Aaron warned. "Don't go out there!"

"They're fuckin' up Malcolm!" I yelled. "They're beating on him!"

"We gotta protect his kids and his wife," Aaron said. "There'll be another day for this fight, but it isn't this one."

"These motherfuckers can't push us around in front of our office!" I shouted. "This is our hill! This is our territory! There's no better time!"

"We got these kids and babies in here!" Aaron said.

That calmed me down, so cooler heads could prevail that night. Obviously, a shoot-out wouldn't be a good idea with babies and a pregnant woman in the building.

Still, I was all too ready to throw down. I was tired of how they murdered our leaders. Tired of how they ran roughshod in our community. We were going to defend our community and stop them from pushing us around.

So, the pigs got Malcolm into the back of the car, got his van up on the tow truck, and pulled away. Sometime later, we bailed Malcolm out and got him reunited with his family.

This was just another daily confrontation that we had to deal with involving the pigs, as they were on us every moment. Whenever we left the office and drove away, we were prepared to take back routes or side streets, because we were constantly being followed and hounded by the FBI. This was the life of a Panther, and it was the norm.

A few days after Malcolm's arrest, we got word that a warrant was issued for my arrest for assaulting police officers with a shotgun. Our attorney, John Caughlan, negotiated with the prosecuting attorney, saying that I never actually made it outside the office with the shotgun, and that they had only seen me approaching the door. The charges were later dropped.

To escape the madness, we headed to Randy's pad. Randolph Redmond, an older brother of James and Joyce, was a towering man with a booming voice. Six feet tall and 300 pounds, Randy had a volatile temper. The Redmonds had grown up as a tight-knit family with eight siblings and no father. Their dad had been killed in a knife fight in the Yesler Terrace housing project when they were small kids.

Because they were all light-skinned, they had to deal with the high yellow existence of being Black. They would be tested almost daily, but their toughness made them revered in the community.

When Randy returned from 'Nam, he brought back all kinds of exotic marijuana and always had a ready supply on hand: Acapulco Gold, Meshmican, or Panama Red. Whenever he got a new batch, he invited us over to test it out. He set up the "Red Room" just for us. This large, closet-like area underneath the stairs had pillows all over the floor and against the walls. Red lighting glowed over a huge bong pipe in the middle, with five or six hoses snaking out of the smoking bowl.

He invited us into the pad by saying, "I got you set up in the Red Room. Come in and let me take you away to another place and put your minds at ease."

After we spread out on the pillows, he placed a handful of Panama Red into the bowl, then lit it. He dimmed the red lights while speakers attached to the walls played Jimi Hendrix. Then we puffed our way to a faraway place. Far away from the hectic life of being harassed by the pigs, chased in the streets under the threat of assassination, and stressed by the rigors of doing community work. We entered a more mellow zone that provided some rare, peaceful moments in the life of a Panther.

One evening, Jake went out on a run to get some supplies. After not hearing from him for hours, he finally returned to the office—battered and bruised.

"The pigs caught me alone," he said. "Roughed me up. Threw me out of their car."

"Jake!" we reminded him, "Don't go out alone! We travel in twos and threes. The cops are waiting for any chance to get to us."

That year, George Jackson was working on his second book, *Blood in My Eye*. It was on the heels of the death of his brother, Jonathan, and was far more critical of the oppressive system in the United States. He was gaining international notoriety, and it was around this time that he was named Field Marshal of the Black Panther Party.

Huey was also becoming more comfortable with his role as Servant and leader of the Black Panther Party, now having been outside, rather than running the Party from inside prison. He still had to report to the Central Committee, but he was able to develop revolutionary philosophy that would guide the Black Panther Party.

On one occasion, he was invited to be a guest on the right-wing TV show called *Firing Line*, hosted by William F. Buckley. Buckley was known to have a sharp wit and quick tongue, and could dismantle anyone's argument. As such, Buckley wanted to debate the leader of the Black Panther Party, believing he could counter any argument that we put forward on why revolution was necessary in America. Panthers across the country gathered in front of their TV sets to watch the debate as it unfolded; Huey, time after time, dismantled and befuddled Buckley. It was another example of how Panthers had sound revolutionary theory, and that we weren't just a group of mad, angry militants. We were molded in both revolutionary theory and practice, and we could not be picked apart by a right-wing, armchair psychologist.

Huey's revolutionary theory was growing in legend when he wrote an essay breaking down the revolutionary 1971 film that was written and directed by a little-known Black playwright, actor and filmmaker, Melvin Van Peebles, who starred in *Sweet Sweetback's Baadasssss Song.*

Huey broke down each of the film's themes, spanning how Sweetback grew up in a whorehouse, saved a Black Panther from a racist cop, then went on the run to escape "The Man." All Panthers nationwide were required to see the film, and numerous PE classes used Huey's essay to discuss the links to our own movement.

The movie became a phenomenon despite Hollywood's elites refusing to fund it or show it in mainstream theatres. It grossed more than $15 million (that would be $111,791,111.11 in 2023, according to usinflationcalculator.com) sparking the launch of the Blaxploitation Film Era and numerous films that Hollywood was now ready to bank on due to its success.

But *Sweet Sweetback's Baadasssss Song* was no such film. It was a revolutionary statement on standing up against a racist and oppressive system, which Huey deftly used to further spread the Party's message to the people.

As 1971 unfolded, the rumblings from the Jackanapes were growing. The FBI was intensifying COINTELPRO—now aimed squarely at the BPP. COINTELPRO was started by Hoover in the 1930s to combat what he called "the growing Communist threat."

He used it to bust unions in the 1940s and it was the foundation for the McCarthy era xenophobia in the 1950s, primarily aimed at actors in Hollywood who were blacklisted because they were suspected of being Communists. It was picked up again during the Civil Rights Movement and used to monitor Dr. Martin Luther King, Jr., as well as both Kennedy brothers.

Now focused on the BPP, the FBI's most dangerous strategy was the age-old tactic of divide-and-conquer. Hoover manufactured feuds between the Black Panther Party and the "United Slaves" (US) which resulted in the murders of Bunchy Carter, John Huggins, and several other Panthers. His agents also used it in Chicago to foster war between the Black Stone Rangers and the Black Gangster Disciples following the murder of our Comrade Fred Hampton, because Fred had organized a truce between the two groups.

These pigs had declared outright war against us and were working behind the scenes to foster dissent and distrust wherever they could in the Black Panther Party. The perfect place for this to happen was between those who felt that military action was the way to revolution, as opposed to the part of the Party led by Huey to organize the community by winning the hearts and minds of the people through the community survival programs.

This culminated in an unplanned confrontation between Huey and Eldridge Cleaver, who was in exile and in charge of the international section of the Black Panther Party in Algeria. The FBI had sent letters to both Eldridge and Huey, claiming that each side was planning to assassinate the other. Because Huey was aware of this tactic, he didn't take the bait.

In February of 1971, they were invited to be interviewed in a highly anticipated, nationally televised show, *AM*. The conversation between Huey and Eldridge was supposed to show camaraderie and the organizational skills of the Black Panther Party. But out of the blue, Eldridge confronted Huey about statements made by Panthers on the East Coast, claiming that he was taking control of the Party, casting aside the role of the Central Committee, and threatening to tear the Party apart.

We watched in shock as Eldridge attacked The Servant on national TV. This blatant betrayal of trust became known as *The Split.*

Huey expelled Eldridge Cleaver from the Black Panther Party.

Some Comrades in New York, as well as in San Francisco (who would become known as the Jackanapes), sided with Eldridge. They began attacking Comrades and provoking confrontations. There were huge headlines in the next edition of the Panther paper saying "Expelled" and "Enemies of the People," with names and photos of the perpetrators of this madness. This started another chapter in fighting the onslaught of attacks initiated by Hoover's army of agent provocateurs.

Not long after these incidents rocked the foundation of the Party, we got the news that our beloved Comrade, Sam Napier, had been murdered in New York. Since the RPCC, he had remained on the East Coast, organizing the broader distribution of the Panther Paper. Then some East Coast Jackanapes kidnapped him, tied him to a chair, tortured him, and set him on fire.

This very dire moment in our brief history suggested that we were at war from within. But Huey refused to allow this planned set-up by the FBI to tear apart the Black Panther Party. We would not respond with attacks of retaliation.

Instead, as we were all called to Central Headquarters to attend Sam's funeral, we became more vigilant with heightened security. Since I was distribution manager for the Seattle chapter and had worked closely with Sam, I was asked to be a pallbearer. It was a sad day to bury another one of our Comrades, someone whom I had grown to love and respect, and who was such a dedicated member of the Black Panther Party.

As I stood in the hot sun in Oakland in my Panther uniform,

along with the other Comrades, we waited for Sam's coffin to arrive. I stood at attention as Huey walked by with the rest of the Central Committee. Then I, along with the other Comrades who were pallbearers, picked up Sam's coffin. We took Sam into the church, where Huey delivered the eulogy—a stark reminder that we were constantly at war, and death could come at any time. Many of us wanted revenge, but we had to maintain our cool so that we would not be in open battles in the streets—exactly what Hoover and his minions wanted. Cooler heads would have to prevail this day.

A Comrade's death always strengthened our resolve and determination to build a solid foundation and wage revolution. But it grew tougher with each death: Henry Boyer, Butch Armstead, and Sidney Miller in Seattle; as well as the murders of Bunchy Carter, John Huggins, Fred Hampton, and Mark Clark.

Now, Sam's death hit deeper, perhaps because I had gotten to know him, and he was such a likable guy with a clear understanding of Huey's vision of educating the masses and spreading our philosophy through the voice of the Party, the Intercommunal News Service, and the Panther paper. On the other hand, we had to cope with the brutal nature of how he was murdered, not by pigs or an unknown agent provocateur, but by Panthers who had been our Comrades.

And while I knew it resulted from a COINTELPRO operation to divide us, I was haunted by the profound violation of being tortured and burned by a former Comrade—one of his own. With Fred's brutal murder, my hunger for revenge burned deep in my soul as I continued my revolutionary work with my own incarceration looming in the near future.

All the while, the assassinations continued, one after another, including a leader of the Houston chapter, Carl Hampton, as well as L.A. chapter leader, Elmer Geronimo Pratt—"G" as we knew him—who was being framed for murdering a white couple on a tennis court; he would soon face a long prison sentence.

Dozens of Panther offices had been attacked around the country and we were constantly on alert, but we remained focused; this was the way of revolution, the protracted war that Mao talked about. We were in it for the long haul and took the good days with the bad.

Later that spring, Central Headquarters organized the Revolutionary Intercommunal Youth Festival in Oakland, and chapters from across the country brought kids. This announced to the world that these attacks would not defeat us, and that continuing our revolution required educating our youth.

Several neighborhood kids wanted to take the journey, including Shirley's children—three or four of Andre's brothers and sisters—and they had Moon Pie's approval. This would be their first trip outside of Seattle and the state of Washington. Giving the Party permission to transport their children 800 miles to attend a once-in-a-lifetime event was a testament to the community's trust in the Party.

Aaron's wife Donnie allowed my nephew, Aaron Patrice, to travel with us, and came along while Jake and I drove a vanload of kids to the festival in DeFremery Park, which the Party had renamed Bobby Hutton Memorial Park. They enjoyed revolutionary-themed activities, as well as piñatas. I loved helping the kids swing sticks to crack open the papier-mâché pig and make treats pour out. This was one of the bright moments in that year of growing tension.

My free time was running out, however, following my conviction of the trumped-up charge of armed robbery. I would soon report to prison to serve my sentence. We had submitted a brief appeal, which bought some time.

I was dating this sister, a former *Jet* magazine centerfold model, Beverly, who had two kids. Knowing I would soon be locked up, I spent more time at her house, with Aaron's permission to take a break from duties.

Did I want to enter the prison system? Aaron and I discussed this question, as I contemplated fleeing to Cuba. Many Comrades had fled there via the Panthers' well-established escape route—our version of an Underground Railroad, if you will. When the Party was expanding across the country, several Comrades from California made their way to Seattle, because we were close to the Canadian border. We set up an operation with some hippies who could move people out of the country undetected when needed.

"I want to get on the train and leave the country," I told Aaron.

"You need to deal with this," he said. "There's an appeal pending. So, you have a chance to get out."

My appeal was denied. I didn't want to go, but I needed to follow orders and keep the faith. Many Comrades were dealing with prison, and I was prepared to do the same.

While I was preparing myself for incarceration, a shocker happened during the trial of Chairman Bobby and Ericka Huggins in New Haven, Connecticut. Judge Harold Mulvey, against everyone's expectations, announced to the courtroom that he found it impossible to seat an impartial jury, effectively ending the trial and throwing out all charges, and releasing them from custody. Sadly, I could not celebrate their release from prison, as I was soon heading there myself.

CHAPTER 26

Time Stands Still - Life in Prison

Shortly after my 21st birthday, I found myself in a profound and ironic contradiction—a revolutionary "surrendering" to the pigs and imprisonment.

Getting on the Greyhound bus to travel to Eugene, Oregon, to report to the Lane County Jail was a solitary journey. Unlike my last trip there during my trial, when my Comrades and attorney surrounded me, I was alone, heading into the unknowns of incarceration.

My thoughts about prison life had been limited to what I had read in books, primarily from Comrade George Jackson, one of the Soledad Brothers who was now the Field Marshal of the Black Panther Party. In his essays on prison life, George described the mental games that guards played, the constant attempt to foster dissension among inmates based on skin color, and the perpetual threat of attack. He also explored the opportunity to organize inmates into a single force to fight oppression.

During the long bus ride, I contemplated this and reflected on my Comrades and our times together, the struggles we had, the battles we fought, and the way we had each other's backs. I longed to be with them.

As for Beverly, I enjoyed our time together, and her two small children were delightful. But I'd only known her a few months, and that made it difficult to establish a meaningful or deep relationship. And though she lived in the housing projects in High Point, and knew the struggles of the lumpenproletariat, she was not a revolutionary at heart, nor was she a Party member. So, it would be best to let her go emotionally.

When I arrived in Eugene, no one met me, as the Panther chapter had closed and our Comrades had moved to Seattle. As I walked alone from the bus to the Lane County Sheriff's Office, where I turned myself in as a political prisoner, I hoped that my appeal would come through and my imprisonment would be brief.

I was placed in a holding cell alone for several days, waiting for transfer to the prison. I actually couldn't wait to get to the prison, because at least there, I would be out of this small cell, and amongst inmates as part of the prison population at the Oregon State Correctional Institute, or O.S.C.I. This medium-security prison had walls and fences that were not as big as the wall down the street at the Oregon State Penitentiary.

We called it "the big house," and my six-year sentence precluded me from being housed there, amongst brothers with more serious crimes, including life sentences, or "murder beefs," as we called them.

Finally, when I was transported to prison, I walked through the gates and headed down the walkway to the entrance where, once inside, I was unhandcuffed and photographed.

Processing began with me placing my belongings in a manila envelope.

"What size are you?" they asked, before providing my prison uniform: underwear, white t-shirts, and a khaki-brown shirt with matching pants. I tried on several sizes for the right fit.

They also gave me the rundown on the rules of the prison

system, the dos and don'ts, how much money I could have on the books, and where I would be staying.

"Now you have to get a haircut," they said.

I wasn't too keen on this. I hadn't cut my hair for several years, after growing out my afro, as I became aware of the righteousness of my own skin color and my hair. This coincided with Stokely Carmichael awakening awareness of the Black Power Movement and our celebration that Black is Beautiful. All of this roiled in my mind as I stepped into the barber area where, to my surprise, a brother greeted me.

"We've been expecting you," he whispered. "We heard a big Panther leader was coming to the prison from Seattle."

"Right on," I said.

"I'm Donnell Allen. They call me Dog. What do they call you?"

"Deacon," I said. "And I want to keep my hair as it is."

He glanced at my afro and nodded. "Don't worry about it. We'll wet your hair, pat it down, trim the fuzz, and make it look like you got a haircut." He took a couple snips around the back and packed down my hair.

This gesture from this brother that I had never met before that moment made me feel like I was in the company of Comrades. This was my first conversation with a brotha inside the prison, and I felt I could trust him.

"Are there other brothas in here?" I asked.

"Yeah, a Panther from Portland is in here. Albert 'Big Red' Williams. You'll meet him later."

"I look forward to meeting the brothas," I said.

Then I was led to Cell Block D, where Dog Allen happened to stay. At the time, O.S.C.I. had no two-man cells; each cell housed a single inmate. My five-foot by seven-foot cell had a small bed, a toilet with no seat, and a desk. There was also a lamp and a socket in the wall for headphones for listening to the radio station that was piped in by the prison system.

I later had an opportunity to go out on the yard, where Donell began introducing me to some of the brothers. First was Albert "Red" Williams, a "high yellow" brother with a reddish-brown afro, who was about the same height as me. As it turned out, he was a Comrade, having served in the Portland chapter of the Black Panther Party, which had been under our jurisdiction. While I knew the Captain of the Portland chapter, Kent Ford, and his wife, Sandra, I had not met many of the chapter's brothers and sisters.

When Red introduced himself, we shook hands with the Black Power handshake and said, "All power to the people." I felt much more at home and relaxed now, because I was around a Comrade who had been in the trenches. Red had experienced a police attack on the Panther office in Portland, in the cops' attempt to disrupt the Party activities, including the children's breakfast program and free dental clinic. During the attack, Red's intent was to defend the headquarters. So, he grabbed the shotgun from the Officer of the Day's desk. Police shot him. After he recuperated, he was convicted of assault and given time at O.S.C.I.

I was introduced to more brothers—Kelsey Turner and Big Frank—feeling an immediate camaraderie.

During my first few days there, I focused on orienting myself to prison life. I was assigned to a work detail in the construction shop with masonry materials. This seemed like as good a place as any. I wasn't down for making license plates or anything else that would benefit the prison system or anything that could be sold outside the prison. Being inside the masonry shop meant that I could work on projects that perhaps would benefit inmates inside, so I thought it was a decent fit.

I needed to feel my way around, learn the rules of the game and the turf, so I started hanging out with Dog and Red. They would instruct me on who was cool, who to stay away from, and which guards to watch out for. We started meeting to quietly and discreetly discuss organizing the inmates and how we could set up political education classes for those who were willing to attend.

We knew the implications for organizing inside a prison, as we were all too familiar with Comrade George Jackson, and the repercussions of his organizing in the California penal system. Though we were not in a facility as notorious as Soledad or San Quentin, we wanted to educate inmates on the prison industrial complex that had forced them into lives that led them to prison, so we began to quietly organize and set up PE classes.

There were also other ways to utilize your time in prison, including sports, and of course, the iron pile. I had never lifted weights before, but was about to work out with the brothers and pack some muscle onto my thin frame.

Meanwhile, I quickly learned about eating prison food. For instance, when the cooks prepared a strange-looking mixture, the inmates named it "kitchen surprise," because they wouldn't know what they were eating until they could actually taste it, and even then, they couldn't be sure.

At least this prison was adjacent to a farm, which provided fresh eggs and meat, not the scraps that I had heard about in other prisons. Plus, many of the cooks were brothers who put their own flavorful twists on the food, so it wasn't half as bad as I had feared.

Meanwhile, I was always thinking about my Comrades back in Seattle and around the country, and what they were dealing with as the fight continued: the attacks on our offices; the attempts to murder us in our sleep; and the efforts to discredit our programs or harass kids coming to eat breakfast. I kept in touch with them by writing letters, reporting what was happening inside the prison.

I also kept in contact with my parents and Beverly. After a few weeks, I couldn't wait to get a visit from someone, and

Beverly came down with her kids. During our nice, long visit, we talked about what was happening back home. This provided some connection back to Seattle, and while she had started working in the breakfast program at High Point, she was not in contact much with my Comrades or what was going on with them and the cadre, so I still felt disconnected. This was a long journey for her, especially with two little kids, so it would be hard for her to keep coming back. She gave me pictures of her and the kids, and I put them on my mirror in my cell. It allowed me to keep an image of someone that I'd been close to. And, of course, the brothers would look at her picture when they leaned into my cell and comment about how beautiful she was.

"She was a *Jet* centerfold model," I bragged. "She's holding things down till I get out." I said this, knowing that she would probably end it soon. This was, of course, part of the prison culture, to let people know that you had folks back at home. It was also a way of declaring your sexuality so that no one got the idea that you would be bait for someone on the prowl.

As the weeks rolled by, I wondered if there was ever any real likelihood of an appeal, but I held onto a faint hope that, somehow, I was getting out any day now. I was waiting to hear if my lawyers were able to successfully challenge my conviction, which would then grant me an appeal bond, allowing me to leave prison, pending further outcome. This hope kept me going at first, but as the weeks passed, reality hit that I would probably have to stay awhile.

So, I began going through the motions of learning the craft of masonry. This included understanding how to build things out of bricks and mortar. I studied how to: lay bricks so they would be level; design an object, like a fireplace or barbeque; mix the mortar; and put it all together. Our first assignment was to construct a fireplace. But first, we had to build a barbecue grill, which would teach us how to use correct angles and how to level the bricks.

Dog was on the same crew as me, and when we built our first barbecue grills, Dog's construction looked like a rickety old fence that could collapse at any moment. Mine looked sturdy and level. It appeared that I had taken naturally to this masonry thing.

I attributed my attention to detail to lessons learned from my moms and pops, especially their "do it right or don't do it at all" mentality that was drilled into us when we were doing housework. Poppy used to have us make our beds up so tight that when he dropped a coin on the blankets, it had better bounce or it had to be done all over again. It was the same when we waxed the floors on our hands and knees, as he orchestrated the whole thing while listening to the operatic voice of Cio-Cio-San in *Madame Butterfly*, as if he were the grand maestro.

Now my skills were paying off.

"Yours looks so good, man," Dog joked. "I want to take my picture next to it, send it home, and say I built that."

Since he had cut me some slack when he patted down my afro to avoid the prison-mandated haircut, I said, "That's cool." So, we both laid claim to my barbecue pit.

The next big project was to build a fireplace, as if it were inside a home. I didn't want to do what everybody else did, so I wanted to create something that reflected my individuality, as well as my connection to the Black Panther Party.

"Sarge," I asked the instructor, "can you get me white concrete bricks that I could dye any color?"

Sergeant "Sarge" Jones was a middle-aged white guy who had worked in the prison system for some time. He had seen prisoners come and go, and he had an eye for someone with special talent. He liked the idea that I wanted to do something different.

So, he found the concrete bricks and gave me access to the colors that I requested—powder blue, just like our Panther shirts. I dyed the bricks Panther blue and made a large fireplace with a raised hearth and powder blue tile that I had requested to sit on the hearth. My beautiful masterpiece drew praise from the team and Sarge.

"I don't know what you have," Sarge said, "but whatever it is, you ought to bottle it and sell it."

I had no intentions of sticking around, nor did I intend to become a brick-layer, as I was determined to get out and get back to my Comrades.

In late summer, on August 21st, we heard the devastating news that Comrade George Jackson had been murdered in San Quentin. The details as reported by mainstream media were sketchy: four prison guards were killed, and George was shot while trying to escape. I knew that there was some sort of set-up to get George killed and that the way it was being portrayed was to serve as a cover-up for whatever conspiracy had occurred.

Years later, I would read the report by London-based investigator William Darden, who had flown to the U.S. immediately upon hearing of George's death to piece together the real story. George did, in fact, want out of prison because he knew the prison administration wanted him dead for two reasons: 1) his organizing; and 2) he had escaped assassination when he was not in the Marin County courtroom where Jonathan took over and died in a hail of bullets. George was convinced they were going to murder him at some point, if he didn't escape.

But the prison administrators had gotten wind of it, and unbeknownst to the guards, agent provocateurs got involved in planning his escape. They were quietly setting in motion a plan that would involve George getting a pistol, which was actually smuggled in by guards, along with a small vial of what was supposed to be nitroglycerin, to blast a hole in the wall of San Quentin prison, enabling George to escape.

However, it was all a ruse, so they could shoot him dead in the prison yard. They did this realizing that they would put guards at risk, and some of them were actually killed in the process. But their main goal was to end the life of a revolutionary who was threatening the prison industrial complex with his organizing skills, which were known throughout California's penal system. He had halted gang violence between Black prisoners and Latino prisoners. The prison system could not let this continue, because it disrupted their divide-and-conquer tactics; as long as they could keep the inmates fighting and killing each other, they could control them. So, they needed to get George out of the way.

When I got the news that George was murdered, it was another reminder of the fate of the revolutionary—to die for the people. Here was another Comrade who died at the hands of the fascists, and I was in prison, where I could do nothing about it. I resolved to continue to educate the prisoners as best I could, and to organize along with my new Comrades in prison, to stay alive and live to fight another day.

By the time the fall rolled around, football season was upon us. That meant that the prison blocks would organize their own football teams and play against each other in a tournament, as well as against outside teams. This was the perfect opportunity for anyone who could make the team to take out their aggressions on the civilians who would come in to play against us.

I tried out for quarterback, knowing I had the ability to play that position from my high school days. The coach, however, had his favorite—a white dude who could throw the ball, but not any better than me. One afternoon while practicing, we were in a scrimmage with the first team offense, playing the first team defense. Each side had to play both ways, offense and defense. We had fought hard all afternoon and were deadlocked in a 6-6 tie. The sun was fading fast into the fall skyline and the coach got word from the guard tower that we had about five minutes left. My team was on our own five-yard line after stopping the offense on fourth down. We had one last play before the call would be made for "yard in."

I called one last huddle to go for a play that would show the coach that I should be quarterback. I told Kelsey Turner, the fastest dude on the field, to run a deep end route, and that when he was about 50 yards down the field, to look over his right shoulder on the outside, and that the ball would be there. I also told my offensive line that they needed to keep those guys off me until I could get that ball out.

When the ball was snapped, I dropped back into my own end zone and floated around while they held the blocks. I saw that Kelsey had taken off and was zooming down the field on the pattern that I told him to run. I threw a deep ball that went about 50 to 60 yards in the air to his outside shoulder. When he turned around, the ball dropped in his arms, and he sprinted the rest of the 40 yards for a touchdown.

For all the inmates who were left on the field watching, it was like bedlam, as if we had just won the Super Bowl. As we walked off the field, I looked at the coach and said, "See... your boy can't do that now, can he?"

I knew he wouldn't make me quarterback, because I was all too familiar with how Black quarterbacks had been treated in the NFL. In fact, the NFL had no Black quarterbacks at the time, and while plenty had been quarterbacks in college, the stereotype was that Blacks couldn't lead a team, and therefore couldn't be trusted as quarterbacks. This was a long-standing, unspoken policy in the NFL, but I knew that the brothers could play that position. I didn't hold it against the white dude who was our quarterback. I just wanted to make my point, and I did.

I was just happy to be on the football team. I was on the starting defense and played middle linebacker, which meant that I had an opportunity to level the civilians who were coming in to play us. I relished that opportunity and played with the same ferocity as my other fellow inmates. The brothers nicknamed me Deacon after the famed defensive lineman "Deacon Jones," and it stuck. From then on, they simply called me Deacon.

The civilians never took it personal, and we never made it personal; it was just an opportunity to blow off steam and release some of the pressure of living a prison life. Around this time, I began to wonder about back home and what was going on with Beverly. It had been weeks since I had heard from her, and I realized that she couldn't face telling me that the relationship was off.

The brothers had always told me about getting a "Dear John Letter," which meant that your girlfriend or your wife was leaving you for another man, because you were in prison and just too far away. I decided that, rather than wait for her to write me a "Dear John Letter," I would write her a "Dear Jane Letter." I didn't want to be crass or mean-spirited, because I knew the day would come when she wouldn't be able to make the trip, or simply needed to move on.

So, in the letter, I explained that I understood why she hadn't written or returned for another visit. I also emphasized that I knew it was hard for her, and that she needed to move on, and that I did not hold any grudge against her. I wished her a good life and well-being. I would not compromise my life as a revolutionary, which meant that I was destined to die for the people, and upon my release from prison, I would resume the struggle for justice.

Around that time, I got word that my appeal had been denied. It was actually a relief, because I could stop looking to get out "any day now" and focus on doing my time. I settled into my work in the prison, which was doing political education with my new Comrades, watching each other's backs, and surviving the day-to-day monotony of prison life by trying to improve myself physically and mentally, while being a part of the prison family.

On September 9th, 1971, inmates took over Attica Correctional Facility in New York, holding 42 staff members hostage. The men were protesting inhumane conditions and treatment, and were demanding change. As the Attica Prison Rebellion unfolded, we were glued to the TVs in the day rooms of our cell blocks when we were not on the yard or attending to our routines.

As it was televised to the world, we related to the rebellion's leaders as they expressed their desire to be treated like human beings and not like animals. The conditions at Attica were horrendous, not like the pristine conditions in O.S.C.I., but we could relate to the mental depression of being housed in cages. They were like spokesmen for all prisoners and became our Comrades. We also knew that their rebellion was in support of George Jackson's murder, which had triggered an unspoken tension at O.S.C.I.

As the Attica rebellion continued for days, many different negotiators were called in to try to end it. Inmates requested that Chairman Bobby Seale come in, speak to them, and negotiate a settlement to guarantee better treatment and conditions for the prisoners. But before Chairman Bobby could visit, Governor Nelson Rockefeller obtained permission from President Richard Nixon to send in corrections officers, state police, and National Guard soldiers to end the standoff. They did this with gunfire, killing at least 43 people, including civilian employees and correctional officers who were hostages.

The bloodbath left 33 inmates dead, making the Attica Prison Massacre the deadliest prison revolt in history. It was not lost on us or anyone else that the prisoners who died were mostly Black and Latino.[6]

The morning that this occurred, the prison captain at O.S.C.I. called Red and me into his office.

"If anything starts," he told us, "we're gonna shoot you and Red first."

Red and I looked at each other, then the captain.

"Well," I said with a nonchalant expression, "do what you

gotta do." My life had been threatened before, and Red had been shot. So, this didn't faze us. Then we walked out.

When we got to the prison yard, all the white prisoners lined up on one side, and all the brothas and Latinos went to the other side. The mood was somber and no one was sure what would happen.

Now, everybody stood around, wondering, *Are we gonna riot or fight?*

The Black and white prisoners generally got along. Most of the time, these groups, including white nationals, stayed to themselves unless we were on the football field, basketball teams, or softball teams in the spring. So, after hours of just standing there, the yard-in call came and everybody quietly lined up in a gesture of solidarity to return to their cell blocks to live another day in the life of an inmate.

The warden tried to ease the mounting pressures of prison life by bringing a Blues concert into O.S.C.I. The lineup featured Muddy Waters, Big Mama Thornton, and John Lee Hooker. It was my first time really listening to the Blues, and seeing them in person made it all the better. They rocked the prison that night, and made it possible for the inmates to feel good about their own blues in an ironic sort of way.

The brothers had also taught me to play pinochle, which was a more complicated version of bid whist. We played with whatever goods that we could get from the commissary—cigarettes, candy, cookies, or potato chips. Since I didn't smoke, I had no interest in cigarettes. Our codenames for the prizes were "Wham Whams" and "Zuzus." Friday night was commissary night and everyone got their Wham Whams and Zuzus to play in the various card games or domino tournaments in each cell block.

That was where I learned to talk smack; in the hood, it's known as "the dozens," and if you couldn't stand the heat, you had to get out of the kitchen. When I first arrived, I played in the lighter games, such as tonk, or spades, or even hearts. To play in the more sophisticated games, you had to know your stuff, and so I had to watch and learn. Eventually, I started playing bid whist, where most of the betting would take place before you could elevate to the pinochle tournament.

I also honed my skills on the domino table and learned to talk high-level smack without offending anyone. This gamesmanship was how brothers passed the time, competing without physical contact while building a little comradery among the inmates.

On nights when I was alone in my cell, I wrote letters to Comrades and my parents. After lockup and lights out, I plugged my headphones into the jack to hear the late-night tunes. This was the only time when we could get soul music. Our favorite show came out of L.A., featuring everybody's favorite DJ—the Wolfman, or as everybody knew him, "Wolfman Jack." He started his show with a wolf-like howl that sounded something like a soulful lycan about to launch into a barrage of R&B music. I listened to the songs of the day by The Jackson 5, Al Green, the Chi-Lites, Blue Magic, and the Delfonics.

My favorite song at the time was by the Dells, "The Love We Had Stays on My Mind." It was probably every other inmate's favorite song to reflect on the lost loves that we had all experienced after receiving Dear John Letters while in prison.

The nighttime guard in our cell block during the week was a tall, lanky, blond dude whom everyone suspected was gay. "Judy Blue Eyes"—our nickname for him that referenced the Crosby, Stills, and Nash song—walked the tiers, checking on inmates. When he was on the far end of the tier, some inmates would call out "Judy Blue Eyes" as a warning he was approaching. We all believed he was lurking, looking for an opportunity to catch a glimpse of one of us doing our business.

While trying to sleep or listen to music, we heard his slow, click-clack coming down the concrete tiers, peering into each cell. And that was how the nights went: soul music, Judy Blue Eyes patrolling the tiers, and everybody waiting for the dawn to come, for a new day, for a chance at redemption—either on the football field, the basketball court, or eventually, at the domino table.

CHAPTER 27

And She Walked Back into My Life

Late that November, a few weeks after sending my Dear Jane Letter to Beverly, a letter arrived out of the blue from someone whom I'd long forgotten: Dee Dee.

Our first conversations back in early 1970 at Summer Liberation School now seemed long ago, when suddenly, here she was again. I smiled, remembering her cute innocence, along with her raw beauty and keen interest in the Party and liberation of her people. Dee Dee's letter immediately lifted my spirits, which were still clouded by disappointment after my appeal was denied.

"Do you remember me?" Dee Dee asked in the letter. "I went to the Panther office when I heard you were a political prisoner who was incarcerated in Oregon. So, I asked for your information to write to you."

This was like a breath of fresh air from the outside, a connection to some sanity of life, which was totally unexpected and completely caught me off guard.

We started corresponding through letters, and she also divulged that the young woman who had given her the tour—T-baby, back in 1970 when we first met, the young sister who had temporarily been in our keep before going back to the juvenile corrections center—had claimed that she was my girlfriend. That had stopped Dee Dee from reaching out to me. I had wondered about her sudden disappearance, but tending to Panther business, dating Beverly, and preparing for prison had consumed my time and attention.

Now, here she was again, like a ray of sunshine on my gloomy, soggy day. We began to establish a bond and a relationship that, unbeknownst to either of us at the time, would last for the rest of our lives.

Dee Dee provided a brief glimpse of life beyond the revolution for the first time, as someone to look forward to meeting on the outside, to hold onto, and to fight for—beyond my Comrades and the struggle. This made prison life seem to move forward at a quicker pace.

Still, the fight for liberation remained primary in my mind. The Comrades whom I had left behind were in the death fight, and I couldn't be with them. I longed for my carbine and the day-to-day struggle of organizing in the community, selling Panther papers, and inspiring Revolution among the masses.

I often wondered who of my Comrades would be murdered next, who would be trapped by the police in gunfire or caught in a pre-dawn raid. I wished that I could be there with them for the good fight.

I began lifting weights, as many of the brothers did, to keep in shape. I had never lifted iron before, but eventually I built more muscle mass, and my body got used to the tearing down of muscle and the soreness that followed. I began to get into prison shape.

In early '72, Aaron told me, "All the Seattle Comrades, along with all chapters across the country, are being transferred to Central Headquarters." Huey had decided the Party needed to reinvigorate the Movement by "building the base of operation," which he learned from the revolutionary practices of Mao Tse-tung and the People's Liberation Army.

Following all the attacks on chapters across the country and the partial split in the Party, Huey believed it was necessary to pull all the strong members out of each chapter to build this base of operation in Oakland.

At the same time, they were making plans to run Chairman Bobby for mayor of Oakland and Elaine Brown for city councilwoman. I had wondered if this was the right move, stripping not only our chapter, but all chapters across the country of their most vital fighters and community organizers. I was a revolutionary and would support whatever directives came out of Central Headquarters. I was determined to "walk the line," keep moving forward, and not get distracted from my goal of getting out of prison wholly intact.

Agent provocateurs could suddenly shift things in prison with some bullshit scheme, as had happened to Comrade George when he was sentenced to one year to life, for a $70 gas station robbery, which turned into multiple life sentences on trumped-up charges while incarcerated.

Though I was not in one of the rougher prisons, such as San Quentin or Soledad, I knew to stay vigilant all the same. I had inquired about the possibility of applying for early parole, which basically meant that I needed to keep my nose clean; I was agreeable to doing that, as long as I didn't have to compromise my principles.

As spring approached, I was given the opportunity to get outside the prison walls. I had excelled on the masonry team and had been asked to build handball courts inside the prison, and then to do some work right outside of the gate. Because of this, I was given minimum security clearance to do other assignments, which included building a rock stairway in the warden's garden for his wife, who was partially disabled. I considered this a humanitarian service for her and not for the warden.

Around that same time, unbeknownst to me, the governor of Oregon was moving to find a way to grant me clemency and commute my sentence. Tom McCall was a liberal progressive politician and my case had come to light due to the efforts of my Comrades and lawyer, John Caughlan.

One afternoon, I was called off the yard and told that I had a visitor from the governor's office. I was directed to go to the visitor's center, where I was escorted to a private room, unlike the visiting room where we normally received visitors. There, a small, slender white man in a blue suit gave me his card and said he was from the governor's office. Full of suspicion and distrust, I sat down at the table across from him.

"The governor is preparing to offer you a clemency hearing," he said, "in order to grant you clemency so you can get out of prison."

I looked back at him and said:

"You can tell the governor that the only thing that I'll accept from him is an unconditional surrender by his government for the atrocities committed against the people, and nothing less."

Then I added: "And I'll make no negotiations for my release unless he's prepared to sign an unconditional surrender on the part of the government."

This man looked astonished and bewildered. He didn't know what to say and left the meeting with no commitment from me. That was the last I saw of him.

I was still a member of the Black Panther Party—a revolutionary—and I was not about to make any deals with government agents. O.S.C.I. had become my new community, and my Comrades were the small cadre of inmates whom I had come to know and hang out with. We watched each other's backs and made sure there were no potential conspiracies to get us jammed up.

Red was a fearless warrior who had proven himself in the Portland BPP office shootout. I was also a fearless warrior, thanks to my roots in the Seattle office, where we had faced down the pigs on numerous occasions. As a result, our egos sometimes clashed. But we knew not to take it to the next level, which would have delighted the guards and the administration. So, we took it out on the basketball court, the football field, or the domino table.

Whenever he was about to slam down the winning domino, throw the winning touchdown pass, or score the winning bucket, he would say, "Did you think you could win?" and that became the mantra of many of our Comrades in prison. If we were lucky enough to hit that game-winning shot at the end of a game of horse, or score the winning touchdown, it was our way of wolfing at each other.

Prisons are like a road stop on the way to the rest of your life, and this prison was no different. Many of the brothers would do their time, only to hit the revolving door, because outside awaited the same traps that landed them in prison. They came from broken families, broken homes, or broken dreams. Many of them were told that they weren't worthy, or they couldn't achieve this, or they couldn't achieve that, so they turned to either crime or drugs.

One brother in particular could play just about every instrument that existed. I marveled as he played the guitar, then switched to the drums, moved to the piano, played the sax, jammed on the trumpet, rocked the bass, and wrote music. Yet here he was in the hole that this country calls prison. I don't know what he did when he got out. I only know he had the talent to be a Quincy Jones or Stevie Wonder, and wondered if he would ever see that side of life or make it.

Other brothers were highly skilled at playing sports, including a dude named Leon, who had wavy hair—the leftover remnants of his conk or "do," as we used to call it back in the hood.

This hair-straightening process was what Stokely Carmichael had talked about in his Seattle speech that had inspired so many young Black people to wake up back in 1967; he talked about the fact that we didn't love ourselves, so we did everything to try to make ourselves white, which included straightening our hair instead of wearing it natural or in an afro.

Leon had been a pimp and a player, and he had the looks of an Adonis—tall and muscular, with a keen intellect. I could see how he could easily charm women. On the basketball court, he was like a LeBron James or Michael Jordan. He had moves that you would only see in a professional basketball game, and he always wore this smile like he knew he could dunk on you, shoot over you, or just drive around you at will. What a waste of raw talent.

Prisons are full of lost dreams and hopes and wasted talent. There's no real rehabilitation that ever happens, unless it's done from within or by oneself. Only those of us who could see the light at the end of the tunnel, envision the bigger picture, and imagine ourselves in different circumstances, would actually ever make it.

I was one of the fortunate ones; I suppose it came from being in the Black Panther Party as a revolutionary. We imagined a world where people mattered, and could be who they wanted to be, and achieve our dreams, regardless of the color of our skin. Revolutionaries see the bigger picture. We see the possibilities and we starve for it, crave it, and will do anything to achieve it.

Being willing to die for the people, to achieve liberation by any means necessary, is what we believed, and that's what gave us a vision for the future and allowed us to push forward and struggle for a better existence.

Red was one of those guys that I believed could see the bigger picture, but there's no telling how many times he was told by a teacher or a counselor that he wasn't good enough or that he couldn't make it. We called it "Death by a Thousand Cuts," and in today's world, it's known as microaggressions. Black, brown, Latino, Indigenous and Asian people, women, LGBTQ people, and even poor whites all experience the mass of cuts/ microaggressions.

I wondered how many of my new Comrades would succumb to the microaggressions of the system. Years later, I heard that Red had died of a drug overdose after battling drugs for most of the rest of his life after he got out of prison. It was a sad ending to a life that held so much promise.

In prisons across this country, 40% of inmates are Black, even though African Americans make up less than 13% of the nation's population. This is the ending that the prison industrial complex has in store for Black and brown communities: putting them in the wastelands of America known as the prison systems with no hope of rehabilitation.

CHAPTER 28

Short-Timer

Later that spring, I was told that I could participate in the Little League Baseball Umpiring program. It allowed me to go on outings with other inmates, who were approved for the same duty, where we would umpire Little League games from the six-year-olds all the way up to the 13-year-olds.

I had a parole hearing coming up later that summer and was being given the opportunity to show I was ready to re-enter society, or prove myself through these programs. While I didn't see them in any way compromising my stance as a revolutionary, I was cautious as I entered into these situations. The opportunity to work with kids again was like a tonic to my starved need to serve the community. The fact that the kids were mostly white had no bearing, because as servants of the people, it was our responsibility to look after the youth and to nourish them. These kids needed as much nourishment as any small children.

The first group of kids that I had the opportunity to umpire were the T-Ballers, six- and seven-year-olds who used light bats and hit the ball off a tee. They had no pitchers and our role was to make sure they had fun while playing and learning the game, so we gave them as much slack as we could. Part of the process of nurturing them was not always calling strikes when they missed the ball altogether on the tee.

As I moved up through the leagues to the 13-year-olds, the highest level, it became more important to call accurate balls and strikes. One young kid stood out and drew a lot of attention because of his skilled pitching. All of the inmate umps wanted to call his games, because he made our jobs easier with his precise pitching. His name was Pat Payton, and whenever I was behind the plate, I would watch out for his fireball, fastball, or side-winder curve when it came across the plate. It left little doubt whether it was in the strike zone.

As an umpire, I had to be neutral, so I couldn't say, "Good pitch."

But I could do one hell of a "STEEERIKE!"

And after the game, I always had the opportunity to say, "You're going to be in the big leagues one day, kid." This nurturing experience replenished me.

These games happened in various local communities near the prison, and the more I got out, the more leeway that I was given. Following the season, the umps were rewarded with a trip to Portland to see a concert featuring Joe Cocker. This flamboyant, white soul singer had Black backup singers belting out songs like "With a Little Help from My Friends" and "You Are So Beautiful." It was a show that reminded me of the days when I was in the band, playing my horn to the blaring sounds of soul music.

Following that successful outing, I was granted a leave, which was one of the steps leading up to my eventual release. A brother who was a professor at the University of Oregon would come in periodically and talk to the brothers or give them insights into ways to increase their education. He took a couple of us out on a leave to connect with some of the Black students from campus in Eugene. This first leave was a daytrip, and he took us to his apartment. We sat, talked, and had a rap session about the Black politics of the day while listening to jazz.

Among the young women at this gathering was the former girlfriend of a Panther in the Eugene chapter. He was being chased by the government and was no longer around, and she had recently had his child—an infant girl. As she breastfed her baby, I couldn't help noticing her beauty. She was Native American, from one of the tribes in the region, and had beautiful, cream-colored skin, long dark brown hair, and big, oval brown eyes.

I tried to be discreet, but having been in prison for a year or so, it was hard not to stare. Later we all had dinner with jazz playing in the background. When it was time to go back to the prison, I told her that I would be in touch if I ever made it out again. Later that summer, on the Fourth of July weekend, I was granted another leave—this time for three days on an overnight visit. I ended up in some students' frat house as they were preparing for a Hippie Fest that weekend.

I later learned that this Hippie Fest was starting in its first or second year, and would actually continue for at least the next 45 years as a gathering of hippies from across the United States. People gathered and could attend live music, sit around and smoke some brother rugy, and buy local hippie crafts.

I spent that first night at the co-ed student house, but I wanted to get into a different location around some brothers and sisters. I reached out to Ray, a brother left over from the Eugene chapter. Ray used to take the Comrades up into the hills surrounding Eugene for target practice. He was also a deer hunter and taught the Comrades how to slaughter a deer and use the venison for food provisions, such as steaks and burgers instead of beef. He was very resourceful and still down for the revolution, so when I reached out to him, I asked about the young Native American woman. He took me by her house; she immediately welcomed me in and I stayed the next three nights. She lived alone with her infant daughter and didn't have many friends. I don't know if she had been separated from her family, but having a child from a Black man could have caused her difficulties.

She welcomed me in because I was a connection to the revolutionary who had left her behind. We had both been members of the Black Panther Party—I still was—and so there was an instant bond. She was tender and gentle and reminded me of the softer side of life that I had not experienced for some time. It was a healing time for us and we enjoyed that weekend together—walking outdoors and discussing life and the revolution.

Soon after that "test outing," my parole hearing came up. I was ready to rejoin my Comrades and get back to the fight, but I gave straightforward responses to the parole board's questions. I sensed that they had been contacted by the governor, because they were all too eager to grant me early parole. I had been a model prisoner from what they could see, and besides, no revolution was going to take place in O.S.C.I.

A few days later, my parole was granted and I was being called a "short-timer," the term for inmates who were getting ready to join their communities and try to make a life. For me, that meant re-immersing in the revolution.

After I was granted parole, I was sent to the "Farm," the last stop for inmates on the way out the door. This minimum-security facility had cells that were more like dorm rooms. The "Farm" supplied the prisons in the area with meat and dairy products for the inmates and guards. I was put on outside duty, cutting the grass around the facility. This aggravated my allergies, so I was relieved to get inside duty in the kitchen.

One of the head cooks, Luther, had a southern way about himself and a down-home style to fixing food. When he cooked green beans, they were seasoned, not bland. For my last day,

Luther said he was going to fix me a special meal. He took me inside the cooler, which was full of steaks for the guards, whereas the inmates got the other cuts of beef that went into the stews, burgers, and the infamous "kitchen surprises." Luther showed me the filet mignon.

"Pick two," he said.

I chose two fat, juicy ones.

"How do you want them prepared?" he asked.

"Medium well," I said, "with a couple of eggs and some hash browns."

As he prepared the meal, I was licking my chops, knowing that I was eating the guards' prime meat. Just as I took my first bite and dipped it in the egg, one of the guards who had it in for me walked into the kitchen. He was furious that I was eating the prime, select-choice filet mignon.

"You're gonna be transferred back to the prison and go to the hole," he said, not knowing that I already had my release papers.

The next morning, I was standing in the release room in my street clothes, collecting my personal belongings from that day 14 months earlier. The guard walked in, looking angry.

I simply turned to him, said, "Bye!" and left the prison for good.

CHAPTER 29

Changing of the Guard - A Different Reality

I couldn't wait to leave the state of Oregon. Ray had picked me up from the prison, drove me to get a bite to eat, and took me to the airport.

"Things have evolved," he said. "Expect a different scene when you get to Seattle."

I knew things had changed, since my Comrades had been transferred to Oakland while I was incarcerated, but I had no idea of what to expect. Rosita was the only Comrade left behind to operate the programs with a new cadre of community workers. She had stayed in touch with me and communicated about the programs, as well as what was going on with the new 'rads, as we called each other, but I knew this would be a different reality.

Gone was the massive fortress that we had built to protect us from the pigs. Gone were the sandbags, the thousands and thousands of rounds of ammunition, the gas masks, the bulletproof vests, and the steel and plywood sandwiches on the windows. Most of all, gone was my day-to-day interaction with trusted Comrades whom I had been in the fight with, who I knew would take a bullet for me, or I for them, who I knew would back my play if I challenged the pigs. This would be a new era, because I was on parole and had a whole list of restrictions that would follow me around for the next couple of years.

As I was about to board the plane, I turned to Ray and gave the power salute, hoping to see him again soon.

"All power to the people, Comrade," I said.

In Seattle, Rosita met me at the airport and took me to my parents' home, which, according to my parole terms, would be my home location for now. I reconnected with Mommy and Poppy. They were like old Comrades themselves. They always cooked in the free food giveaways and free community dinners and picnics, and they were always supportive of Aaron, my younger brother Michael, and me. They had come down to Oregon to see me on a number of occasions and always remained supportive, so it was good to see them and reconnect.

Later that day, Rosita picked me up and introduced me to the new Comrades. They all seemed so young. I was only 22 years old at the time, having joined the Party when I was 17, but these Comrades were like kids to me. Even though they were young adults, they seemed raw and untested. However, I was eager to meet them because they had been working hard to keep programs alive by selling Panther papers and working in the community.

I spent time getting to know Arthur Harris, Maurice White, Waymon Earls, O'Neill McClinton, and Maryland Jackson, who had worked in the Party, an old friend from the neighborhood, Leonard Dawson, who had spent some time in the Party in the early years, and then, along with Joanne Moten and others. Eventually, I would be introduced to Comrade Ron Johnson, who was different from the other new recruits. He was from L.A. and had joined the Nation of Islam in Compton, California. He was my age and had been tested by the streets of a rough city. Ron would be somebody that I would lean on and build a close relationship with, because he understood life at a deeper level. Eventually, he would become my most trusted Comrade and lieutenant.

Rosita put me in contact with Milton Norwood, the leader of our quasi-military support group, the Black Contractors. Norwood was a general contractor and had job sites across the Central District.

I needed a job to satisfy one of the conditions of my parole and he hired me immediately as a laborer and brick mason, since I had learned that trade in lockup. While I would not have the freedom to sell papers and interact with the community and my Comrades right away, this would at least buy me some time while I worked as a construction worker, until I could get free of my parole officer. The next most important priority on my list was to go see Dee Dee. The last time I had seen her was several months before I had turned myself in, and my only recollection of how she looked was through the pictures that she had sent while I was in prison. My most recent memory of seeing her in person was the last time we had been together. Now free, I drove to her home where she was staying with her grandmother, and when she walked outside, she looked like the most beautiful woman that I had ever seen. She had a full-blown afro and was dressed like a Black hippie, consistent with the early 1970s: bell bottoms, bright colors, and big hoop earrings. She was stunning. We embraced and said hello.

"I'm on my way to visit my mother in Spokane," she said. "I'll be back in a couple of weeks."

"Have a safe trip," I said. "I look forward to seeing you when you come back."

Meanwhile, my adjustment to freedom didn't take long. I reconnected with several people in the community, and Marilyn was like an old Comrade from back in the day. She knew all the places to take me to reconnect with my people.

After a few days, I started on the first of a series of job sites where Milton had assigned me. One, ironically, was the old synagogue directly across the street from the old Panther office. When I got there, the building was completely gone! I was stunned.

Only the People's Wall remained. Created by Dion Henderson in 1970, it surrounded our office as a testament to the struggle of the Black Panther Party. It was covered with images of Angela Davis, Huey Newton, Bobby Seale chained and gagged to a chair, Little Bobby Hutton, and the New York 21. The wall also had images of jazz great Charlie "Bird" Parker, Malcolm X, and Emory Douglas' drawings with a sister holding a gun and enjoying good times while preparing for an attack from the police.

As I settled into the job that day, Milton had me laying brick work and doing some tuckpointing. I had learned well from my time in prison and he trusted me to do this job. I did a number of odd jobs like that until he was given the opportunity to bid as a subcontractor on a larger scale project that would last more than a few weeks. Once he had secured the subcontract, I would be on that site for the next six to 12 months. It was the kind of stability that enabled me to go to my parole officer and say, "See, I'm working."

As a reintroduction to the community, the new 'rads suggested I attend some of the community events happening that summer, one of which was the Black Community Festival held at Judkins Park. Arthur Harris, one of the young 'rads, had arranged for me to speak at the festival. As I took the stage, I looked out at hundreds of young Black people in the park who had no recollection of who I was or what the Black Panther Party stood for.

I suddenly realized how things had dramatically changed since the "old days." The large crowds that used to gather at rallies or demonstrations were filled with activists and revolutionaries ready to dismantle the fascist system, launch revolution, or at least vociferously voice their support. This was, of course, not a rally, but a summer festival celebrating Black heritage and the community, yet it seemed like the right place to provide a little "PE." The youthful crowd seemed disinterested or not into it, wanting instead to get the band back on the stage so they could get to partying.

A new era had dawned during my short time in prison. We needed to rekindle the flame to fire up the community. So, I began laying out a strategy to agitate and capture the hearts and minds of the people as we were instructed to do in 1968 when Bobby Seale organized the "Free Huey" movement, which was the spark that grew the Party nationwide.

I didn't know how to accomplish this, but I needed to get around my seasoned Comrades, so I flew to Oakland, hoping to meet with the Chairman and get some new direction. Some Comrades picked me up from the airport and took me to the new Central Headquarters, which was now on East 14th Street. This sprawling building was the hub of activity, including newspaper production.

It was a much larger operation than I had ever seen at Central, because Huey had organized the base of the operation by calling in Panther chapters from across the country to assist in running Bobby Seale for mayor and Elaine Brown for city councilwoman.

I ran into Valentine while he was working on garbage pickup duty. We couldn't rely on city services for our needs, so we had our own garbage truck pickup that went around to various locations, such as houses and offices, then made dump runs to keep the areas clean. Those areas included the many cadre houses around headquarters. As the garbage truck was pulling up to Central, Valentine saw me and shouted:

"Hey, Comrade!"

At that moment, he collapsed and went into convulsions. It startled me. I knew he had epilepsy, but I had never actually seen him have a seizure. He was driven away in an aid car and later recovered. His attack was probably caused by his keeping a hectic schedule, multitasking, and forgetting to take his medication.

As things began to wind down for the afternoon and Comrades started coming in from their duties, I ran into my brother, Aaron. We went to get a bite to eat and a drink, so we could talk about everything that was going on. Up to this point, I had not been given any detail or discussion with anyone about the move to Oakland, the "Base of Operation," and how things were working with all our Comrades here now.

Aaron told me that when everyone came to Oakland, their rank in previous chapters did not matter. As a result, Aaron was no longer the Defense Captain, but part of the rank-and-file. That alone gave me pause for thought, because Aaron had proven himself as a leader in the Party, and it was hard to imagine that he was not at least in some leadership role, however large or small. He said he was working under his now former wife, Donnie, and that she was in charge of his day-to-day assignments.

When this first happened and she gave him an order to sell papers, he told her to go fuck herself. For that, he was called in front of the squad and was mudholed—which meant getting your ass kicked by a group of people. When he told me that, I was furious.

"If anyone ever tries to mudhole me for some bullshit," I said, "I'd kill every one of them." Of course, I understood that the Comrades were just following orders. And I didn't mean it literally, but still, I was upset.

He quickly hushed me up and said, "Don't say that. If they hear you, you'll be in trouble."

I knew something was not right, but chalked it up to the

revolution and said no more about it. I had been on the opposite end of mudholing in the past when I led the Goon Squad in Seattle, and we would routinely discipline wayward or reactionary brothers in the party. Although, that was different; we were a young organization at the time and there were a lot of crazy niggas joining the Party, and they were doing stupid shit like robbing stores and beating up women. We had to weed them out of the Party, which meant, most of the time, we ended up kicking their asses. But that was a totally different situation.

Aaron was a trusted Comrade who, as the leader of our chapter, had paid his dues, and had fought the fight. He deserved more respect. Not that I thought he deserved any special treatment. He was a soldier in the "People's Army," as we all were. Like everyone else who came to Oakland from around the country, he was committed to serving the people in whatever role he was asked, but it felt unjust the way it went down.

I was probably more angry at Donnie. What had led to her being put in that position? Was she being used as a pawn by someone else? Years later, Aaron would tell me that he suspected it was Huey who had put Donnie in charge of him, in an attempt to run him out of the Party. But Aaron was a fighter and would not allow that to happen. I hung out with several of my former Comrades, both from Central and Seattle, and tried to get a feel for this new "Base of Operation" and why it was important to the revolution. It would serve as an important framework and guidance for me to reorganize activities back in Seattle.

When I returned to Seattle, Dee Dee had come back from Spokane. I began seeing her on a regular basis, and it wasn't long before I had made up my mind that I was going to ask her to marry me. She had no idea that I was that serious about her.

"Do you want to go to my parents' home to meet my mother and father?" I asked her after a few weeks.

Surprised, she agreed. After the visit, I asked: "Will you

marry me?"

"Yes!" she said, sharing later that she was shocked and had no idea that I would propose. After going through a difficult time with a previous relationship, she hadn't thought about marriage.

Now engaged, we were like kids in a candy store, full of excitement about being together. We were not going to marry in a traditional way. No tuxedos, white dress, or fancy wedding party. This would be a Panther wedding that had meaning to what life was like for young revolutionaries. Prior to the actual wedding date, we got our marriage license and set an appointment to go to the church that I had grown up in, Grace Methodist Church, where Reverend Brown would perform the formal ceremony in the sanctuary.

That evening, it snowed as I gathered at the cadre house with Dee Dee, O'Neal McClinton, who would act as my best man, and Marilyn, who would serve as the maid of honor. We had to walk from the cadre house to the church, so I put Dee Dee on my back, O'Neal put Marilyn on his back, and we walked the two blocks through the snow as we smoked a little brother rugy. We were all giddy and happy when Reverend Brown saw us.

"Marriage is serious!" he lectured. "You need to make sure this is what you want to do and be serious about it."

"We understand," I said. "We're young, but we're serious about taking this step." We were having a good time and we were happy as we performed the ceremony and were pronounced man and wife. Then, O'Neal and I put Dee Dee and Marilyn on our backs, and we walked through the snow to the cadre house, where we had our own little private party, smoking the brother and sipping on some brew.

Later, we planned our Panther-style wedding ceremony, which would take place at the Mardi Gras, a popular restaurant and lounge that had been a nightclub in the 1950s and '60s. It was owned by Aaron's father-in-law, Morgan, as we called him. He had seen the best of the jazz scene in Seattle back when Duke Ellington, Billie Holiday, Count Basie, John Coltrane, and many of the jazz greats routinely stopped in Seattle to play at either the Birdland or his place at the Mardi Gras.

Morgan had met many greats throughout the years, and sat and talked in his bar with Kareem Abdul-Jabbar and other superstars who would stop in the community on their way through Seattle, whether it was playing a basketball game or being in a concert. Morgan had a big heart and he always supported the Party, he always supported his family, and he was gracious enough to allow us to have our wedding in his nightclub.

It was a spirited and lively environment, different from what most people would expect or even consider. The thought of having a wedding ceremony and reception in a nightclub/cocktail lounge would probably never occur to normal folks. But for a Black Panther wedding, it was just the kind of non-traditional setting one would expect from revolutionaries. Traditional wasn't our thing; in fact, the opposite was the case in most instances. It was an unspoken practice, often without having to give it thought, to do things contrary to the ruling class.

The large facility could accommodate more than 200 people, and Morgan's longtime friend, confidant, and partner, Margo, the resident soul food cook, prepared an exquisite soul food sit-down dinner. Dee Dee and I wrote our own vows which reflected our revolutionary lives together.

Rosita did the officiating and we were fully dressed in Panther gear—Dee Dee wearing a long, velvet black gown, while I was decked out in a leather jacket, beret, and Panther blue. It was a sight to see, and I can only imagine that it was Seattle's first Black Panther wedding. Supporters, Comrades, friends, and family joined our celebration.

Meanwhile, "Tricky Dick" Nixon had just won his second

nomination for president and, along with his henchman, FBI Director J. Edgar Hoover, COINTELPRO was in full swing.

During the day, I had to work my job as a construction worker long enough to appease my parole officer. There was no way I was going to go back into prison, so I had to stay in full compliance. It was difficult not being able to get back into the full swing of the survival programs and working in the office from day to day. That was all I had known for the past several years prior to going to prison. Whereas, I was not used to going to work for "The Man," so to speak, at the construction job.

What made it easier was that my Comrade and close friend, Milton, was the sub on my job, building a new location for S.O.I.C., Seattle Operational Industrialization Center, a nonprofit job training program to help underprivileged people in Seattle gain job skills. In essence, it was helping the community, which made it easier for me to do the work and get into it from day to day, but I longed for my Comrades, and I longed to get back into the fight and into the struggle for revolution.

On the weekends, I joined my Comrades selling Panther papers, as well as attending and teaching political education classes, but I was eager to be more directly involved.

CHAPTER 30

The New Revolution

After returning to Seattle from Central Headquarters, I began to have a better idea of how this new direction was going to unfold. I spent months reassociating myself with the people that I used to hang out with—the lumpenproletariat and common community folk.

The die-hard revolutionaries, whom I had known as my Comrades prior to prison, were no longer in the mix. The only ones who remained were my brother, Michael, James and Joyce Redmond, and Rosita, but I didn't know her well. It was challenging adjusting to being around folk who didn't live, breathe, and feel ready to die for the Panther mission. The main challenge amongst my new Comrades was figuring out who was worthy of my trust, and who was not.

I also had to adjust to being married. In the Party, Comrades would "relate to," as we called it, or have a relationship with whomever they wanted, without restrictions, as long as it was mutual. There was no ownership of any particular individual. On the other hand, if a person wanted to be in a committed relationship with another Comrade, they would do so, and everyone else would respect that.

The open relationship style that I had enjoyed during previous years in the Party made it difficult to adjust to a committed relationship, even though I loved Dee Dee immeasurably. While I would eventually adjust to this new reality, it would take time before I realized I had found my soulmate and could let go of old expectations of having to be available to other Comrades or women.

In early 1973, while Dee Dee was pregnant, I would often be asked to organize a troop of Comrades to go down to Central to work on Elaine's and Bobby's campaigns. I loved being back in Oakland on those trips among the hundreds of Panthers who were going door to door, canvassing neighborhoods and organizing the community. It felt like the early days of the Party, and I relished those times working on the campaign. Gaining a political foothold in the Bay Area was crucial to moving our agenda forward to engage people in pursuing political power—from a grassroots base, rather than traditional politics.

Even though Bobby and Elaine were running on a Democratic ticket, they by no means represented the Democratic Party's principles. Instead, their platform was based on our "Ten-Point Program," including "our wants and our needs" to:

- control the businesses and institutions within our community;
- make sure that people had decent healthcare;
- provide a relevant education to our youth, teaching them to believe in their abilities while exposing them to the "true nature of this decadent society" and their role in changing it;
- stop police from murdering innocent Black, brown, and oppressed people; and dismantle the prison industrial complex.

This was the platform of our political efforts and the Black Panther Party. While we may have changed our approach to achieve these end goals, it was still the same revolution—by any means necessary—and we needed to engage our community and the political system that had been so unjust, unfair, and stacked against our community. We needed to change this dynamic.

While neither myself nor any other Seattle Panther would be running for office, we were committed to strengthening our programs in Seattle and to supporting the base of operation in Oakland, as was laid out by Huey and Bobby. So, I met with the Comrades and established three priority goals:

1. strengthen our existing programs and make them have a deeper impact in the community;

2. retool the free medical clinic that was operating on a limited basis and needed expansion to become a large-scale Community Medical Center;

3. and establish (as a long-term goal) a school similar to the Oakland Community Learning Center that was already in operation.

The Oakland Community Learning Center evolved because so many Panthers were coming into the Bay Area to support the base of operation. Sisters and brothers got into relationships that produced more babies, creating the need for a more organized childcare and educational system. The Party was not about to turn its kids over to the U.S. public school system.

Instead, the Oakland Community Learning Center was led by Ericka Huggins and a cadre of Panther educators who had previous experience teaching. The curriculum resulted from the

Ten-Point Program, calling for an education that taught us the true nature of our society. The school's leaders were seeking accreditation so that the young people could receive proper credit for graduation and college. At the same time, they would be educated on our terms, not those set forth by the education system that was steeped in racism.

Seattle desperately needed this school as well, and opening one became part of our long-range plan by first laying a foundation for its successful operation.

When election day came, we were all full of anticipation. The polls showed Bobby neck-and-neck in his race for mayor. At the end of the day, Bobby's race was so close with the other mayoral candidate, that a runoff was announced. The final vote count was so close, that within itself, this result was a victory, because, in fact, he forced a runoff in the election. The next round of voting would not happen for another couple of months.

With Elaine losing her bid for the city council seat, the effort would concentrate on Bobby winning the mayoral position. Meanwhile, Elaine had established herself as a powerful force, someone to be reckoned with in the Oakland political arena. As she cultivated connections, she wielded a strong influence across the city where control of the Port of Oakland was at stake.

Later that spring, Bobby lost the bid for mayor, but that laid a foundation for the eventual election of the first Black mayor of Oakland, Lionel Wilson.

CHAPTER 31

At Once a Revolutionary - Leaving Friends Behind

During the summer of '73, I attended the first year of the University District Street Fair on 42nd and University Avenue, which was the early battlegrounds of the anti-war movement.

A guy selling t-shirts in a booth caught my attention. He was smiling—it was David. I hadn't seen him since we were 16, some seven years earlier.

But his smile wasn't quite as big as before, and it was hesitant. Not a smirk, but just kind of a half-smile, like he wasn't sure what I was going to say.

"Hey, David, what's going on!"

He barely spoke. His vibe seemed to say, *Why are you talking to me? I thought you hated white people.* His expression and the feeling it evoked in me, seared into my memory.

Fast-forward 15 years, at my 20-year high school class reunion, where I searched the room for him during the cocktail party before the dinner; I hoped to say hello and reminisce over old times. I didn't see him until I visited the candle-lit table with photos of classmates who had died. I scanned the pictures—and one was David. I stopped in my tracks.

I couldn't believe that he had died. I felt cheated out of an opportunity to offer some clarity around the unintended separation in our friendship and our lives. As I made the rounds amongst my classmates, I asked if they knew anything of his passing.

"All I know is, he died in a boating accident," one classmate said.

Another added, "He slipped on a sailboat, and hit the back of his head. That snapped his cerebral cortex and had died instantly."

That sounded just like the David that I knew, always prone to accidents. Not that he was careless, but he lived life carefree.

As for Mark, I don't recall the last time I actually saw him. Perhaps it was at graduation. We may have wished each other good luck, but our transition had occurred long before then. His brother, Paul, died of cancer before his 21st birthday, and Mark had already moved to Los Angeles, having received his million-dollar trust fund that was set up by his grandfather. The rumor was that he had used the money to purchase a Moog synthesizer and that he was doing music down in La-La Land.

He never attended class reunions, but years later, when I became a business partner with a new company, I realized that the insurance company we used for business liability was the same company that was owned by his father, Sprague Israel. After his father died, Mark inherited the business, being that he was the lone surviving heir. On a number of occasions, I reached out to him through his business associates in Seattle, and asked that he give me a call or let me have his number or an email address, but the response has always been the same:

"He doesn't want to talk."

So, I'm left wondering, if back in 1967, when he first became aware that his best friend was now a Black activist, and eventually a Black Panther in '68, and knowing how the press distorted the true meaning of the Black Panther Party, that maybe he and David thought I had gone crazy and suddenly decided to hate white people. That was the image that America tried to project on the Black Panther Party. Would Mark ever know that I never stopped loving him or David as friends, and that I had never adopted a hate for white people?

As I look back on those years, I cherish my time with them during that age of innocence as we were growing up, running the streets, and throwing eggs at cars. Those times when we played war in the streets, laughing, while dodging imaginary bullets. The times when we played football on the field and danced to *West Side Story* and argued over who was better—the Rolling Stones or the Beatles.

I now imagined that they must have thought I was crazy, all the time, but in the back of my head, I loved them anyway. Years later, it would occur to me that, without intent, I had lost my childhood friends. What I realized was how there really had been a major transition in my life in 1967, something I had never thought about, a true death of the innocence of my childhood.

CHAPTER 32

Fatherhood and Continuing the Fight

Since much of my time during the first year of my release was spent working to fulfill my obligation to hold a job, I had a limited time in the office with the Comrades.

I spent my days working with Milton, constructing the new headquarters for S.O.I.C., and we were building it from the ground up. This gave me time to observe the actions and activities of my Comrades and the office, and get a thorough understanding of where we needed to refocus our efforts.

During this time, I noticed that the medical clinic was not getting much traffic from the community. It was only operating a few days a week and it wasn't reaching out into the community enough to provide the kind of services that were so lacking. I also observed that we could do more to stimulate revolution by having a voice like we once had on issues critical to the Black community. As I began working with the Comrades, I began to get a feel for whom I could rely on, and the level of commitment they had to the struggle. One of the people who emerged as a trusted Comrade and confidant was Ron; he could handle whatever challenge that was thrown in his direction. He was also good at articulating the struggle and the need for revolution. For that, he would become my one and only lieutenant.

Another Comrade was Carolyn Downs, a sister who previously had been in a relationship with Arthur Harris. They had a daughter, Trena, but were no longer together. Arthur had also become a trusted Comrade; he had been in charge of several functions including distribution of the paper and the breakfast programs. Carol had obviously learned many things from him as she was an extremely hard worker and could take charge of any program or duties.

By the time summer rolled around, I was beginning to get back into the swing of things. My parole officer was satisfied that I had a stable job and the check-ins were not as frequent.

In the meantime, Dee Dee had become very pregnant, and by the end of summer, Frelima Ebony was born. She was named after the organization that was fighting for liberation in Mozambique; its acronym was FRELIMO. We already had two children by the time she came along. Her older brother, Merrill, who is named after Dee Dee's father, and Samora Monque, who was named after the leader of FRELIMO, Samora Machel.

Merrill had been staying with Dee Dee's mother in Spokane and we would soon have to go get him, as she didn't want to let him go after becoming attached to him. Our family had grown overnight, it seemed, and the reality of an expanding family and fighting the revolution was front and center. I needed to find the time to continue leading the effort while also making time to spend with Dee Dee and the kids.

But Dee Dee was in the struggle as well; she, too, was a revolutionary. While she would find time to serve in the breakfast programs and sell newspapers, she also became the quasi-Panther mother, taking care of all the Panther kids while the Comrades were out in the community. She often had six or seven kids to look after, including Ron's two boys, Kenyatta and Ranu, Rosita's son, Rodger, and Carol's daughter, Trena. She was up to the task.

Dee Dee also taught the kids how to read and write before they entered the public school system. And because she participated in the weekly PE classes and was an avid reader, she instructed the kids about our people's history and the Panther philosophies, to prepare them for the outer world.

And being that she was often the only person with the kids, she needed to know self-defense. So, I put her through the same training that we had provided for our Comrades in the early days. I would blindfold her in a dark closet, then have her take a weapon completely apart and put it back together, load it, and be ready for action. That way, she could defend herself if I were not there, and she was prepared to protect the kids to her death.

We had always been taught to do a thorough analysis of the conditions within our community in order to properly serve the needs of the people. It was during this analysis that I made the decision to close the free medical clinic. It was apparent that the people needed total healthcare and not just a twice-a-week clinic.

"We need to find out, what is it going to take to build a comprehensive Family Medical Center?" I asked my Comrades. "And how can we improve the free busing to prisons program?"

We expanded the Busing Program to all four male prisons in the state—Monroe, Shelton, McNeil Island, and Walla Walla State Penitentiary—as well as the women's prison in Purdy, Washington.

We also returned to the Vanguard position to lead and support other struggles. In 1972, a group of activists had taken over an abandoned school on Beacon Hill; one was former Franklin High School teacher, Roberto Maestas. The activists had asked the city for permission to use the old Beacon Hill Elementary School for much-needed programs serving the

Latino community. When the city refused, they occupied the building, so we met with them to offer our support.

Roberto was joined by three other activists: a former Panther, Larry Gossett; a respected leader in the Asian community, Bob Santos; and Native American community leader, Bernie Whitebear. They became known as the Gang of Four. It was critical for us to reestablish ourselves as part of the revolutionary collective of activists in Seattle.

The Panthers also expanded our work around sickle cell anemia testing. The Party had launched a national campaign to increase awareness around this little-known disease that primarily affected the Black community. Young Comrades had done an effective job of pushing this program out and using city funds to employ young people during the summer. The Summer Youth Employment Program had 10 kids organized into a troop, which went out into the community to do sickle cell anemia testing and blood pressure screening.

Valentine had organized the Seattle Chapter's Sickle Cell Anemia program before he left for Oakland. With Rosita, he organized a massive testing program in the state prison in Walla Walla. Valentine also worked with a medical technician who eventually adapted an electrophoresis instrument for use in sickle cell testing. Prior to that, sickle cell tests were done one at a time. This instrument allowed us to do many simultaneously, putting the BPP at the forefront of revolutionizing the fight against sickle cell anemia.

The Summer Youth Employment Program was another way for us to attract more workers to our ranks. While many started as high school students, they eventually supplemented our cadre so that we could do greater outreach and have a larger impact on the community. Arthur Harris was largely responsible for putting this program in place. He was good at organizing the young people and had made a solid contribution to the efforts of the Party. Eventually, he and the others would all become Black Panther Party members, and Central Headquarters acknowledged their hard work.

We were almost back to full strength, as it was back in the old days, and we were selling large numbers of the Panther newspaper. While our tactics changed slightly and we were no longer hunkered down in bunkers preparing for attack, we were still focused on raising the consciousness of the people and stimulating revolution. It was challenging to keep the Comrades focused on the day-to-day struggle.

Around this time, we got a call informing us that The Servant was stopping in Seattle on a flight that was en route to Denmark. We were to meet him at the airport during his brief layover. This was the perfect time to introduce the young Comrades to Huey, so they could see our living legend. They had never had contact with any national leaders of the Party, so this would inspire them to continue as dedicated, hardcore Panthers.

Being a Party member was not a nine-to-five gig. However, many of the new recruits had other responsibilities, such as taking care of a family or furthering their education. For example, Morris White was a young intellectual who was enrolled in pre-med to become a doctor. He saw this as an opportunity to become a doctor in our free medical clinic and serve the community, so I encouraged him to continue his studies.

Other Comrades, like Wayman Earls, had families and needed to provide for them. Our chapter could not take care of our Comrades' living expenses, as Central Headquarters did, thanks to the sheer numbers working there, and the ability to raise large amounts of money to support the campaigns of Chairman Bobby and Elaine Brown. Our operation was much smaller, but we had an enormous impact in the community, which continued to recognize our efforts. Whenever there was a police shooting, the community looked to us for leadership, and we were always on the spot.

CHAPTER 33

The Chairman Leaves

Following Elaine Brown and Bobby Seale's campaign defeats for mayor and city councilwoman, plans were made for Elaine to run for city council again.

One afternoon, we got the news that Chairman Bobby had left the Party. We received no information about why it happened, but it was a shock to everyone, especially me.

None of the new Comrades were around when we had first started the Party under the leadership of Bobby Seale. He had guided us in those early years as we became the first chapter outside of California, and later as he built chapters across the country. Bobby held the torch for the Black Panther Party while Huey was in prison and Eldridge was in exile.

The devastating loss of his leadership for the Party sparked a mass exodus of hundreds of Comrades who had come to Central Headquarters to build the base of operations. Comrades also left chapters across America.

I never contemplated leaving the Party, because I knew it was bigger than one person. Yet I still had questions. How could the Chairman leave after knowing how committed he was to the struggle and how much he deeply cared about the Comrades and the Party? It just didn't make sense. The next question was, *Why?*

Unfortunately, there was no way to ask that question without somehow insinuating distrust or challenging our Central Committee. We had to just let it go and stay focused on the tasks that lay in front of us. Chairman Bobby had instructed us well in those early years, as he did with the Comrades across the Party, with true political education, daily reading, and the understanding of being a true revolutionary. Without his leadership, we wouldn't have gotten as far as we did, especially given that Huey was in prison and Bobby had taken the Party to a national and then international presence.

March of 1975 brought another grim reminder of our purpose.

Joe Hebert, a cousin of Comrade Ron, was murdered by a Seattle police officer. He was shot while holding his car keys, which led the cops to claim the same excuse that we've always heard: that his keys were mistaken for a gun.

Joe's family retained our lead attorney, John Coughlan, to represent them at the police inquest. Like Huey's attorney in Oakland, Charles Gary, John was often referred to as the "White Panther." John had surely earned that reputation as a longtime fighter for human rights, starting in the 1950s, when he fought for workers' rights. He had been labeled a communist by the same COINTELPRO that was now targeting the Black Panther Party. He had never stopped fighting and was a tireless servant of the community and the people. Intelligent and crafty, he knew the tactics of the prosecuting attorneys because he had been a prosecutor in his early years, something that many attorneys who end up in private practices do in order to gain that level of knowledge; he knew exactly how to counter their arguments in the courtroom.

Ron worked closely with him on this case, and together they were able to identify all the holes in the police officer's arguments. Their main focus was the trajectory of the bullet; Ron and John constructed a prop with a Styrofoam wig head and, using a clothes hanger, they showed the trajectory of the bullet. The police claimed when they shot Hebert, that he had turned on them with a knife, so they shot him in the forehead, and he fell backwards.

Ron and John proved that the cops had turned him over after he was shot. Through our own investigation, we found that the exit wound was really in his forehead and the entry wound was at the back of the head at a downward trajectory. When presenting this to the jury, it provided graphic evidence that Joe was shot in the back of the head, execution style.

This was reminiscent of what had happened when Comrade Fred Hampton was murdered in Chicago. While the district attorney was holding a news conference stating that there was a shootout between the Panthers and the police, and that members of the Party had been killed, ACLU lawyers were simultaneously conducting a straw test at the site of the murders and found that all the bullet holes had an inward trajectory, with the exception of one bullet, which came from an officer firing through the walls on the other side of the apartment, proving that it was a shoot-in.

In our case, the verdict came back as unjustifiable homicide against this cop, Alan J. Earlywine. That meant Earlywine had murdered Joe, and though we secured this verdict—the first-of-its-kind in the shooting of an unarmed Black man—the prosecuting attorney, the racist Charles O'Carroll, refused to prosecute, going against the verdict and setting the cop free. This was the pattern that had gone down in countless shootings of innocent Black and brown people across America, and a continuation of what happened during slavery with slave-catchers shooting their captives and donning a badge in the defense of racist segregationists.

The Party got involved in another case in August of 1975, when Joann Little, a 20-year-old sister, fled her jail cell in Beaufort, North Carolina, after killing the white deputy sheriff who had attempted to rape her. Little used the jailer's icepick weapon against him in her desperate fight to resist. When Little surrendered to authorities, citing self-defense, she was arrested and put on trial for murder.

The Party raised funds for her defense. I had been coming in and out of Central Headquarters on various assignments, and was summoned to be on the security detail for the large fund-raising rally that was being held in Oakland. When I arrived at the site, I was given a weapon so that I could monitor the crazies that might show up. Along with the rest of my Comrades, we showed support for the sister who ended up eventually beating the charges, in part because of the broad support that she received to raise funds for her defense. It was a historic campaign that saved her from execution or life in prison, and was one of the first successful efforts to assert the right of Black women to defend themselves against white rapists.

While traveling back and forth from Central, I had struck up a relationship with a couple of Comrades, including a brother named Tex from Texas, and Deacon, a Comrade working at the Oakland Community Learning Center. As with all my Comrades, we had a close bond. Later that year, I heard that Tex had been killed in a botched raid that Aaron was a part of. I didn't get all the details; I only heard that it was an action being carried out by the squad and he had been killed in friendly fire. Not much was ever said about it, because of the nature of the action, but I knew Aaron was close to him and it was a sad day.

Deacon would also be murdered while protecting kids attending a dance at the community school, and at least I got a chance to say goodbye, as did all of the Comrades. Death continued to be a constant companion that we could not escape.

Another grim reminder was Cindy Small, one of the sisters who was working day and night during Elaine's campaign. Cindy fell asleep at the wheel and crashed her van, dying instantly.

In Seattle, we returned focus to one of our original programs, community control of the police and began organizing efforts to create a mandate for cops to be held accountable. This was the first of its kind in Seattle, and today is known as "community policing." The primary intent was to hold cops accountable for their actions, and to build a sense of trust by requiring police officers to live in the communities that they patrolled. We would begin working with local community organizations and I secured an appointment to serve on the Church Council of Greater Seattle's Police-Community Relations Task Force by working through one of our progressive white supporters, Carrie Sheehan. Our goal was to submit our plan for their support.

Carrie was a longtime activist throughout her life, with a strong commitment to community and social justice. Among other things, she had dedicated her life to women's and human rights, as well as prison reform. She introduced me to the Church Council of Greater Seattle's Police-Community Relations Task Force.

Later that spring, I got a call from Central Headquarters, informing me that there would be an all-Comrade picnic in one of the large parks in the Oakland area. It was a time for all the Comrades to come together with their kids, many of whom were enrolled in the Panther's school, the Oakland Community Learning Center. We were one of the last remaining chapters invited to come down and participate. We made plans for as many Comrades as possible to go down to Oakland. This included Dee Dee and all the kids, since it was a family event. It would be the first time that I traveled to Central Headquarters with Dee Dee and my family.

When we arrived, Joanne, our sister, told Dee Dee that she

and the kids could stay with her. Plenty of cadre houses were available for the other Comrades to stay in, but Joanne wanted Dee Dee to stay with her.

The picnic was a huge success, as many Comrades who had stayed on after the Chairman's departure gathered in the park. I was summoned to Central Headquarters to meet with members of the Central Committee. This included: Elaine Brown, who was now Chairman of the Black Panther Party; Ericka Huggins, director of the Oakland Community Learning Center; and Larry Hinson. I was there with Simba, the Comrade who was now in charge of the L.A. office.

The L.A. leadership had been decimated, first after the assassinations of Bunchy and John, and later following the frame-up of Comrade Elmer Geronimo Pratt. Known to us as "G," he had been framed for murdering a white couple on a tennis court in Los Angeles, which was absurd. He was sentenced to 25 years to life in prison. Years later, attorney Johnny Cochran would take up his case, disprove all the evidence against him, and establish that it had been a fabrication all along. After 25 years in prison, G was freed.

He sued the city of Los Angeles and other agencies, received a large settlement, and promptly moved to Tanzania. There, he met up with Pete and Charlotte O'Neal, who had opened a Panther cadre after going into exile in the early '70s. Pete had been framed on a robbery charge and was facing prison time; rather than enter the penal system, he and Charlotte, his Comrade wife, went into exile and joined Eldridge in Algeria at the international branch of the Party. After things fell apart with Huey and Eldridge, they moved to Tanzania, establishing many of the same programs that the Party was running in the "belly of the beast," back in the U.S., in a small village where they would take up home. They had been invited by the president of Tanzania to be his guests, and he welcomed these revolutionaries into his country.

In the meeting, Simba and I gave reports on our activities in our respective chapters. Simba went first and claimed that not much was going on, other than selling some papers. He had no report on programs or other community organizing. After he finished, I laid out the work that we were doing in Seattle:

- Feeding 2,000 kids a week across the city in our five free breakfast programs. Providing groceries to the community in our free food program, which was the precursor to food banks that would later develop in our city. Transporting families to visit inmates in five Washington state prisons, including the women's prison at Purdy, as part of our free busing to prisons program. Teaching children in our Summer Liberation Schools. Testing people for sickle cell anemia through our Summer Youth Employment Program (SYEP), in which we paid a cadre of high school students to do community outreach. Selling hundreds of Panther papers weekly, making us one of the top-selling chapters outside of Central Headquarters.

I went on to mention that we had launched plans for three major projects:

- Reorganizing the free medical clinic into a full-service Family Medical Center. Establishing a school patterned after the Oakland Community Learning Center. And working to get the community control of police program on the ballot.

Ericka Huggins immediately told me, "You can't have a school." She then proceeded to tell me why I couldn't organize a school and take on that type of responsibility.

I was stunned, thinking, *That's what we're supposed to be doing, organizing in the community and taking the lead from Central Headquarters.*

It was the first time that I had been discouraged by leadership in our efforts to "capture the hearts and minds of the people" and organize in the community. We had done our analysis, and we knew that Black kids needed an alternative to the school system. Building a school was in line with point number five of the Ten-Point Program, which stated:

"We want education for our people that exposes the true nature of this decadent American society. We want education that teaches us our true history and our role in the present-day society."

But I chose not to react, and decided to follow orders and stay in line with the Central Committee. Yet in the back of my mind, I knew that Chairman Bobby would not have discouraged our efforts. Unfortunately, he was gone, so I fell in line.

CHAPTER 34

Comrade Ron

As we returned to Seattle, I was determined to keep the Comrades focused and moving forward. I put the idea of a school on hold, as we had plenty of work to do in the community and could build on the efforts we had been focused on.

We had put a lot of effort in building relationships and coalitions across the city with groups like: El Centro De La Raza, led by Comrade Roberto Maestas and his wife, Chata; Radical Women, led by Clara Frazier and Gloria Martin; the Socialist Workers Party; Lacy Steele with the NAACP; Larry Gossett, a former Panther at the Central Area Motivation Program; and at BSUs on campuses across the city.

The UW campus was like a second community for us, as it was a staging ground for a lot of our organizing. It was also a primary location for our fundraising efforts. We had established ourselves on campus largely due to the breakfast program and enjoyed enormous support from the students. We knew which days to show up, usually on Thursdays and Fridays, and what times to be out across the campus when classes were changing, with students filling up the walkways. We were selling Panther papers as well. Students would take a paper and put in a donation, but many times they would just simply put in donations and skipped the paper.

In any event, we were doing political organizing by educating the young folks and by getting donations for the programs. This was just another example of us being among the people, because many of the students were Black and they were struggling to be accepted on campus. Our presence reinforced the fact that they belonged. The white liberal students were also emboldened by our presence, because it made them stand up to the conservatives.

The UW campus was a small city of 30,000 students, and we made sure that we had a well-known presence. One afternoon, when we got on campus, we got wind of the fact that the BSU president was planning to bring Ron Karenga to speak on campus. Karenga was a known FBI informant, who, along with his goons, facilitated the murders of Bunchy Carter and John Huggins. Their murders would never be forgiven, and Ron was well aware of how I felt about it, so we confronted the BSU president at the student center known as the Hub.

The Hub was where all the action happened on campus, and where students would converge for lunch and to hang out. Thousands of students were there at various times of the day, so it was a perfect place to sell papers and collect donations. Ron was a trusted Comrade, and I knew he would always have my back. He was my lieutenant, second in command, enforcing any directives that I might issue, and I had let it be known that no Karenga Tang would be speaking at the UW campus, as long as we had anything to say about it.

When we confronted the brother in this huge lunchroom cafeteria, he took a swipe at Ron, but missed.

Ron punched him in the face, knocking him down.

Ron's donation can went flying through the air, with money

scattering everywhere. Students began picking up the coins and returning them to cans while Ron and I dealt with the brother.

When we finished with him, he was clear that there would be no Karenga on campus. During the second wave of the lunch hour, the UW pigs had gotten wind of the confrontation, even though it had happened hours before. They confronted Ron and were about to arrest him with all of the students looking on. As they were handcuffing Ron, I jumped in the middle of the fray.

"You better arrest me, as well," I said, "because, either both of us are going to jail, or no one is! Put the cuffs on me, too."

The students were all revved up at this point, and the crowd around us had swelled to a few hundred. The students were chanting and supporting us. It was a standoff, and the shit was about to go down.

"We didn't cause any trouble," I told the cops. "And the students have our backs."

The pigs uncuffed Ron. They left, defeated.

The students cheered for us.

This was one of many actions that solidified the bond between Ron and me; this would be significant later. Of all my Comrades, he would always have my back, and for that, I trusted him the most. Perhaps it was because he was older and had been through the struggle as a member of the Nation of Islam in L.A. before coming to Seattle and joining the Party. Whatever it was, I knew he was ready to throw down without hesitation.

As we approached the dawn of 1976, the bicentennial of the U.S.—Babylon, as we called it—we continued to challenge the status quo in the community. One of our constant supporters was the editor of a local Black newspaper, the *Medium*. Connie Bennett was the sister of the newspaper's founder, Chris Bennett, and they both actively supported the work of the Party. Connie was a tough sister—fine as wine with big green eyes, she tolerated no nonsense and sported a big afro.

And she routinely wrote articles about how we were helping the community.

Early that spring, the *Medium* newspaper announced that it was starting a new recognition called the Unsung Hero Awards, and nominations could come from the Black community. The Children's Free Breakfast Program and the Seattle chapter were nominated to compete for this honor. We were excited that, after seven years, the Black establishment was acknowledging our work, because we were perceived as the anti-establishment Black community organizers. Our struggle was about helping those at the bottom.

We had no expectation to win this award, but the nomination increased our credibility. The evening of the ceremony, all the Comrades went to Mount Zion Baptist Church, which was Seattle's largest Black congregation and the bedrock of the established Black community.

The pastor was the Reverend Samuel B. McKinney. When we first started our free breakfast program, we had gone to Dr. McKinney and asked him to host one of the breakfast program's sites. His response was that they already fed kids in their daycare center. However, it wasn't for the community, and he turned us away.

We did not have a good relationship with churches and pastors. We had attended some Mount Zion services, but felt more comfortable at First A.M.E., which also had a large Black congregation. Reverend Cecil Murray was a progressive-minded pastor, so my Comrades and I attended his church on a regular basis.

Now, it was ironic that we were up for recognition for the Children's Free Breakfast Program in Dr. McKinney's church. The evening began with speeches by Seattle's Black dignitaries, which included Sam Smith, one of the first Black legislators to serve in Olympia, the state capital, and Seattle Mayor West Uhlman.

As the evening went on, each community organization

shared slideshows about the programs that were nominated. For most people there, the anticipation mounted, as the announcement of the winner hung in the balance. Even more exciting was that the ceremony was being broadcast live on the local NBC-TV affiliate channel, King 5. Finally, as the master of ceremonies stepped up to the podium to announce the winner, we were all set to hear someone else's name called.

"And the winner is," he said, "the Black Panther Party's Children's Free Breakfast Program."

We were as shocked as everyone else!

"Will Elmer Dixon please come on the stage to accept the award," the emcee said.

As I stepped up to the stage, the Black dignitaries and mayor were gone!

"They must've gone out the back door," someone said.

Connie handed me the award.

"First, I want to acknowledge my Comrades," I said. "This is not my award."

I had not prepared a speech, so I spoke from my heart and soul.

"Our struggle as Black Panthers continues, and this is just a small step. We aren't looking for recognition. But we are very grateful to the *Medium* newspaper for recognizing the community efforts of my Comrades. I also want to acknowledge the women in the community who cook in the breakfast program and understand the importance of kids being fed before school."

As I scanned the audience void of our city's Black leaders, I said, "The struggle for freedom and liberation is ongoing. This is in no way a celebration of victory, but an acknowledgement that our struggle is a just one, in light of the attacks that continue to come our way from the FBI. We still need revolutionary change and will coninue providing our survival programs. Finally, I want to express my undying love for my Comrades and for our people. We, the Black Panther Party, will continue to serve our community until freedom from oppression and justice are guaranteed for every Black, brown, and oppressed people in America!"

It was expected that the city's leaders would congratulate the winner, but they had slipped out the back door, quickly and quietly, because they were not going to be seen on live TV handing the Black Panther Party an award.

Receiving this acknowledgement in front of a televised audience was an implausible moment in our history. I could just imagine the FBI and the cops fuming as we were standing there getting the award. We didn't need this recognition to know that we were relevant and correct in our struggle for justice, but it was still sweet vindication for the work and sacrifices, for the attacks, for the murders of our Comrades, and for our call for revolution.

The irony was that Mayor Uhlman had refused to give the ATF permission to use Seattle cops to attack our office six years earlier. I later learned that, while he was in D.C. for the national mayor's conference following that incident, President Nixon had instructed one of his henchmen, White House Chief of Staff Bob Haldeman, to uninvite Uhlman and his team to the presidential dinner. Now Uhlman was sneaking out the back door instead of giving us our due.

But this made no difference to us. Our reward was that the broader Black community was recognizing our work.

CHAPTER 35

Storm on the Horizon

It was a warm spring day in 1976 when my plane touched down in Oakland. As we glided across the runway, I wondered how the conversation would go with Elaine Brown. Such a request, to meet with the current head of the Central Committee, really wasn't unusual. I had often been called by Chairman Bobby and other leaders of the Black Panther Party's Central Committee to discuss the operations of some particular event.

Still, I was curious as to why she wanted to see me now.

Aaron had relayed a request from Elaine, asking if I could be one of her personal bodyguards when she was running for city council. I asked him to relay to her that I couldn't at the time, because running the Seattle chapter was demanding my constant presence. Elaine had made this request a few years earlier.

Was she upset that I had turned her down?

Perhaps she was contacting me now because of a recent conversation after Ericka Huggins called me.

"Norma told me that you are not feeding your kids red meat," Ericka had said with an accusing tone.

I replied: "I told Norma that we had stopped feeding pork and beef to the kids in the breakfast program a few years ago, because we found out that red meat can cause cancer and other diseases."

We went back and forth about whose responsibility it was to remove meat from both my kids' diets and from the breakfast program. There was no resolution, because I believed it was not only my call, but also the responsibility of my wife and myself to decide what we would feed our kids. And as head of the chapter, it was my responsibility to decide what to feed the kids in the breakfast program.

But for me to be called to Central Headquarters, I knew something more urgent was on the agenda than a minor tiff I had with the director of the Party's school.

In the past, whenever I was called to Central, I always came promptly, no questions asked. In fact, during the early days, when Chairman Bobby called up and insisted that we get down there right away, we immediately hopped in the car and drove 800 miles to the Bay Area. At the time, Central Headquarters was located on Shattuck Avenue in Berkeley, and we did the 12-hour drive, non-stop.

In recent years, it was much easier to just hop on a plane, especially if I were traveling solo. So, after receiving Elaine's call, I simply flew down and had the brothers pick me up from the airport, then drive the short distance to East 14th Street, the current location of Central Headquarters.

I knew most of the Comrades at Central, which was a large, sprawling office, unlike the previous Central Headquarters, which were either in a house or a storefront location. The influence of the mid-70s was evident in the way we dressed: bell bottoms, afros, and colorful jackets, some of them leather.

It was a normal, busy day and the 'rads were performing their normal duties, working on the latest edition of the Black

Panther newspaper, or organizing a community survival program as well as other operational activities. Others were preparing to go into the field to sell the newspaper, the voice of the Party, or do community organizing.

"I'm here to meet with Elaine," I told the Officer of the Day.

"Have a seat," he said. I couldn't resist mingling with a couple of 'rads who were preparing the latest edition of the Panther newspaper. We did the latest version of the Black handshake–twisting our hands in a circular motion, ending with a finger snap, and thumping our heart to show respect. Then we hugged.

I knew most of these Comrades who had been working diligently on the paper over the past six or seven years because I had been the distribution manager for our chapter in previous years. Now, they told me what stories they were working on, and I caught them up on what was happening in the Seattle chapter.

"Elaine is busy at the moment," someone told me. "Go with some of the brothers to a different location, and Elaine will meet with you there later."

"Right on, Comrades!" I said as we hopped into the car and drove away. The Party had houses all over East and West Oakland, and we drove 30 minutes to a cadre house in West Oakland. When we arrived, I stepped inside. Everything seemed normal until one of the brothers told me:

"You're under house arrest, Comrade, and will be kept here until Elaine comes later."

Stunned, I said nothing.

Outnumbered, it would be pointless to try to fight my way out of this, despite my martial arts training. Plus, I didn't want to fight with my own Comrades. So, I let them escort me into the basement to await Elaine's arrival. I had no idea why I was under house arrest, or what my fate would be. But it had to be serious for Elaine to summon me all the way from Seattle and put me under house arrest.

At the time, Elaine was leading the Party as Chairman, serving in Huey Newton's absence. Huey, who had been exiled in Cuba, was grappling with legal matters that would determine whether he could return to the United States. As head of the Central Committee, Elaine was in a very powerful position.

As I sat there alone wondering what could've prompted my arrest, I reflected on the past couple of weeks, recalling my conversation with Ericka and another sister in the party, Norma, who had come to Seattle to attend a nursing conference in Issaquah, Washington. When Norma had arrived, we picked her up at the airport and drove her to Issaquah. After the conference, she came back to Seattle and I took her on a tour of our headquarters to meet the Comrades.

Later, I took her home, where she met Dee Dee for the first time. Dee Dee was in the kitchen preparing meals for the cadre kids, which included our four children and two or three other Panther kids. This was not unusual, as Dee Dee was often required to look after the cadre kids while others were in the field. After the brief visit, I drove Norma to the airport.

"Why wasn't there any meat on those kids' plates?" she demanded.

"We don't feed our kids red meat," I said. "They eat chicken, fish, and ground turkey, and from time to time, Dee Dee simply fixes them a vegetarian meal."

She replied, "You cannot not feed those kids meat!"

"Red meat is a carcinogen," I explained. "It's unhealthy even for adults to eat."

"Those are the people's kids!" she snapped. "You can't feed them that way!"

"These are not the people's kids," I said. "These are my kids. Besides, the people don't feed my kids. We do, and we feed them healthy meals!" Many Black parents have learned unhealthy lifestyles and diets due to years of oppression and poverty. Dee Dee and I had made a commitment to provide healthier food choices to our kids as well as for the children in the breakfast programs.

Later that week, Ericka had called to ask me about my conversation with Norma, and I repeated what I had said to Norma, that we were not feeding red meat to not only our kids, but were also not feeding red meat to the kids in the breakfast program.

Now, as I sat there on the basement floor waiting for Elaine, my conversation with Ericka had seemed normal enough, no harsh words or yelling, as Ericka had a calm demeanor about her. But I wasn't sure, and so I just waited.

Then I recalled that conversation with Aaron about him getting mudholed, and realized that I might soon fall victim to the same fate. I scanned the basement for ways to escape. *If only there was a window, maybe I could jump.* But it was a finished basement with no visible windows. Of course, armed guards blocked the upstairs door. I was being treated like an enemy of the people over some damn bacon!

A few hours later, Elaine appeared with Larry Henson and Ericka Huggins. As they gathered their chairs in a semi-circle around me, as if holding court, I sat cross-legged on the floor, processing the sudden onslaught of charges they yelled at me.

"You disrespected a member of the Central Committee!" Larry accused.

"Disrespected who?" I shot back.

"Norma Amour," someone said. Apparently, Norma was a member of the Central Committee.

"Norma?" I responded with genuine amazement.

I had no idea that Norma was a member of the Central Committee. Even more to the point, I hadn't disrespected her. I had simply stated the fact that my and Dee Dee's children did not belong to the people, they were ours. She birthed them, and she was not a member of the Black Panther Party; she was my wife.

It was apparent that they were not going to hear my side of the story, so I just let them run their Kangaroo Court. I knew they had ulterior motives.

"You're being transferred to Central Headquarters," Larry said.

"I need to take care of a few things in Seattle," I said, thinking about my family and who would run the chapter, as I'd been doing for the last four years since getting out of prison. I knew that no one could step in to lead the chapter, but I needed to buy some time.

"I'll come back in two weeks and report for whatever assignment I'm given," I said.

They agreed and ended the meeting. When I arrived at Central, I ran into Norma. She looked at me with this almost sheepish, coy, guilty grin, as if she knew what I had just been involved in. She spoke to me, and I replied back to her obediently, and left it at that.

When I returned to Seattle, the Comrades were eager to hear what was going on.

"Is there a new order?" they asked. "Did they tell you about a new program? Do you have directions for our operation?"

I called a meeting to explain what had just transpired in Oakland.

"I'm being transferred to Oakland," I said, "but you know what that means. Before I get any new duty assignment, I'll have to face the wrath of the squad and get mudholed. Before I make a decision, I need to hear from you and what your thoughts are on how you think I should handle this."

Because I trusted and respected their opinions, I had always included them in decisions on anything of significance.

"I don't think you should go, Comrade," Ron said. "It would only put you in danger and disrupt everything that we've been working for."

"I need to think about it," I said, knowing that if I did not return to Central, we would most likely end up splitting away from the Black Panther Party. We would take over the programs and continue to run them separately without the support of

Central Headquarters and the Party. We would no longer have access to the Black Panther newspaper to educate the community. They were prepared to go that path, and they knew that we could successfully run the programs and community organizing without the aid of Central.

Ever since I had returned from prison, it had become clear that our past organizing had prepared us to run an independent organization/chapter. We had re-established the chapter as a viable force in the community, by starting new programs such as the pest control program, expanding the blood pressure screening and sickle cell anemia testing, and launching a prison tutoring program.

We had proven that we could operate on our own. But operating independently held a different meaning for me. Unlike the other chapter members, my time in the Party dated back to the founding of our organization. Unlike the newer members, I had molded my life around the single idea of revolution. I remained committed to Party principles and to my Comrades unto death, convictions that had been tested many times over, during police and FBI attacks, and my time served in prison.

My life was baptized in the blood of my fallen Comrades: Fred Hampton, Little Bobby, Bunchy, John, and many others, including Seattle Comrades, Butch Armstead, Sidney Miller, and Henry Boyer, who fought alongside me against the pigs, knowing we always had each other's backs.

Since joining the Party at age 17, I had been indoctrinated with our principles from other revolutionaries like Franz Fanon, and according to the Marxist theory of dialectical materialism: "Material conditions entail contradictions which seek resolution in new forms of social organizing. Meaning, one can be both part of the problem and the solution."

I had always aimed to be part of the solution, and now it seemed the best solution was serving my community with my

Comrades in Seattle. The Party was the only thing I ever knew. Consequently, leaving the Party had far different ramifications for me, personally, and what it would mean for my life going forward without being attached to the Panthers that had formed my life for the last eight years.

I had no intentions of moving my family to Oakland, whether I returned in two weeks or not. If I did return, it would be like abandoning my children and Dee Dee to fend for themselves. The decision weighed on me heavily. It would alter my life and that of my Comrades forever.

That night, I told Dee Dee what had gone down in Oakland.

"I'm not going to make this decision without your input," I told her. "You know how important you and the kids are to me, and how important my work is with the Party."

Dee Dee responded: "Elmer, you know I would never tear you away from the Party. While at the same time, our task in life is to make sure that our children have a solid foundation. So, if I need to, I would move to Oakland to keep our family together."

But we both knew that this would not be the case. We would be separated, just as Aaron and Donnie had been split. We talked about what it would mean for the children for me to be away from them. We also talked about my years of dedication to the Party and to the community, and that it should count for something. But what it came down to was bigger than me, us, or even the Black Panther Party. It was about what we had built in the community in Seattle and the opportunity we had in front of us to continue to make a difference.

The next morning, the office was bustling as usual. The summer youth employment programs were in full swing, and we had three teams of 10 youths preparing to go out into the field. After I checked on everything, it was time to call Elaine. Upon hearing her voice, I immediately advised her that I would not be returning to Oakland.

"I want to talk to The Servant," I said.

Agitated, she said, "Huey isn't in charge. You just get your ass down to Oakland!"

I replied calmly, "Me and the 'rads are taking over the operation of the Seattle chapter and running the survival programs on our own."

Before I could finish, she started screaming, "You motherfucker!" and hung up. Phoning back a few minutes later, she warned, "Motherfucker, I'm coming up there!"

"Well, then, come on!"

CHAPTER 36

The Standoff - Elaine Arrives in Seattle

Earlier that spring, as we were preparing for our summer programs, our fourth child was born. The third of three daughters, she came into the world as Angola was achieving its liberation. So, we named her Angola Chimurenga. Chimurenga translates to "liberation" in Angola's language, so her name meant "Angola's liberation."

Ironically, that's what was about to happen to the Seattle chapter.

After I told Elaine to come to Seattle, we knew that she would eventually come, but we didn't know when, so I prepared the cadre for what would eventually happen.

Elaine would not travel without bodyguards, known as "the Squad." This elite group that had been assembled by Huey was tasked with keeping out-of-line Panthers in check, while enforcing some of his strategies to disempower drug dealers. Every member of the Squad was highly trained in martial arts and weaponry, and was not to be fucked with.

"Elaine is coming to Seattle on Saturday," Aaron told me by phone, as he had been serving as one of Elaine's personal bodyguards. "I'll be with her." I wondered which members of the Squad would be coming.

On Saturday, we felt ready for their arrival, because we had been going over plans. We had just returned to the office following a normal day of selling papers in the field, when the call came.

"We're here," Aaron said.

"'We,' who?" I asked.

"Elaine and me," he said.

"Who's with you?" I asked.

He didn't answer, but in the background, Elaine was talking to someone with an elevated tone and pace.

"Where are you?" I asked.

"We're at the airport," Aaron said.

"It doesn't sound like you're at the airport," I said.

"Well," Aaron added, "we're just coming over, so we'll be there soon."

I knew they were most likely armed. I also figured that the hotel was likely a staging area where they could make final plans, and because they couldn't bring weapons on a plane, the rest of their team must have traveled by car to bring weapons.

I immediately pulled the essential Comrades together: my brother Michael, Wayman, Morris, Joanne, Carol, and Ron.

"Elaine and others are coming," I said, "and they're probably armed."

We had been through this drill and now was the time for final preparation. I laid out a plan to defend ourselves, with an option to allow Elaine and her team to withdraw. I didn't want a gunfight with members of the Party, especially with my brother in harm's way. Nor did I want to endanger the lives of my Comrades. But we had to make a stand.

"You still have the option to leave," I said. "I won't hold you accountable."

They were committed and chose to stay.

Still, as I looked at each Comrade, I knew that only a few of them were mentally ready. Ron and Michael were the only two that I trusted in a firefight. Morris was a revolutionary theorist, as was Wayman, but they had never fought a battle in the trenches. Joanne was a solid Comrade, as was Carol, but they knew nothing about armed struggle, let alone facing down people with weapons.

Michael had been around the Party since he was 16, and had been there when we were under possible attack from the pigs; he knew how to defend himself. A disciplined Panther, he had done community organizing under the direction of one of our section leaders, Bobby White, and had good contacts in the community. He had recently worked with some of the young Comrades in weapons training, and I trusted his knowledge of weapons as he was a member of a local gun club in Issaquah, a rural suburb of Seattle. Ron was my most trusted lieutenant, and we had been in skirmishes before, so he was someone that I could depend on.

I sent Carol home to be with her daughter. I called Dee Dee and explained what was happening.

"Put the kids into bed and be prepared to defend the apartment in case there's overflow from whatever's about to happen," I told her. "I don't believe the Comrades from Central would come to our house, and I won't lead them there, but I want you to be ready."

I looked around at the Comrades, wondering, *Who should get which weapon?*

As we sat in the backroom office upstairs, I passed around a bottle of Tanqueray for those who needed or wanted a shot.

"Show no fear," I said. "I'll do the talking. Just stay ready."

I gave Michael the shotgun and stationed him in the back of the office, behind a swinging door near the lab that we used for sickle cell testing.

"Don't come out unless it's time for action," I told him.

Ron had his .9 millimeter in his shoulder holster and Joanne had a .45 in her purse. Morris also had a handgun, and I put my trusted .357 Magnum in the drawer of the desk where I would sit during the meeting. Upstairs was Wayman Earls, armed with an AR-15, the civilian version of the M16.

I had also placed a stack of my last five or six monthly reports on top of the desk. I had been required to submit them to Central Headquarters, to report our actions, including confirmation that we had taken red meat off the menu for the children's breakfast program. I wanted to establish that there should have been no surprise that we were not feeding kids meat, specifically my own, because I wouldn't feed children in the breakfast program anything that I wouldn't feed my kids. This was the bone of contention that had originally started with Norma challenging how Dee Dee was feeding our kids at the house.

When the team arrived at the office, it was Aaron, Elaine, Larry Henson, and Flores. Larry was on the Central Committee, but Flores was a gunman, and I knew it.

They came in, and we greeted everyone as typically we would: "Hello, Comrade. Power to the people!"

Larry said, "Why don't you show us the office?"

I knew he wanted to case the place to see how things were set up.

"Sure." I showed him the main room where the office was, the next room, which was the study room, the area where the food bank preparation was made, and then the back where the lab was.

Michael was positioned behind that door and I knew he was holding his breath, not making a peep, so that he wouldn't be detected.

When we returned to the foyer, Larry wanted to see the upstairs.

"There's nothing up there but a couple of exam rooms," I said. "Let's just start the meeting."

Larry got agitated and said, "He won't let me look around."

"Let's just sit down and meet," I insisted. "Are we going to do this or what?" I went to my spot behind the desk. Elaine sat in the chair at the back of the room, while Ron, Morris, and Joanne were strategically placed where they could observe Larry, Flores, and Aaron.

As the meeting started, I pointed to my weekly reports, which were stacked on the desk. I started explaining every activity, including the removal of red meat from the breakfast program diet.

"If those reports had been read," I said, "they would have known that was the case."

Larry again became agitated. "Are you saying I didn't read the reports? Are you saying that I was lying?"

Flores approached and put his hand on his weapon in his belt.

Shit was about to go down.

Aaron put his arm on Flores to stop him and said, "Let's not get excited."

Ron was prepared to draw down. Elaine was sitting in her chair, nervously striking a match, trying to light a cigarette.

"I don't want any gunplay," she said. "I don't want any gunplay."

At that moment, Wayman, who was positioned upstairs, nervously rattled his weapon.

Larry said, "Somebody's upstairs."

They knew they were surrounded and that we had our own weapons. No one dared to move, as the next movement would probably trigger a gun battle.

"This meeting is over," I said.

Elaine got up and Aaron ushered her out, while Larry and Flores backed out of the office. If they drew their weapons, we would draw ours. And if a gunfight erupted, they were outgunned and outnumbered.

Michael had already drawn down a bead on Larry Henson and was prepared to come out blasting with the shotgun. As they backed out of the door, Larry started screaming:

"Let me go get that motherfucker! Let me go get him! I want to kill that motherfucker!"

We had already hit the floor, turned out the lights, and drawn our weapons. If he had come back in the door, he would have been blown back out into the street. But they pulled Larry back and got into their cars and sped away.

Checkmate.

CHAPTER 37

On Our Own

The next day, the shock of no longer being a member of the Black Panther Party began to set in. Since that spring day in April of 1968, at Little Bobby's funeral, my whole life had been dedicated to the Party and the people.

It seemed like a lifetime: building close-knit relationships with my Comrades; living and fighting as one; enduring the deaths of so many; persevering under the constant threat of assassination; and staring death in the face—together. It was a loss too deep to comprehend at the moment.

For the immediate future, it felt like we were standing alone, but I knew the community would continue to support us. I didn't know what the coming days and weeks would hold, except that we knew we were still revolutionaries and still very much in the struggle. I decided not to make any broad announcement to the rest of the group or the community, but to wait and see how things would begin to shape up.

For my Comrades, the meaning of this abrupt break with Central would have a different meaning. They were relatively new to the struggle, having come to the Party after those years of confrontations and standoffs with the pigs. They hadn't experienced living in fortified cadre offices, wearing uniforms, mourning the deaths of Comrades, or covering each other's backs.

The standoff with Elaine was something they had never experienced: the prospect of an armed confrontation. I wondered whether it was wrong to put them in that situation, even though they had decided to take a stand with me. I chose not to second guess myself and stand strong with my decision.

The most important thing was to keep our position in the community strong. We would continue the programs as if nothing had happened, by serving the community, body and soul. Our main focus was to make sure that there would be no retaliation and for us to stay on guard. We didn't know if the Squad or some individual would strike back at the rebuff that we had handed Elaine and her team. So, we made a commitment to guard each other's backs and to continue operations as before.

We maintained our programs, with the only difference being that we no longer had the Black Panther newspaper to sell when we went out to raise funds, or to use as a method of educating the community. When we showed up on the UW campus and the street corners where people were used to seeing us, we simply continued collecting donations in large cans labeled, "The Children's Free Breakfast Program."

This was not unlike what we had normally done anyway. Most of our contributions, particularly on campus, came from students who wanted to support the Children's Free Breakfast Program. Sometimes people wouldn't even take a paper, but would instead simply put money in the can. Now it was like they didn't have to bother with taking a paper, but just simply make their donation. In fact, contributions increased. On a typical morning on campus, our four-person team easily collected $1,000 in donations.

Huey had always emphasized the importance of the Panther paper as a tool to educate the community and stimulate revolution.

Now, we had to improvise. We had built relationships with several Black publications in the community, the most important of which was the *Medium*. Connie continued her support for the programs, just as she had always done, and we relied on her backing us. I built on that relationship and collaborated with her to continue getting important issues in front of the community.

The next few weeks were challenging. Two of the Comrades who were with us at the standoff, Morris and Wayman, had gotten cold feet and began to doubt whether we had made the right move. One afternoon, they wanted to confront me, but erroneously went to my parents' house looking for me. When my mother told me that they had come to her house, I was furious. Not because they were looking for me to question the standoff, but for the fact that they had gone to my parents' house and confronted my mother.

Ron and I were at the Panther office when Morris and Wayman showed up. My instincts to protect my family kicked in.

I punched Morris squarely in the face as he walked in the door.

He reeled back, then came towards me as if to continue the fight, but he was woofing and wasn't throwing any blows.

"Never go near any member of my family again," I threatened, "or I'll blow your ass away!"

Days later, Wayman and Morris drove to Central Headquarters, where they begged for forgiveness. They tried hanging around Central for a while, but no one trusted them. Yet they were still given the opportunity to come to Seattle to try to re-establish themselves and sell the Panther paper.

They made the mistake of trying to bad-mouth me, Ron, and other Comrades, but nobody on the street was buying it. They would soon leave town again for Central. They lasted only a few months there before leaving the Party altogether.

We continued building on our coalitions. Eddie Rye was head of the Central Area Metropolitan Program, CAMP. A popular, flamboyant community leader, he was always organizing in the community. We worked with him, and later, Larry Gossett, to hold Saturday Pancake Breakfasts at the center to raise funds. Donnie had left the Party months earlier, and I started reconnecting with her and my nephew, Aaron Patrice, Aaron's son. She was working at CAMP and we became close again.

In the meantime, Ron and I began to reorganize the operation. We had a cadre of young Comrades who were ready and willing to continue the programs of the Seattle Black Panther Party, despite the fact that we did not have that official title. I set a plan in motion to build on the programs that we had already established, while growing new ones.

One of the most critical elements of the plan consisted of three foundations: the rebuilding of the Sidney Miller Free Medical Clinic; the establishment of a community school; and the development of a community control of police plan that could be adopted and made operational.

To broaden our operation, it was important for us to establish ourselves as a non-profit 501(c)(3). We had already been exploring this prior to the breakaway and now pursued these efforts in earnest. We would have to organize a board of directors and make sure that we had the financial capability to do all the necessary reporting to keep ourselves out of trouble. Organizing the board of directors was actually quite easy. As Black Panther Party members, we had been highly visible in the Black community, and since we had won the "Unsung Hero Award" earlier that year, we had established some measure of increased respectability.

We met with progressive leaders across the city. I started with folks with whom I already had a relationship, as well as those who were doing good work organizing in the community. They included Dr. Bob Flennaugh, a Black dentist who was well-respected in the community, as well as the local church institutions; he would later become the first president of our board of directors, and Vivian Caver, a local community leader.

I also reached out to Dorothy Hollingsworth, the first Black woman elected to the Seattle school board, who was well respected throughout the district. She was also the mother of a young man with whom I had gone to school, Raft Hollingsworth.

I had another meeting with Dr. Michael Washington, who was the lead dentist at the Odessa Brown Children's Clinic and had worked on my children's teeth. These, and others, were examples of established and respected Black leaders within the community, all of whom had agreed to serve on the board of directors for the newly formed Sidney Miller Community Service Center.

Naming the center for our fallen Comrade maintained our recognition as the Black Panther Party. This was the foundation from which we operated, but make no mistake, the community still knew us as the Seattle Black Panther Party. No separation or distinction ever occurred in their minds. While we had broken away from Central Headquarters, we were still, in essence, revolutionaries and Party members on our own turf. Many people still saw us as the Vanguard, defenders of the community. We had never fully shifted the community's view of us as a Defense Force, a reputation that began in those early days when a mother called Aaron and asked us to go to Rainier Beach to defend her kids.

Chairman Bobby had instructed us to not respond to every such request, but it had been difficult. Even now, those requests still came. When sisters called us because their husbands or boyfriends were beating or abusing them, we paid the dudes a visit. By the time we left, they understood they needed to keep their hands off or suffer the consequences.

A well-known and respected member of the community, Milly Russell, had been working at the University of Washington

School of Medicine to recruit Black medical students and other minority students who were interested in the medical field. She was a good friend and a staunch supporter of the Party. One afternoon, she called to say that her 19-year-old daughter, Pat—who was pregnant—was being abused and threatened by her boyfriend.

"You call Elmer," Milly told her.

Pat Russell, now dean at City University of Seattle, vividly remembers that time.

"I was involved in a horrible relationship," she said during an interview for this book. "The police weren't doing anything to protect me. It was 1976, and I was a young, Black, single mother. They couldn't have cared less. I had actually taken out a restraining order, but thought nobody would do anything about this. In fact, I was in the municipal building and was in the elevator with the officer who had responded the night before, after my boyfriend had beaten me."

Pat said the officer asked her, "Are you going to go through with it?"

And she said, "No."

With a straight face, the cop said, "Then we'll have him on murder."

Pat realized the police would leave her for dead.

"And I thought, 'Okay, end of talking with you people,'" Pat recalled.

The first time she called me, she was dazed and beaten. I took her to the hospital.

Then, another time, as she was trying to escape her abuser, he attacked again.

"He hit me in my stomach," Pat said, "and shoved me in the car. So, I called Elmer."

When I got the call, I assured her, "We're coming. You tell that nigga, if he puts his hands on you, that he's gonna come through us."

Ron and I arrived with our .9 mm and .45. If we had to pistol whip him, we were ready to make the point that, "You will never hit her again!"

Pat was terrified. "This person I was involved with was there. I was really frightened at that moment, because Elmer came in and said, 'Hi,' and sat down. I remember being petrified. If they left before he did, I was in physical danger. But they didn't leave. They protected me. [My abuser] sat there and got a real attitude. He didn't say a word. He got up and left. He was my boyfriend, the father of my daughter."

Ron and I camped out in Pat's apartment over several days, armed and waiting for the dude to show up. But he must have gotten the message and never came back, nor did he ever bother her again. The Party had long established the fact that we would defend sisters against abuse, and this legacy would not go away.

Pat was amazed. "No police would do that. Nobody was going to sit there to make sure I wouldn't be beat to death. That's where it was going. Elmer was fearless. The guy left and didn't come back. Elmer spent the night with me, platonically, to make sure that I was okay."

Pat remembered how my Comrades and I were a comforting presence in the community.

"He was always there," she recalled. "Always caring, the Panthers were always there. They were the heart and soul of the Central District. They took care us. They fed the community. They made sure we were medically taken care of. There was no other place to go. Going to the police was stupid. You would end up a murder victim or you'd get arrested."

We kept in touch with Pat to make sure she was okay.

"When I was in the hospital having the baby," Pat said, "the Panthers showed up. Sometimes I didn't have to call; they checked on me. And they brought a toy for the baby."

Pat recalled that we helped her over a period of several years.

Years later, when she was director of an adult basic education program, she called on my help once again.

"I was getting bombarded with racism," she said. "I knew Elmer was doing diversity training. I called him. I introduced him to board members. He ended up on their all-white board of directors, where as a member, he could make a difference to stop the kind of racism I was experiencing."

As Black Panther Party leaders in the community, many people believed we were going above and beyond the call of duty. In fact, Chairman Bobby told us, "You can't respond to everything. We have a revolution to organize!"

We had to figure out where to intervene and how to redirect people to get the help they needed. The problem was, the institutions that were supposed to help and protect people were often the problem. So, we took it upon ourselves to help as many people as possible. But we couldn't be all things to all people, all the time, and this tugged heavily on us.

For example, when a Black mother kept calling and saying that her kids were getting beaten up at Rainier Beach High School, and the principal was doing nothing to stop the violence, Aaron said we could not help. But she kept calling, and we paid the principal a visit.

"Either you stop this," we told him, "or we will."

The beatings stopped and the woman's teenagers were finally safe.

Another time, a woman called and said her landlord had taken the door off her apartment because he wanted to kick her out. We went over and reattached the door. We weren't going to leave a woman with babies in an apartment with no door.

Similarly, in 1968, one of Seattle's most respected gospel singers, Pat Wright, was attempting to purchase her home, but the racist realtor refused to sell to her. She asked us to step in. We visited the realtor, who was eventually run out of the neighborhood, because she was a racist and part of the illegal redlining scheme. Pat was delighted to purchase the house across the street from our parents' home.

She would later create the Total Experience Gospel Choir, which became renowned across the country. During a series of concerts in 1977, a choir member was receiving suggestive notes from an anonymous person and feared she was being followed. So, Pat asked us to travel with the choir for a brief time to ensure her safety. We just couldn't escape the fact that people wanted us to be their security. We didn't mind, because Pat was a community institution and we would do anything to protect her and the choir.

Our legacy as protectors was as strong as ever as we embarked, in 1977, on this new phase of work to protect and empower the Black community.

Providing quality healthcare to our people remained a top priority. And we did that by developing the foundation for the new Sidney Miller Free Medical Clinic, which was a huge undertaking that we were prepared to move on. I had put forth the idea that we needed a more well-rounded clinic, thus the idea was to build a Family Medical Center that would offer a full range of services for families. Previously, the clinic offered only limited services, such as the original "Well-Baby Clinic."

First, we needed a building that we owned and could not be evicted from. We had already hired an attorney, Bob Betts, to finalize our paperwork for the 501(c)(3) and to represent the organization in any legal matters pertaining to our status as a non-profit. Bob introduced me to a millionaire, Jim Hemmingway. Jim owned several properties across the city and was retired, but still very involved in personal philanthropic projects. He would spend four or five months in the Seattle area, and the rest of the year on his yacht, traveling the world. When Bob brought this guy up, I told him, "That's just the kind of person we're looking for," and asked him to arrange the meeting.

Jim was a no-nonsense, casual kind of guy, who was very laid-back. He had heard about the Black Panther Party programs and supported our mission to provide quality healthcare to the Black community. We began meeting to discuss one of his buildings located in the CD that ironically was a block from the original storefront Black Panther office on 34th Avenue. It was a grocery store when we were growing up, next to a gas station on 34th and Pike Street. It had been unused, except for a small portion upstairs that was rented to the first vestiges of cable TV called Viacom, which would become Comcast years later.

The deal that Jim put together would involve us purchasing the building, with him making the down payment, and he set it at a price where we could afford the payments with no stress. Since Viacom had rented from Jim, we would become their landlords. I still chuckle about that to this day, to think that we were once Comcast's landlord. The deal included them paying their rent directly to Jim's company; the amount was the bulk of the portion of our mortgage payment, so we had to pay only one dollar a month for the building payment. We all thought that was a pretty sweet deal; we had a big building that was going to house the new medical center, and our mortgage was a dollar a month.

Over the next couple of years, we planned the structure for the new clinic. This included forming a new coalition with four other free clinics in the area: the Aradia Women's Clinic; Sea Mar clinic, which served the Latino/Chicano community; the International District, or ID, Clinic, serving the Asian community; and Country Doctor Clinic, serving low-income whites. Together we formed the Community Healthcare Service Network, and our first order of business was to appoint someone to establish the framework for us to collectively apply for a National Healthcare Service Grant, the first of its kind in the nation.

These clinics had been organized by Dr. John Green, including the original Seattle BPP clinic named after Sidney Miller, so we all had Dr. Green in common. This allowed us to forge a tight relationship and build a bond that would enable our new clinic to come alive again.

One key individual working with me on this project was Carolyn Downs. Carolyn was a community worker and Panther who worked in every aspect of our operation. During the transition period when the original Comrades were transferred from Seattle to Oakland to establish the "Base of Operations," Carolyn was among the community workers left in Seattle to continue working in the survival programs. She cooked at the various breakfast program sites, ran the Summer Liberation Schools, cooked in the free feeding programs, and helped organize bags of groceries for the free food giveaways. She was an integral part of our operation.

Now, we faced many obstacles for the development of this new clinic, so we set a target date for 1978 or 1979.

Our food program expanded because the need for food in the community had grown as a result of the mini recession in the mid-1970s, following the mess that Richard Nixon had left behind and the ensuing gas price meltdown. Many people were left without basic sustenance to feed their families.

To help them, we expanded our network for collecting food. Charlie's Neighborhood Grocery across the street from the office was a prime source, connecting us to a variety of potential suppliers. The owner introduced us to the dairy farmer who supplied the store with eggs. We met with the farmer, and as a result, he donated a couple hundred dozen eggs every week.

He also turned us on to the produce brokers who operated on the Seattle waterfront, where produce was brought in from local growers across the state. Thankfully, they gave us boxes of fresh produce that included all sorts of vegetables (lettuce, tomatoes, etc.) that we could put in our grocery bags.

We had a long-standing relationship with Gays Bakery. As kids, Aaron, Michael, and I used to go there and see Rosa, a clerk in the Gays Bakery Variety Store, to get donuts for a nickel a piece. Then, they donated to the Panthers' breakfast program. Now, they gave us hundreds of loaves of bread every week that we used both for the breakfast programs and the free food bank.

We had also established a connection with the local allied grocers, who donated canned foods.

So, each week, we gave away several hundred bags of groceries to the community, just as we had done while operating as the Party, only now in an expanded operation. We continued to enjoy support from community members who volunteered. And we attracted an eclectic group of colorful individuals who helped with the food program.

We had been organizing community dinners on special occasions, Thanksgiving, spring dinners, and summer BBQs for the past several years. Carol had always worked with the community cooks who volunteered. One was Pearlie, who was from down South and was always available to do some down-home cooking. She made the best pie and cakes, including a buttermilk pie like the one my Aunt Doris used to make, and she made the first 7-Up cake that I ever tasted. Another sister was an older woman by the name of Lulabelle Parker. Lulabelle was from Arkansas and carried a .38 pistol in her purse. She was a fiery woman, especially having survived the South, and was not to be messed with.

An older gentleman, Mr. Jones, sometimes acted like he was in charge when he came in to organize the grocery bags for the food program, and often bumped heads with Lulabelle. It was a challenge to keep them separated and stop Lulabelle from shooting him.

I got to know each of them and would sometimes drive

Lulabelle home after the food program was finished. She'd asked me in to have a meal. How could I refuse, knowing that she had that good southern cooking? She used to always put a plate in the oven to warm it up before she put the food on it; this was an old southern tradition that I later adopted in my own meal preparation.

Another lady, who was nearly 100 years old, was Mrs. Barnes. A proud woman, she walked up to the office with her cane to get her bag of food.

"Mrs. Barnes, you don't need to come to the office," we told her. "We'll bring the food to you."

This idea inspired us to establish a food delivery service to several elderly residents across the CD.

These relationships were what made serving the community all the more rewarding. These were the faces of the people for whom we had sacrificed our lives and now served, body and soul. Life as a Panther went on. We just didn't have the official title.

We established a prison tutoring program utilizing 50 or more students from the University of Washington, who went inside the prison at Monroe to provide tutoring so that the inmates could obtain a GED upon their release. Since the prisons weren't doing rehabilitation, we were doing it instead.

One of our breakfast programs was at the Yesler Terrace housing projects, where Ron lived. Since he had taken charge of that site and was the primary resource in that community, he had gotten to know the people well. He was approached by some sisters who had complained about the rats and the roaches in the apartments. He brought that concern to me in our weekly meetings, and we discussed what to do.

After he laid out the problem—the analysis, as we used to call it—we agreed that we needed to investigate the proper way to exterminate roaches. We realized that Raid was not the way to go, because the roaches would drink that stuff up like milk.

We went to a local extermination company and asked them about using their product. They were using a commercial roach poison called Pyrethrin, which was very dangerous if not used properly. They also had a program where they would train their employees how to use the material safely.

I turned to Ron and said, "Comrade, you're going to school." We had been talking about starting a free pest control program, but had not discussed it in detail. Now we were about to put theory into action, but we had to make sure that we knew what we were doing.

Yesler Terrace would be our testing ground, as long as we did it with respect to the environment and the people who lived there, which was most important. On the first go-around, Ron sprayed one of the apartments that the sisters had complained about, and while we killed most of the roaches, many of them escaped and ran to the apartment next door.

The Yesler Terrace housing project had been built during World War II to house military staff, like most of the housing projects in Seattle. They were a complicated maze and network of units which were attached in groupings, so we had a daunting task. Ron approached the Seattle Housing Authority representative who was in charge of Yesler Terrace and told them that we wanted to rid the housing project of roaches through our free pest control program. We got their blessing to move forward and coordinated with them to craft a plan to attack the problem across the whole complex in an organized fashion.

We would go from unit to unit, moving families out temporarily for a day, and then going on to the next unit of apartments, one by one. This was the systematic approach that Ron had organized to basically exterminate roaches from all of Yesler Terrace. When the dust settled, we had successfully launched our free pest control program and word spread throughout the community.

We began to get requests from individual homeowners in

the CD. These included a large house on 31st Avenue South. We told the homeowners that we needed to examine the house to set up our strategy. When we arrived, we were shocked that the house was three stories with multiple bedrooms, almost the size of a small mansion. Housing had become cheap in the CD as a result of the white flight that had occurred back in the late 1950s and early 1960s, and this was one of the large homes that a Black family was able to purchase.

After mapping out our strategy, we put on our hazmat suits and donned our masks, then began the process of moving the roaches into a central area. Ron started by squirting a shot of Pyrethrin through a long, narrow hose attached to the can into the cracks along the baseboard and on the ceiling. It was like World War III had broken out, as thousands of roaches scurried from underneath the walls and behind the refrigerator. We realized we were in a battle, as the house was so infected, that we would spend hours in there killing roaches. This would become one of our most significant new programs that the community would benefit from.

Meanwhile, we had attracted new Comrades to our ranks, including Damita Edwards and longtime Comrade Marylin Jackson. Marylin had come into contact with the Party back in '68, but was too young to actually join. She used to hang around Willie Brazier, but we had to make sure that we left her out of operations because of her age. She resurfaced in '72, around the time that I had gotten out of prison, and was a longtime friend and respected member of the Party.

I met Marilyn while I was speaking at the predominantly white Newport High School in Bellevue. I was quoting the *Red Book* and Chairman Mao, inspiring Damita to join our ranks as a community worker. She and her friends were a rowdy but hard-working bunch, serving in many of the programs, including the bussing to prisons program. Damita became one of the tutors at Monroe prison, where the inmates gave her the distinction as an "honorary convict," which I'm sure her parents would not have appreciated if they had found out.

Another young sister who became a dedicated Comrade was Rene "Pookie" Chambliss, the niece of Chris Chambliss, a well-known baseball player for the New York Yankees, the Seattle Mariners, and other teams. She was another rebel who marched to her own drum beat and was a hard-working member of the crew. She loved riding motorcycles, and tragically, was killed on her way home one evening while riding her new cycle. It was hard on the Comrades, and a reminder of how death was ever present, even now, in our new reality.

We expanded our Summer Youth Employment Program. Sponsored by the city of Seattle, the program placed up to 10 high school students in summer jobs with organizations that gave them job experience.

Prior to this, we had enabled young people to work on our sickle cell anemia testing and blood pressure screening program. By adding two more groups, we became the only organization in the city that had three different Summer Youth Employment Programs running at the same time.

One was an environmental cleanup project which was an offshoot of the free pest control program. Because we couldn't have the young people handling poison, we put them to work eliminating vacant lots that were covered with blackberry bushes, which were breeding grounds for rats. They removed garbage and debris, discarded furniture, tires, and sticker bushes, helping to rid the neighborhoods of dangerous rats.

The third group of students served as assistants in the Summer Liberation School, which we expanded to a broader summer school program. This alternative school was patterned after the Party's "Oakland Community Learning Center" that we had been planning for years, but had been rebuffed by Central Headquarters.

Now, we renamed it the Summer Youth Institute, and rather than hire high school students, we engaged University of Washington students who were pursuing education as a career. The department director who administered the Summer Youth Employment Program was Don Dudley, the original owner of the Black radio station, KYAC. He was a good friend and staunch supporter, so we worked with him to build a different structure into our summer youth program; we wanted to hire UW students at a higher salary than high school students and appoint one of them to serve as the director of the summer institute.

We also collaborated with him to bring in local sports celebrities to hold clinics for the students throughout the summer. One of those was Slick Watts, the starting guard for the Seattle SuperSonics, which had recently won Seattle's first world title. This successful collaboration laid the foundation for our school.

As we expanded the free transportation to prisons program, we needed a reliable bus. Using funds collected from our efforts in the field, we purchased an 18-passenger van, which could take larger numbers of people to visit their loved ones who were locked up in the state's five prisons. When the word got into the community that we were transporting loved ones to the women's prison at Purdy, and since very few men went to visit the sisters, we drove busloads of their children to the prison.

One of the new riders to Purdy was a little girl, about two or three years old. Her mother had gotten in trouble with the law and no one could bring her baby to her, so we did it. I would pick her up from her grandmother's house and have one of the older kids hold her while I drove a van filled with 18 to 20 kids up to visit their mothers twice a month.

These were the things that we continued to do in service to the people who needed us. The people only knew us as the Panther Party, so we continued to operate as such, without claiming that we were Black Panthers, only going on our reputation in the community.

Once we secured the National Healthcare Service Grant from the government, we moved forward with our plans to reopen our Medical Clinic. The process included hiring Dr. Colin Romero as our lead physician, a physician's assistant, and other support staff to run the clinic. And we hired Joyce Redmond, the former co-captain of the Panther women, to be our bookkeeper. They would be vital in helping us lay out the clinic's design, put up walls, paint, add furniture, and basically set the whole operation in motion.

Along the way, in 1978, Carolyn Downs was diagnosed with cervical cancer, and would eventually succumb to the disease shortly before the clinic was scheduled to open. I petitioned the board of directors to change the name from Sidney Miller, the name of the original clinic in remembrance of our fallen Comrade, to Carolyn Downs. In 1979, the Carolyn Downs Family Medical Center was born and would eventually become the only original Black Panther Clinic in operation 50-plus years after it originally opened in 1970.

Me with my brother Aaron Dixon, author of the 2012 book, "My People Are Rising: Memoir of a Black Panther Party Captain."

Doing business as a Diversity, Equity and Inclusion consultant and president of Executive Diversity Services. Here I'm outside PepsiCo's headquarters downtown Chicago.

Speaking about my life as a revolutionary and diversity consultant at JAMK University of Applied Sciences in Jyväskylä, Finland.

Teaching a class about diversity at JAMK University of Applied Sciences in Jyväskylä, Finland.

With Rosa Parks. Dee Dee is on the left.

My brother Aaron's son Aaron Patrice on the left, with my son Merrill.

Enjoying a pool party at our Seattle home in 2005. From left, our daughters: Samora, Frelima, Genise and Angola. Seated beside me is Dee Dee, whose youthful looks often made her mistaken for one of the kids.

With Ericka Huggins at the unveiling of the Huey P. Newton bust at a park in Oakland, California, in 2021.

A nice moment with James Brown during our 30-year friendship. That's Aaron on the left.

My original Panther weapon—an M1 carbine—on display in the Northwest African American Museum in Seattle for the Black Panther Party's 50th anniversary. The FBI broke into my apartment and they claimed it was an automatic weapon. They confiscated it to conduct a test fire that showed it was not an automatic and I picked it up.

Delivering a TEDx Talk at the University of Tulsa in 2023 about my life as a revolutionary who became a global diversity consultant.

I started competitive bodybuilding at age 40. This photo was taken at a competition around 2003 or 2004 when I was 53 or 54. Healthy eating and fitness remain a top priority for me and my family.

Me in 2021 serving breakfast at the People's Free Breakfast Program, which is run weekly by young people and former Panthers at the BPP 55th Anniversary in Defermary Park, Bobby Hutton Park, in Oakland, California.

Me with Heidi, a former student at JAMK, and George Simons, my training partner in Finland and at universities in France. We have worked together at several SEITAR Congresses across Europe. He's an expat living in Mandelieu-la-Napoule next to Cannes, France.

In Belgium at a SIETAR Europa dinner in 2019. Across from me is Steve Crawford, who brings me to Finland every year.

A fun moment after speaking to a community organization in Jyväskylä, Finland.

With former police sergeant and diversity advocate David Walsh in Dublin, Ireland in 2022.

With me are City of Berkeley, CA, Training Manager Wilhelmina Parker and Senior EDS Consultant Santalynda Marrero. The former BPP Central Headquarters was just blocks away on Shattuck.

In Paris, France, with a collective of Black women expats who invited me to talk about the Black Panther Party. In front of me is a longtime friend, Kathleen Demaron.

My beautiful wife of 50+ years.

With my wife Dee Dee in Hong Kong.

I was nominated for the prestigious Gold Medal of Honorary Patronage, given by the oldest student organization in the world, "The Udon," at Trinity College in Dublin, Ireland. I accepted on behalf of our fallen comrades and all members of the BPP. Past recipients include Desmond Tutu, Ruth Bader Ginsberg, Whoopi Goldberg, and many others.

In 1968, I dispatched a group of Panthers to protect our lawyer, Mike Rosen, when a rally at Garfield High School following the arrest of Aaron and Curtis erupted into a riot. Mike and I reconnected many years later. From left: my brother Michael Dixon, my brother Aaron Dixon, Mike Rosen's wife, me, and Mike Rosen.

CHAPTER 38

Afterlife - Dawn of A New Day

By late 1981, the operations began to wind down. Linda Richardson, a longtime Panther, introduced me to her brother, Cliff, who told me about a business concept called AMWAY. I'd never heard of it, but decided to take a look. It was based on getting other people involved in building a business that could earn them income while generating income for yourself.

This was a critical shift for my mindset and my workstyle. For the last 12 years, I had only known the life of a Panther, committed to struggle, dedicating all my time to the Party, and then to running our newly formed non-profit organization, the Sidney Miller Community Service Center.

It never dawned on me to take a salary as the executive director, because as Panthers, we didn't expect to be paid. Dee Dee had already enrolled in a local job development organization, S.O.I.C., to learn a new job skill that enabled her to land a position at Virginia Mason Medical Center. She was the wage-earner, while I contributed $1,000 per month, which was a stipend that I gave myself for running the community service center.

We had a bunch of kids at home, and I needed some greater means of supporting them, so Dee Dee and I were open to hearing Cliff Richardson discuss this opportunity.

I took to the AMWAY business opportunity and loved the idea of helping people start their own businesses as a way to rise out of poverty. Fortunately, this this would allow me to build some financial security for my family.

We had some initial success and invited Ron to join, but as we soon found out, many of the organization's leaders had right wing politics and a political agenda. And any success was based on being able to inspire others to dream of riches, something contrary to revolutionary philosophy and damn-near impossible for the people I knew. We were community organizers, not wealth-builders, so it was a difficult transition to attempt, even if we put our own spin on it to build community.

One benefit for me personally was being exposed to different books than I had been reading. Books by individuals who talked about positive thinking and imagining and dreaming about what it was you wanted out of life and that was a good thing for people who had been oppressed for most of their lives.

I also started reading books like *The Power of Positive Thinking* by Norman Vincent Peale and *Think and Grow Rich* by Napoleon Hill.

One book that I particularly related to was *The Magic of Believing* by Claude M. Bristol, a World War I veteran whose poverty inspired him to research and write about the power of believing. Bristol's writings reminded me of what Stokely had said all those years ago in '67 at Garfield, stating that the reason Black people didn't have freedom was because they didn't love themselves.

Bristol's book was all about self-belief. I thought of the youth we had been targeting for our school and how it applied to them becoming leaders of the future. As Panthers, we always believed that we could make a difference and dreamed of revolutionary change for the people. We had faced insurmountable odds in challenging the biggest bully in history, the U.S. government, standing up to our oppressors and demanding freedom by any means necessary. The learnings from these books only reinforced what I had always known: that it was important to believe in myself and believe in my abilities.

But I also knew I didn't want to be a part of the 40/40 Club; working 40 hours a week for 40 years, then retiring with a gold watch and riding off into the sunset to die. That was literally what happened to my dad. He died at 60 years old and was never able to enjoy the fruits of his labor for so many years of work.

For me, now, I needed to start somewhere. I had no real vision of where my life was headed, but I didn't want to follow the mediocrity of what would be considered a normal life. Our lives as Panthers were anything but normal, and I knew that much greater opportunities than a 40/40 lifestyle waited for me to apply my skills to help people and support my family all at once.

I started applying for positions, building my resume from my experience running the Community Center for the past six years. My objective was to first secure, then find a path to freedom from the nine-to-five routine. I just didn't know how it would play out, so I just imagined it happening. I landed a position as branch director of the Al Davies Boys and Girls Club, a perfect position for me, as I had always loved working with the youth in the breakfast program and the Summer Liberation School.

Al Davies had originally been the Downtown Tacoma Boys Club, formed in the 1940s by white businessmen who needed a place for their male kids to hang out. Built in the heart of downtown Tacoma, long before the migration of Blacks from the South, the wealthy lumber barons had no idea that when they established endowments for the club, that Black people's kids would be the beneficiaries of their gifts. By the time the investments matured, the center of the city was the heart of the Black community in Tacoma, known as the "Hill Top."

By the time I had got to Al Davies, one of the capital funds had already matured and they had built a new club. I also learned that other funds had been established; one for capital improvement, and one for ongoing operations. They had even built a camp at the foot of Mount Rainier in the 1950s that had been unused for years. Not only was the camp going unused, but it had been neglected and in need of repair. The operating funds were being diverted to the other clubs in the area as a security blanket to cover budget shortfalls. It was clear that I needed to bring those funds back to the club it was intended for, so I set out to do so.

But it wasn't easy; the executive director, Jim Hatch tried to block me every step of the way.

When I asked for $13,000 for new football uniforms, Jim said he would oppose my request during the next board meeting. So, I invited the parents to testify in the board meeting, by bringing in a couple of kids to illustrate that they were using wrong-sized uniforms.

After Jim made his statement to oppose funding new uniforms, a young, white businessman on my board leaned back in his chair, puffed on his cigar, and said:

"Hell, I like football!"

His declaration had a domino effect around the room. Everybody voted to give the money to the football team. That began a series of changes when the executive director opposed my proposals to get the money back into the Boys and Girls Club, but I always won. As a result, I got approval to spend $10,000 to $15,000 for new wrestling mats for the wrestling team. And for the photography club, we cleaned up a dark room that wasn't being used, we bought cameras so the kids could learn photography skills. We also purchased video cameras for recording events. When we put on an elaborate talent contest in which the neighborhood kids could showcase their talents, they competed for a prize.

I also set in motion a plan to recapture the summer camp with the goal of giving more inner-city youth the chance to experience nature and the outdoors. It was exciting that these programs were benefitting Black kids who otherwise had few, if any, opportunities to learn new skills and enjoy recreation in a safe and nurturing environment.

When I proposed returning the boxing club to our facility, Jim was on a mission to stop me. The Tacoma Boxing Club had a rich history of creating Black Olympians. At the 1972 Olympics, Sugar Ray Seales won a gold medal; in the 1976 Olympics, Leo Randolph won gold; and in 1980, Johnny "Bump City" Bumpus made the Olympic team. They were all boxers from Tacoma. The Tacoma Boxing Club had been training at Al Davies as its home, but someone made the decision to remove them from the club.

The boxing club was critical to the Black community and its identity, because of the recognition it brought as a model for success to young people from the Hill Top. Sugar Ray Seales and Leo Randolph were heroes and fixtures in the community. Relocating the boxing club to Al Davies became my top priority, and it would require all of the community organizing skills I had learned in the Party to get it done.

But when I proposed that we restart the boxing club to Jim, it became apparent that he was either a closet racist or was just ignorant to the importance of successful role models to Black kids. His response to the idea was to say:

"We're not trying to make kids into professionals."

I responded, "If we're not trying to teach kids how to be professionals, then what are we trying to teach them? To be mediocre with no goals in life?" I cast a sharp look and declared, "I'll see you on the boardroom floor."

At the next board meeting, I brought in members of the community, former boxers, including Leo Randolph, and the boxing coach, "Sarge," who was an active member of the U.S. Boxing coaching staff.

Jim didn't have a chance. The board unanimously approved the reinstatement of the boxing club back into Al Davies.

By the time I was finished disrupting their plans, we had re-outfitted our football teams in proper gear (three teams had been using the same equipment), started a wrestling team, and organized a photography club, complete with cameras and video equipment.

I knew from that point on that Jim was probably going to find a way to get rid of me, but I decided that my performance would never be the reason.

Every year, the three clubs jointly held a large fundraiser and a silent auction at the Tacoma Dome to raise money for the upcoming year's budgets. It was my second year with the club and I launched into raising items for the auction. In the middle of the auction planning, the annual retreat for the branch directors, including Jim, was about to be held in Hawaii. The organization would pay our travel expenses and we would pay for our wives.

I informed Jim that I thought it was important for someone to stay behind to continue to procure items for the auction and saw no reason for me to spend club money to take myself on a boondoggle to Hawaii. I said I would stay behind and organize the auction while they were away. He couldn't argue with that because he knew how important the auction was.

While they were sipping Mai Tais, I continued to find items for the auction, including a mink stole and other valuables, by walking the streets of downtown Tacoma, hustling—something my Comrades and I would do while raising funds and supplies for the programs.

"Use what you got to get what you need," we used to say.

In the end, the auction turned out to be a huge success. All the budgets were secured for all three clubs, and Al Davies still had access to its investment funds. While I believed all along that kids throughout Tacoma, regardless of race, should benefit from these investments, the kids on the Hill Top were more disadvantaged and deserved some equity to allow them to catch up in the race of life.

As part of his quest to get rid of me, Jim ended up writing a negative and bogus performance evaluation for me, regardless of my efforts. This put me on the spot to move to Tacoma, a point that I said I would consider when I was hired. He knew that I didn't want to uproot my family and was applying the pressure.

"I'll resign if you change the evaluation to reflect my work," I said. "And most importantly, if you agree to a 'hands off' policy for the boxing club to leave it at Al Davies."

He agreed, and with the boxing club secure, I moved on.

EPILOGUE

From Revolutionary to Interculturalist

Up until age 32, my entire adult life had been as a member of the Black Panther Party, a community activist, one of the Party's many "people's servants."

The same was true for thousands of my Comrades who had unselfishly committed their lives to the struggle for human rights and justice—many dying—while others continued to languish in prisons, after being falsely accused or after committing some revolutionary act. We knew nothing else.

We served out of an undying love for the people, knowing that ours was a righteous cause. My life journey as a revolutionary did not begin on that spring day in 1968, when we first met Chairman Bobby and, later, gazed into the coffin of Little Bobby Hutton.

It had begun years before: growing up in the era of the Civil Rights Movement; seeing the images of the beatings on the Pettus Bridge; hearing the wails of those four little Black girls' parents as they realized they would never see their children alive again; seeing afros and Black is Beautiful; witnessing news reports of the countless assassinations and insurrections in

Watts and Detroit; and even playing Army in the streets as an 11-year-old, as if protecting freedom from the invading Nazis.

The foundation for my life as a revolutionary was laid by the lessons from my parents, especially my father, who displayed a fierce loyalty and protection of his family, as if he were a Panther papa, who always stood for human decency, respect, and standing up for the little guy. Fortifying this foundation with equal power was my mother, who protected her young and was steadfast in her defiance to the racism she encountered while growing up in places like Chicago and Mississippi, or when we moved to Seattle and was being denied employment because of her skin color.

They both taught us by example, to respect people for their character and not the color of their skin. These were among the many lessons that prepared me to be a member of the Black Panther Party, and for my life beyond.

I grew up in the melting pot, or rather, the salad bowl, of a community in Madrona where I and my siblings, enjoyed friends who were Black, white, Latino, Chinese, Japanese, and Filipino, all blending together as if making a perfect stew of cultures and flavors.

I drew insights from the diverse collection of my parents' friends, and the broad influence of their music: Dizzy and Dinah, The Duke and The Count, Amad Jamal and Paul Desmond, Madame Butterfly and the Tales of Hoffman, and Nelson Eddy and Jeanette MacDonald, and Poppy's beloved Ella Fitzgerald.

All this molded my character, and that of my siblings'.

It was natural to ascend into leadership positions in the Black Panther Party, an organization that was all about building a movement that spoke up for the forgotten, the abused and oppressed, the downtrodden, and the lumpenproletariat, who had been used as steppingstones by self-serving exploiters to build their own wealth.

This was an era for heroes who would rather die standing than live on their knees. We witnessed more assassinations of our leaders than in any other generation before or since. Coming into the Party, we had been unwittingly pre-positioned to know death as no stranger, leaving us without fear so that we could stand in the face of the biggest bully in history, telling them:

"Up against the wall, motherfucka, we've come for what's ours."

I suppose this defiance of authority or power eventually led me to stand up to Elaine and her own brand of power. Yes, she had a taste of it, as she wrote in her book, *A Taste of Power*, but power can corrupt even the best of us. I hold no grudge against Elaine, Norma, Ericka, or the Comrades who came to Seattle that day—least of all, my brother, who was there with the intent of protecting me. I continue to have immense respect for Elaine's brilliance and Ericka's profound grasp of the needs of our community. They both continue to serve.

We adhered to a revolutionary code and lived and fought as freedom fighters against insurmountable odds. We were bound to make some mistakes along the way, some which were more easily forgiven than others, and I knew of many Comrades who had yet to find it in their hearts to do so. Finding some measure of peace, I was able to move on, and with my Comrades, celebrate all that we accomplished and what we stood for.

I eventually took a job as an Equal Employment Opportunity Officer with the Seattle Parks Department. Superintendent Walt Huntley hired me after reminding me that Aaron and I had once stormed into his office with shotguns when he was head of Model Cities, and we demanded that he stop ripping off the community.

While he may have thought we were crazy, he knew we had the community's well-being at heart. Now, years later, he looked past that and gave me an opportunity to play a different role while continuing to advocate for oppressed people. I was initially hired as a Training Manager, but he also designated me as the department EEO Officer, directing me to recruit women for non-traditional positions, to retool the sexual harassment policy, and to protect them. The role was a natural fit and I relished it.

I began by training all department staff to know their responsibilities in preventing and not engaging in sexual harassment. My most critical task, however, was investigating incidents of sexual harassment and recommending the appropriate penalties based on the severity of the offense.

In the "old days" as a Panther, I would have cut them no slack and gone directly upside their head with the butt of a gun, but these were different times, and I was in a civilian population, not a revolutionary army.

I essentially became the last line of defense for women who were being targeted at a time when sexual harassment was rampant in the American workplace. I quickly gained the reputation as the new *sheriff* in the department, standing up for women who previously had no voice or recourse.

As fate would have it, a high-level manager in the construction shops was accused of harassing one of the women in his department. It was a lower-level offense, and I counseled him and suggested a verbal warning. When he offended again with a different woman, I escalated my suggested punishment to a written reprimand. He was well-liked by most of the crew workers and was somewhat insulated. When he offended a third time, and in a more egregious way, I had no choice but to recommend his termination, which was upheld in a hearing.

This role eventually led to me being recruited to join two women, Donna Stringer and Linda Taylor, as they were establishing a new business to provide diversity training to their clients. This led me on the path to becoming a diversity consultant and trainer, conducting diversity and inclusion training to organizations across the country, including Fortune 500 companies and the likes of Indra Nooyi, the first woman of color to lead a major U.S. corporation. Nooyi, at the time, was being groomed to replace Steven Reinemund as the future president and CEO of PepsiCo and PepsiCo International.

I had come a long way from facing down cops in the streets, standing up to a brutal racist government alongside my Comrades, fighting for justice and freedom. In a way, this new fight for equity in the workplace was the continuation of our struggle for freedom and justice in an unbalanced society. Now, my work focused on helping leaders in companies I once cursed to shift the dynamic and make their operations more inclusive and equitable.

Now, I was being paid to do it by the very ones responsible for the change.

My life had come full circle, and I continue to improve an unjust society, choosing to stand and fight rather than live on my knees.

References

Goldstein-Street, Jake. "50 years ago, the Seattle Freeway Revold kept apart the Central District from being ripped apart." *Capitol Hill Seattle Blog*. September 21, 2018. http://www.capitolhillseattle.com/2018/09/50-years-ago-the-seattle-free-way-revolt-kept-the-central-district-from-being-ripped-apart/.

Wikipedia. "El Centro de la Raza." Article. Last modified November 20, 2022. https://en.wikipedia.org/wiki/El_Centro_de_la_Raza. Joe Brazil Project. "A Love Supreme Live in Seattle." Posts. Last modified 2021. http://joebrazilproject.blogspot.com/.

Rothstein, Richard. "A 'Forgotten History' Of How The U.S. Government Segregated America." Interview by Terry Gross. *NPR*, May 3, 2017. https://www.npr.org/templates/transcript/transcript.php?storyId=526655831.

End Notes

[1] Intelligent Channel, YouTube, "Marlon Brando Eulogizes Black Panther Bobby Hutton (1968)—from the Education Archive," https://youtu.be/1g05Sb9CcnE, last accessed April 25, 2023.

[2] Louis E. Tackwood, *The Glass House Tapes* (New York: Avon, 1973), https://www.amazon.com/Glass-House-Tapes-Louis-Tackwood/dp/0380012154.

[3] "Afeni Shakur," Article, Wikipedia, last modified December 31, 2022, https://en.wikipedia.org/wiki/Afeni_Shakur.

[4] Huey P. Newton, *Revolutionary Suicide* (New York: Penguin Random House, 2009), https://www.penguinrandomhouse.com/books/300589/revolutionary-suicide-by-huey-p-newton/

[5] Freedom Archives.org, "The 50th Anniversary of the August 7th Marin County Courthouse Rebellion, https://freedomarchives.org/projects/the-50th-anniversary-of-the-august-7th-marin-county-courthouse-rebellion/, last accessed April 26, 2023.

[6] "Attica Prison riot," Article, Wikipedia, last modified December 29, 2022, https://en.wikipedia.org/wiki/Attica_Prison_riot.

[7] Louis E. Tackwood, *The Glass House Tapes* (New York: Avon, 1973), https://www.amazon.com/Glass-House-Tapes-Louis-Tackwood/dp/0380012154https://www.amazon.com/Glass-House-Tapes-Louis-Tackwood/dp/B000OJL8L2.

[8] "Afeni Shakur," Article, Wikipedia, last modified December 31, 2022, https://en.wikipedia.org/wiki/Afeni_Shakur.

[9] "Animal No More, Eric Burdon Goes to the Blues," NPR interview by David Dye, June 29, 2006, https://www.npr.org/2006/06/29/5286723/animal-no-more-eric-burdon-goes-to-the-blues.

ABOUT THE AUTHOR

As a revolutionary who co-founded the Seattle Chapter of the Black Panther Party in 1968, Elmer Dixon wore a beret, a leather jacket, and a holster holding a loaded gun.

Today, as president of Executive Diversity Services, Dixon continues his lifetime mission as an agent for change within the board rooms and auditoriums of some of America's top corporations. Dixon also speaks around the world and most recently gave a TEDx Talk in Tulsa, which is available to watch on YouTube.

He is one of the most sought-after leaders in the field of Diversity, Equity, and Inclusion, and demand for his services has tripled since the social justice protests began in 2020.

Dixon has led his Seattle-based company's teams in training people in more than 200 companies that include Microsoft, United Airlines, The MacArthur Foundation, Pepsico, Goodwill, JCPenney, and many more. The scope of a single training is vast, according to this testimonial by Vickie Pryor, former Manager of Onboard Service Training for the world's largest air carrier, United Airlines:

> "EDS trained 38 managers to partner with 38 EDS trainers in order to provide Diversity Awareness training for over 16,000 flight attendants in seven cities and three countries. After training, 91% of participants said they had learned something they could apply to their work performance immediately."

Dixon's training had similar success when EDS partnered with PepsiCo to conduct a top-down, three-level educational process aimed at developing an inclusive organizational culture. This provided training for more than 65,000 employees and managers.

Dixon draws from his life-on-the-line commitment to human rights during the Black Power Movement of the 1960s and 1970s, to instruct and inspire people in corporate America as well as on college campuses and in organizations around the world, about how to create and sustain Diversity, Equity, and Inclusion.

Starting in 1968, he was a Black Panther Party leader for 14 years, at times living and working in a bulletproof bunker with an arsenal of weapons to protect against constant threats from government-sanctioned violence that killed many Black activists—including Panther leader Fred Hampton, as shown in the recent movie *Judas and the Black Messiah*—during the 1960s and 1970s.

All the while, as the Party expanded to chapters in 68 cities with thousands of members, Dixon worked to nurture and protect the Black community in Seattle. He oversaw programs that included: the children's free breakfast program, a health clinic that still exists, a free groceries program for families, and armed patrols to protect Black people from police violence.

Dixon is has been a regular guest lecturer at JAMK University of Applied Sciences in Jyvaskyla, Finland for the past 12 years on topics related to Strategic Diversity Management, Cross Cultural Competence and Team Development. He has taught regularly at Espeme, an undergraduate program of Edhec Business School in Lille and Nice, France.

As a member of SIETAR (Society for Intercultural Education Training and Research) Europa—a global organization that facilitates communication and respect between and among people of different cultures to improve intercultural relations—Dixon speaks regularly at the SIETAR Europa Congresses and on university campuses around the world and is currently the President of SIETAR US. He has visited more than 40 countries.

A former body builder, Dixon also volunteers with community organizations serving young people from a range of cultures. He also enjoys spending time with his family, speaking to schoolchildren, watching movies, and traveling and is currently writing a series of children's books chronicling his life as a Black Panther and revolutionary to inspire future generations to stand up for freedom and human rights.

Elmer Dixon is available for speaking engagements, book signings, DEI trainings and media interviews. For more information, please contact him at edixon@executivediversity.com.

APPENDIX

Black Panther Party Required Reading List

The Autobiography of Malcolm X by Malcolm X

Malcolm X Speaks by Malcolm X; George Breitman (Editor)

Black Reconstruction in America—Souls of Black Folk by W.E.B. DuBois

The World and Africa by W.E.B. DuBois

Africa's Gift to America by J. A. Rogers

World's Great Men of Color by J. A. Rogers

Africa's Gift to America, World's Great Men of Color: 3,000 B.C. to 1946 A.D. by J.A. Rogers

Native Son by Richard Wright

The Black Muslims in America by C. E. Lincoln

The Colonizer and the Colonized by Albert Memmi; Jean-Paul Sartre (Introduction by); Susan Gibson Miller (Afterword by)

A History of Negro Revolts by C.L.R. James

Myth of the Negro Past by Melville Jean Herskovitts

The Negro in Our History by Carter Godwin Woodson; Charles H. Wesley

The Strange Career of Jim Crow by C. Vann Woodward; William S. McFeely (As told to)

Before the Mayflower: A History of the Negro in America, 1619-1964 by Lerone Bennett, Jr.

Black Bourgeoisie by E. Franklin Frazier

From Slavery to Freedom—Negro in the United States by John Hope Franklin; Alfred A. Moss; Alfred A. Moss

I Speak of Freedom by Kwame Nkrumah

The Lost Cities of Africa by Basil Davidson

Black Mother, the Years of the African Slave Trade by Basil Davidson

The Other America by Michael Harrington

Studies in Dying Colonialism by Frantz Fanon

The Wretched of the Earth by Frantz Fanon; Constance Farrington (Translator); Jean-Paul Sartre (Preface by)

The Nat Turner Slave Revolt by Herbert Aptheker

American Negro Slave Revolts: A Documentary History of the Negro People in the U.S. by Herbert Aptheker

American Negro Poetry—Story of the Negro by Arna W. Bontemps

Black Moses (The Story of Garvey and the UNIA) by E.D. Cronin

Garvey & Garveyism—The Philosophy & Opinions of Garveyism by Marcus Garvey

MUNTU: The New African Culture by John Janheinz

Blues People by LeRoi Jones

Ghana by Kwame Nkrumah

We Charge Genocide by William L. Patterson

Rules of the Black Panther Party

Every member of the **Black Panther Party** throughout this country of racist America must abide by these rules as functional members of this Party. **Central Committee** members, **Central Staffs**, and **Local Staffs**, including all captains subordinated to either national, state, and local leadership of the **Black Panther Party** will enforce these rules. Length of suspension or other disciplinary action necessary for violation of these rules will depend on national decisions by national, state or state area, and local committees and staffs where said rule or rules of the **Black Panther Party were violated**. Every member of the Party must know these verbatim by heart. And apply them daily. Each member must report any violation of these rules to their leadership or they are counter-revolutionary and are also subjected to suspension by the **Black Panther Party**.

The rules are:

1. No Party member can have narcotics or weed in his possession while doing Party work.
2. Any part member found shooting narcotics will be expelled from this Party.
3. No Party member can be **drunk** while doing daily Party work.
4. No Party member will violate rules relating to office work, general meetings of the **Black Panther Party**, and meetings of the **Black Panther Party anywhere**.
5. No Party member will **use**, **point**, or **fire** a weapon of any kind unnecessarily or accidentally at anyone.
6. No Party member can join any other army force, other than the **Black Liberation Army**.

7. No Party member can have a weapon in his possession while **drunk** or loaded off narcotics or weed.
8. No Party member will commit any crimes against other Party members or **black** people at all, and cannot steal or take from the people, not even a needle or a piece of thread.
9. When arrested, **Black Panther members** will give only name, address, and will sign nothing. Legal first aid must be understood by all Party members.
10. The Ten-Point Program and platform of the **Black Panther Party** must be known and understood by each Party member.
11. Party Communications must be National and Local.
12. The 10-10-10-program should be known by all members and also understood by all members.
13. All Finance officers will operate under the jurisdiction of the Ministry of Finance.
14. Each person will submit a report of daily work.
15. Each Sub-Section Leader, Section Leader, and Lieutenant, and Captain must submit Daily reports of work.
16. All Panthers must learn to operate and service weapons correctly.
17. All Leaders who expel a member must submit this information to the Editor of the Newspaper, so that it will be published in the paper and will be known by all chapters and branches.
18. Political Education Classes are mandatory for general membership.
19. Only office personnel assigned to respective offices each day should be there. All others are to sell papers and do Political work out in the community, including Captain, Section Leaders, etc.

20. **Communications**—all chapters must submit weekly reports in writing to the National Headquarters.
21. All Branches must implement First Aid and/or Medical Cadres.
22. All Chapters, Branches, and components of the **Black Panther Party** must submit a monthly Financial Report to the Ministry of Finance, and also the Central Committee.
23. Everyone in a leadership position must read no less than two hours per day to keep abreast of the changing political situation.
24. No chapter or branch shall accept grants, poverty funds, money or any other aid from any government agency without contacting the National Headquarters.
25. All chapters must adhere to the policy and the ideology laid down by the **Central Committee** of the **Black Panther Party**.
26. All Branches must submit weekly reports in writing to their respective Chapters.

8 Points of Attention

1. Speak politely.
2. Pay fairly for what you buy.
3. Return everything you borrow.
4. Pay for anything you damage.
5. Do not hit or swear at people.
6. Do not damage property or crops of the poor, oppressed masses.
7. Do not take liberties with women.
8. If we ever have to take captives, do not ill-treat them.

3 Main Rules of Discipline

1. Obey orders in all your actions.
2. Do not take a single needle or piece of thread from the poor and oppressed masses.
3. Turn in everything captured from the attacking enemy.

The Black Panther Party Ten-Point Program

Written October 15, 1966

1. **We Want Freedom. We Want Power to Determine the Destiny of Our Black Community.**
   We believe that Black people will not be free until we are able to determine our destiny.

2. **We Want Full Employment for Our People.**
   We believe that the federal government is responsible and obligated to give every man employment or a guaranteed income. We believe that if the White American businessmen will not give full employment, then the means of production should be taken from the businessmen and placed in the community so that the people of the community can organize and employ all of its people and give a high standard of living.

3. **We Want An End to the Robbery By the Capitalists of Our Black Community.**
   We believe that this racist government has robbed us, and now we are demanding the overdue debt of forty acres and two mules. Forty acres and two mules were promised 100 years ago as restitution for slave labor and mass murder of Black people. We will accept the payment in currency which will be distributed to our many communities. The Germans are now aiding the Jews in Israel for the genocide of the Jewish people. The Germans murdered six million Jews. The American racist has taken part in the slaughter of over fifty million Black people; therefore, we feel that this is a modest demand that we make.

4. **We Want Decent Housing Fit For The Shelter of Human Beings.**
   We believe that if the White Landlords will not give decent housing to our Black community, then the housing and

the land should be made into cooperatives so that our community, with government aid, can build and make decent housing for its people.

5. **We Want Education for Our People That Exposes The True Nature Of This Decadent American Society. We Want Education That Teaches Us Our True History And Our Role in the Present-Day Society.**
   We believe in an educational system that will give to our people a knowledge of self. If a man does not have knowledge of himself and his position in society and the world, then he has little chance to relate to anything else.

6. **We Want All Black Men To Be Exempt From Military Service.**
   We believe that Black people should not be forced to fight in the military service to defend a racist government that does not protect us. We will not fight and kill other people of color in the world who, like Black people, are being victimized by the White racist government of America. We will protect ourselves from the force and violence of the racist police and the racist military by whatever means necessary.

7. **We Want an Immediate End to Police Brutality and the Murder of Black People.**
   We believe we can end police brutality in our Black community by organizing Black self-defense groups that are dedicated to defending our Black community from racist police oppression and brutality. The Second Amendment to the Constitution of the United States gives a right to bear arms. We therefore believe that all Black people should arm themselves for self-defense.

8. **We Want Freedom For All Black Men Held in Federal, State, County and City Prisons and Jails.**
   We believe that all Black People should be released from the

many jails and prisons because they have not received a fair and impartial trial.

9. **We Want All Black People When Brought to Trial To Be Tried In Court By A Jury Of Their Peer Group Or People From Their Black Communities, As Defined By the Constitution of the United States.**
   We believe that the courts should follow the United States Constitution so that Black people will receive fair trials. The Fourteenth Amendment of the U.S. Constitution gives a man a right to be tried by his peer group. A peer is a person from a similar economic, social, religious, geographical, environmental, historical, and racial background. To do this, the court will be forced to select a jury from the Black community from which the Black defendant came. We have been, and we are being, tried by all-White juries that have no understanding of the "average reasoning man" of the Black community.

10. **We Want Land, Bread, Housing, Education, Clothing, Justice And Peace.**
    When, in the course of human events, it becomes necessary for one people to dissolve the political bands which have connected them with another, and to assume, among the powers of the earth, the separate and equal station to which the laws of nature and nature's God entitle them, a decent respect of the opinions of mankind requires that they should declare the causes which impel them to the separation.

    "We hold these truths to be self-evident, that all men are created equal, that they are endowed by their Creator with certain unalienable Rights, that among these are Life, Liberty and the pursuit of Happiness. That to secure these rights, Governments are instituted among Men, deriving their just powers from the consent of the governed. That whenever any Form of Government becomes destructive of these ends, it is the Right of the People to alter or to abolish it, and to institute new Government, laying its foundation on such principles and organizing its powers in such form, as to them shall seem most likely to effect their Safety and Happiness." *

* *This paragraph quotes the second paragraph of the U.S. Constitution and the first line was quoted by Dr. Martin Luther King, Jr. in his 1963 "I Have a Dream" speech.*

Photo Credits for

The Museum of History and Industry (MOHAI) in Seattle, Washington

MOHAI, Seattle Post-Intelligencer Collection, 1986.5.52275.17A, Joanne Dixon in courthouse lobby surrounded by people during typewriter trial.

MOHAI, Seattle Post-Intelligencer Collection, 1986.5.52275.22A, Elmer Dixon in courthouse lobby surrounded by people during typewriter trial.

MOHAI, Seattle Post-Intelligencer Collection, 1986.5.52333.3A, Panther attorneys at typewriter trial.

MOHAI, Seattle Post-Intelligencer Collection, 2000.107.026.10.02, photo by Phil H. Webber, Willie Brazier.

MOHAI, Seattle Post-Intelligencer Photograph Collection, 2000.107.027.04.01, photo by Doug Wilson, E.J. Brisker.

MOHAI, Seattle Post-Intelligencer Collection, 2000.107.049.32.03, photo by Grant M. Haller, close-up of Elmer Dixon.

MOHAI, Seattle Post-Intelligencer Collection, 2000.107.049.32.10, photo by Cary Tolman, Elmer Dixon speaking at SNCC.

MOHAI, Seattle Post-Intelligencer Photograph Collection, 2000.107.100.18.01, photo by Dave Potts, Attorney Alan Caughlan and others.

MOHAI, Seattle Post-Intelligencer Photograph Collection, 2000.107.136.40.1, photo by Kurt Smith, Garry Owens resting cheek on hand.

MOHAI, Seattle Post-Intelligencer Collection, 2000.107.0246.07.02, photo by Bob Miller, Elmer Dixon in striped pants standing with two comrades.

MOHAI, Seattle Post-Intelligencer Collection, 2000.107.0246.07.03, photo by Bob Miller, Elmer Dixon in press conference in Panther Office.

MOHAI, Photographer Tom Barlet, Seattle Post-Intelligencer, 1969, Information secretary Kathy "Nafasi" Halley at Panther protest with Elmer in forefront.

MOHAI, Seattle Post-Intelligencer Collection, 1986.5.50946.2, Photo by Stuart B. Hertz.

MOHAI, Seattle Post-Intelligencer Photograph Collection, 2000.107.026.10.01, photo by Dave Potts.

MOHAI, Seattle Post-Intelligencer Collection, 2000.107.100.18.02, photo by Dave Potts.

MOHAI, Seattle Post-Intelligencer Collection, 2000.107.049.32.04, photo by Bob Miller.

MOHAI, Seattle Post-Intelligencer Collection, 2000.107.049.32.9

MOHAI, Seattle Post-Intelligencer Photograph Collection, 1986.5.11580.13, photo by Dave Potts.